BYGONE H

BYGONE HEAT

Travels of an Idealist in the Middle East

C. W. R. Long

I.B. TAURIS

LONDON · NEW YORK

New edition published in 2004 by I.B.Tauris & Co Ltd
6 Salem Road, London W2 4BU
175 Fifth Avenue, New York NY 10010

In the United States and Canada
distributed by St Martin's Press
175 Fifth Avenue, New York NY 10010

ISBN 1–85043–662–2
EAN 978–1–85043–662–1

A full CIP record for this book is available from the British Library
A full CIP record for this book is available from the Library of Congress

Library of Congress Catalog card: available

New edition typeset in Sabon by Avon DataSet Ltd, Bidford on Avon
Printed and bound in Great Britain by MPG Book Ltd, Bodmin

Here at rest in ample clover
We rejoice in telling over
Our impetuous May and June ...
We recall without repining
All the heat of bygone noon.
(*The Yeomen of the Guard*)

To Jan, whose company would have enriched these travels;
Andrew, whose idea this was;
Swith, who bore the fiercest heat of the day;
Ed, who came too late; and
Mark, who has travelled further and longer.

Contents

Contents

List of Illustrations

Glossary

(Except where indicated, these words and expressions are Arabic)

abd, pl. abid	servant, slave
Agha-ye man (Persian)	'sir'
ajnabi	foreigner
ana	I
al hamdu lillah/'l hamdu li'llah	thanks be to God
Bakhshish, pl bakhashish	gratuity
bazar (P)	market
bedu [correctly, badawi]	bedouin
burqu', pl baraqi'	body-hugging cover
cadde (Turkish)	street
chay	tea
darnafis (French)	screwdriver
dayr, pl. adyar	monastery
dinar, pl. dananir	dinar(s), the currency of Jordan and Iraq
dışarıya gidiyorum (T)	I'm going outside
ezan (T)	the call to prayer
fallah, pl. fallahun	peasant
farrash, pl. farrashun	servant, messenger
fils, pl. flus	one hundredth of a dinar
flus (pl. of fils)	money
haji [correctly hajj], pl. hujjaj	Muslim who has completed the pilgrimage to Mecca
hanım efendi (T)	'madam'
hubub	duststorm, sandstorm
'id, pl. a'yad	Muslim festival

x

Glossary

'id al Adha	the Festival of Sacrifice, ending Ramadhan
idhan [correctly, adhan]	as for ezan
Incekum (T)	Fine Sand
Al Ittihad	The Union
jallabiyyah, pl. jallalib	nightshirt-like garment
jibli ispanir (English) wa darnafis (French)	Bring me a spanner and screwdriver
jumhuriyyah, pl. jumhuriyyat	republic
kahvecioğlu (T)	Son of the Coffee Maker
Khoda Hafiz (P)	'Goodbye'
al Kindi	the ninth-century Father of Islamic Philosophy
Koffer (German)	box, trunk
Maghrib, pl. magharib	the West; sunset
majlis, pl. majalis	reception area, hall, foyer
muadhdhin [correctly mu'adhdhin], pl. muadhdhinun	the muezzin, who delivers the idhan
müdür (T)	petty official
muezzin (T)	as for muadhdhin
mukhabarat (sing. mukhabarah)	secret police
mutasarrif, pl. mutasarrifun	governor of a province
na'am	yes
nargileh, pl. nargilat	hubble bubble pipe
nesf-e jihan (P)	'half the world'
Ramadhan	the Muslim fasting month
shai	as for chay
Sham	Damascus; Syria
Shi'i, pl. Shi'iyun	adherent of the minority branch of Islam, the Shi'ah, which is the official religion of Iran and important in Iraq
simetchi (T) [correctly simetçi] (T)	breadseller
sokak (T)	street
Subh bikhayr	Good morning
Sunni, pl. Sunniyun	adherent of the majority branch of Islam, the Sunnah
suq, pl. aswaq	Market
Suriyyah	Syria

xi

tell, pl. atlal	hill, mound
vali (T)	as for mutasarrif
Watani al Akbar	The Greatest Nation, Mine
ya sayyidi	'O, sir'
yıldırım (T)	lightning
yok (T)	'nothing doing'

Foreword

Why hanker after countries   *... how couldst thou take such journeys*
Heated by foreign suns?   *into the fanatic Arabia?*
                    (Horace)   (Doughty)

M y eldest son, Andrew, hearing snatches of these Orientalist jottings, suggested that I write them down. The result is not — was not intended to be — a learned work. I was nowhere personally engaged in anything of political or historical importance and accordingly offer little insight into great events. The other Horace being the most superficial of travellers, the book scores very low as a guide. In fact, like *Persian Pictures* and *Eothen*, it is — in the words of the author of the former — 'free from all details of geographical discovery or antiquarian research, from all political disquisitions and from all useful statistics'. It is an account, intended to amuse, of the 30 years I spent working and travelling in Muslim lands. Iraq, a paradise for me, was, by some way, the most enjoyable of them.

In the British embassy in Baghdad, I was one of a large team. My feelings about the other countries where I worked were undoubtedly affected by my membership in them of unattached small groups sent abroad by another organisation, one of whose 'top managers' was in the habit of anticipating that when he arrived at the Pearly Gates St. Peter would look down his nose at someone prepared to admit to having spent the bulk of his earthly working life on its payroll. The relations of the two bodies have been well captured by Olivia Manning in her *Balkan Trilogy*.

The reader may well be surprised at the affection I express for Iraq. I and my colleagues witnessed frequent coups and revolutions, had to feign nonchalance when rebellious units of the air force bombed Baghdad and for most of our time walked a little faster as we passed tanks on street corners. The fact is, however, that even those who went on to diplomatic dream postings — New Zealand and South Africa, for example — would say in after years that there was never anywhere like Iraq. I became more personally concerned for it than anywhere else I went. I wanted Arif to defeat the Ba'th; I desperately hoped that his brother would inherit his power. In the most favourable post-monarchy period for falling in love with the country — one sandwiched between Ba'thist administrations which were extremist compared with those of the simple Arif brothers, — nothing was done in Kurdistan, in the Shi'i south or in the marshes to rival the deeds of those who came immediately before and after them. It helped that our work was exciting. But the country in any case had almost everything in its favour — a delicious climate if you like it hot, wonderful archaeology (not surprising in the Sumerian cradle of civilisation), marvellous scenery between and beyond the Twin Rivers, all the sport one could want and, not least, characterful, interesting and no-nonsense people. For the last thirteen and a half centuries at least, Iraq has usually had dreadful leaders; the Arab distinction between rulers and ruled was handsomely borne out there. The only debit entry was the political tension.

I learned about Palestine in Iraq. Cambridge and McGill somehow managed to expose me to the language, literature and history of the Arabs, and to Islam, without letting slip what I gradually gathered had happened there — the grievous wronging of the Palestinians in particular, and the Arabs in general, by my own country. The Iraqis had of course satisfied themselves on the point long before and, as supporters of the Palestinian case, they and I were completely at one. Such a meeting of minds did not always occur to anything like the same extent in my later countries, where — thanks to Sykes, Balfour and Eden — even pro-Arab Britons could be treated with considerable suspicion.

Rose Macaulay accurately notes in *The Towers of Trebizond* that the Turks find it difficult to comprehend that foreigners may not understand their language. Using Arabic, on the other hand, was something which sometimes had to be fought for, especially in the Gulf. Though my love affair with Arabic has, therefore, brought me — unlike Ronald Storrs — frequent disappointment, the academic path I went out of my way to tread 40 years ago tied me to the Middle East with a firmness I have never regretted. My heart still leaps at the prospect of a journey there. I have a lively scorn for the Edward Said view and thrill to the exoticism of the whole area, whether Arab, Iranian, Turkish or indeed Pakistani. For fear of being disappointed, I have deliberately never returned to Baghdad.

The Middle East has been transformed since, a century ago, Gertrude Bell said, 'The East looks to itself; it knows nothing of the greater world of which you are a citizen.' Even in the late 1970s, a Middle Eastern posting was almost a jail term to those who did not relish the prospect. Contact with home was solely by mail: an international 'phone call was a red letter event or an indication of a grave emergency, the BBC World Service could only be heard erratically, television was out of range, English was little known. To those who wanted to immerse themselves in a foreign culture, this situation was of course ideal. Now, however, intercontinental telephoning is as quick and satisfactory as a local call at home and the BBC is always fully audible and free of inter-ference if expatriates want to hear it. BBC World Service television is available in most hotel bedrooms. A cricketing fanatic finds it anachronistic, and somewhat guilt-inducing, to have coverage of test matches beamed from thousands of miles away to a part of the world where cricket hardly exists and which is both bemused and demystified by this development.

Expatriates who would have had difficulty in indicating on a map the location of their capital city of temporary residence, and even more in pronouncing its name, now have little incentive to try to come to terms with their surroundings. If they are of the overwhelming majority who do not seek to, they can now make considerable headway in English. Specialists have greater difficulty these days in constructing cultural bridges without being thought to be behaving oddly or showing off.

The Gulf is changing fastest of all. When I first went to the Middle East, only a tiny fraction of the island of Abu Dhabi was built-up. Now — while the water in the pipes is still brown and pedestrians still get their feet covered in sand — it has turned into a modern city which will continue to grow in graciousness. Most surprising of all, in your hotel these days you get a complimentary bottle of wine or whisky. Even in Doha, alcohol has recently become available to tourists. (In Karachi, it has to be certified as being for medicinal purposes and a passport has to be produced.) In Al Ayn hotels, pork is a standard choice on the menu. Now you can walk on the grass in Ankara parks without being whistled at by attendants.

Since I am not an admirer of British carping and interventionism, in the pages which follow I have not always succeeded in avoiding the example of Gertrude Bell, who 'seldom erred on the side of charity in describing her companions'. My characters are not, however, invariably true to life and have occasionally been given a minimal imaginative coating to smooth the narrative. I should add that some of my assessments, e.g. of hotels, are the unrevised ones of some years ago, that the chronology of one or two of the events on which I touch has been varied to suit the creative purpose and that, though in principle I still transliterate from Arabic and Persian in the way I learned at Cambridge, an initial letter *'ain* is never reproduced and household names like Khomeini and Nasser appear here as in the newspapers.

Richard Long
Newcastle

Parts of Chapter 18 (pp. 179–81) and 21 (pp. 202–5) have already appeared as 'Letter from Abu Dhabi' (17 August 1979) and 'Letter from Doha' (25 May 1990) in *Middle East International*. Chapter 22 was first published as 'Don's Diary' in *The Times Higher Educational Supplement* on 24 January 1991. All three are here given in their original form.

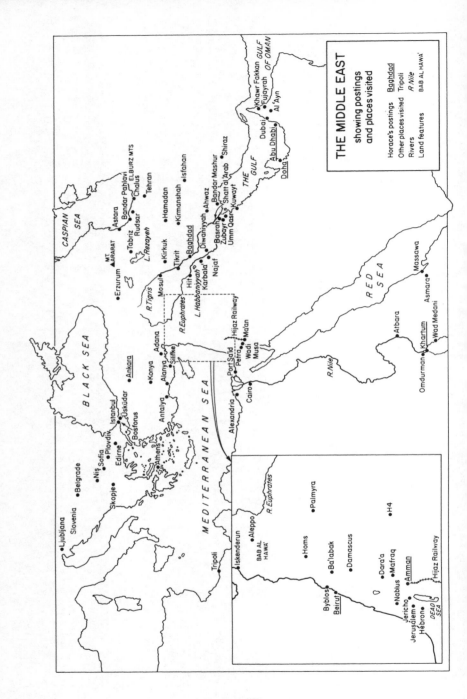

THE MIDDLE EAST

showing postings
and places visited

Horace's postings   Baghdad
Other places visited   Tripoli
Rivers   R.Nile
Land features   BAB AL HAWA'

xviii

1

Damascus Road: Libya

How big the world is... It comes to me as ridiculously presumptuous that I should dare to carry my little personality half across it.

(Gertrude Bell)

... I am really more surprised at being here than I can tell you — surprised at its being me.

(Freya Stark)

Horace left school utterly bored with the French and Spanish for which Cambridge had reserved him a place to be taken up after National Service. He had no definite plan for a change of subjects but began his two years in the army with the vague intention of not allowing things to remain as they were. He had never had the remotest understanding of any of the sciences; his only enjoyment from them had come when the physics master had failed to make his experiments work and thrown his apparatus around the classroom. Unable to stand the thought of more Molière and Lope de Vega, and using as argument and consolation the fact that his father had been academically a chemist, however, he wrote to the senior tutor of his college with the desperate request to transfer, when free again, to a science tripos. It was probably just as well that the reply poured scorn on the idea.

Suez put matters on the correct course. Horace had only been a soldier for a couple of months when the nationalisation of the Suez Canal Company by President Nasser of Egypt saw his regiment painting its trucks to match the colour of the desert he feared to lose his life in; a girlfriend said she didn't want anyone she knew to be in the army at a time like that. Apart from vaguely registering the death in the Canal Zone four years earlier of a son of the family which had lived next door to them then, Horace had

1

hardly heard of Egypt or the Arabs before. But he became intensely interested in the progress of the tripartite attack on the Canal — not least because, if it were over quickly, there would be insufficient time for him to take part and risk the premature closure of his account. More honourably, suspecting that the rights and wrongs of the episode were not as straightforward as was being generally suggested, he found sympathy for the Arabs growing in him. In the event, Suez did not require him, but the climax of his military career 15 months later, sprung from soil already fertile, prepared him for lifelong support for them.

His regiment was part of 24 ('Lightning') Brigade, charged with mounting internal security operations worldwide at a day's notice. But although Aden, Cyprus and Kenya had all suffered internal emergencies of the very kind which it was its *raison d'être* to counter, during the time he had been with it the services of his Lancastrians — to read the Riot Act in colony or dependency — had not been needed. Just when Horace thought he was home and dry and his survival was, together with other less negative considerations, emboldening him to claim that he had enjoyed his spell in the forces, however, his unit suddenly found itself posted overseas.

They mustered on their sloping Durham parade ground, set in a landscape resembling as yet unglimpsed features in the east of Turkey. Horace was immediately ordered back to his quarters to change his beret for the prescribed cap. His skirmishing over regulations had displayed itself at the wrong time as usual. Major Vale, OC 'A' Company and fresh from putting down the natives and hunting big game in colonial Africa, could not quite make him out. 'The cheek of some of these National Service subalterns,' he fumed, uncharacteristically. 'Never seen anything like it, sir,' parroted CSM Wimper, his obsequious side uppermost. (On another occasion, he had observed that it had 'never been done' when Horace ordered his platoon to turn the collars of their greatcoats up in a blizzard. Winning no admiration, 'It has now,' Horace replied.)

The troop train wound its way diagonally across the middle of England, its passengers growing more and more tired and fractious as the winter evening closed in. The standard chaos deliberately created by transport officers, whose shouting made their loss of control no more bearable, greeted them when they arrived finally at Lyneham.

2

Horace had flown once before, but was more apprehensive now than on the first occasion. To his relief, the battalion needed a whole weekend to become airborne. Taking his mind off the coming ordeal, he escaped to Oxford, visiting a lifelong friend who had eluded the army. From the platform of a station where he had to change trains, he watched a 'plane high in the sky and thought, 'I can never do that.' His fears were unnecessary.

Their destination was initially a secret. France had just bombed its restive Tunisian possession and the wilder pundits maintained that their journey was connected with that action. It seemed, however, to be common knowledge that Libya was their target, though their length of stay remained uncertain. In the end, their departure was smooth. After a fitful night's sleep in a cramped, slow Hastings, Horace was finally aroused by the reassuring beat of the engines and the dazzling reflection of a Libyan sun. He had not been warned that 'An imagination that is awake and receptive may catch from that vision an infection that will last a lifetime.' As his eyes grew accustomed to a glare of an intensity never encountered before, he began to make out, far below, the shadowy shapes of fishing vessels. Apparently immobile in a deep blue sea, they were in fact going full tilt for the African shore, which — of a whiteness he could not outface without blinking — began to become clear below. The strand was of a remarkable narrowness and fenced off by a strip of luxuriant and mysterious greenery which almost as quickly gave way to sand stretching as far as the eye could see. He knew that it pressed up against the Mediterranean from a depth of hundreds, if not thousands, of miles.

Now that almost everyone on board was awake and in a mood of keen anticipation, the pilot sent his navigator down to invite Major Vale to inspect the view from the cockpit. Horace, though only wearing one pip, was hurt not to be bidden to accompany him. The journey ended all too soon and, indeed, in Libya. They found themselves, exhausted and bleary-eyed (Horace in addition ecstatic at his flying achievement), in RAF Castelbenito. It was outside Tripoli, the capital of the country, which had only ceased to be an Italian colony during World War II and had been independent for a mere six years. It did not occur to Horace to speculate about the role of foreign military bases in sovereign states.

The exercise, for it turned out to be no more than that, lasted little longer than the unconscionable return RAF flights of the party. Most of their riot-quelling equipment — medieval-looking shields and staves — was delivered in Malta or Spain, hundreds of miles from where they needed it, and did not catch up with them. Their failure consequently to rehearse their tactical role was total.

The weather was so balmy (this was February) that it was easy to credit the fact that Libya held all the world's high temperature records. The whole atmosphere was one of delightful intoxication and excitement. The clarity of the air, the clamour of insects and birds and the unfamiliar colours and smells of Africa enchanted him. Even the RAF camp, though apparently named for Mussolini, seemed romantic. From the moment of landing, Horace felt that Libya was destined to be influential for him. Crucially, his first sight of the Arabic script decided his future.

Meanwhile, the reality of military duty unavoidably required his attention. Major Vale had overcome the effects of the flight quicker than him and, back on the soil of his favourite continent, was in his element and determined to fuss:

'Now then, Horace, you should be with your men.'

'Yes, sir.'

'Where are they billeted?'

'I'm not sure, sir.'

'Not sure? Fine officer you are.'

Horace was confident that they were being well cared for by Sergeant Forest, but had failed, as so often, to ensure that outward appearances were irreproachable. (A few months later, supervising a rehearsal for a passing-out parade from under cover while his men stamped back and forth in a downpour, he was caught and carpeted by another company commander. This one was known as Major 'Gin and Tonic' on account of his addiction to the combination, of which, according to the officers' mess book, 52 once passed his lips in a single evening.) Horace scampered to put the superficialities right.

They had no sooner settled than they were ordered to prepare for re-embarkation, but not before getting through a quick manoeuvre. Major Vale went over the ritual: 'Situation, Intention, Information, Execution.':–

'Tension, you will embus your platoon in trucks E and F. On

being ambushed, you will dismount your men and take up an all-round defensive position. Any questions?'

'How can I control men travelling in two trucks, sir?'

'You'll have to do the best you can.'

Typical, Horace mused, that the ambush drill it would have been heresy to vary at Barnard Castle should go by the board at the first practical test.

When Major Vale had moved on to give orders elsewhere, in defiance of his instructions Horace required the driver of the lorry which was to carry the rear half of his platoon to keep right on the tail of the vehicle in front. The convoy moved off into the Sahara and in no time the exercise encountered an unexpected check. When the ambush was sprung, the pursuing chauffeur turned out to have no usable brakes and the feigned peril of the situation was forgotten in a public interchange between Horace and his superior officer:

'I gave you a direct order to maintain the correct distance between your vehicles.'

'I was not to know, sir, that one had no brakes.'

'Irrelevant, you have wilfully sabotaged equipment belonging to a brother regiment.'

All the rules about not criticising a junior before his subordinates were forgotten as, scorning the army beneath his breath, Horace had to follow Major Vale's lecture to the end. The exercise fell behind schedule and, when it resumed, had lost all its momentum, like an athlete tripped during a race. They traipsed about on the fringes of the Libyan Desert for a while. Horace bumped into an old acquaintance. This son of a law lord-to-be was his platoon under-officer at Eaton Hall near Chester, where National Service infantry subalterns were trained, and had at the last moment taken his position as right marker, normally accorded the tallest in a platoon, because he wore the badges of a Guards' regiment. The haughty Dingin was one of the umpires for the exercise. They recognised each other at once and had a friendly conversation between sand dunes, which proved that Britons were not invariably formal and distant when meeting unexpectedly in the outback.

Largely thanks to the RSM's partiality to hurdlers, Horace had succeeded in avoiding the limelight until the very last event of his

Officer Cadet School training, the concluding 'battle camp' exercise at Trawsfynydd. As the finale to this, however, he had been selected to lead his men in a suicidal assault on an enemy position. In rolling country like the Old Course at St Andrews, but with much severer inclines, he had lost contact with his sergeant and seen his platoon eliminated. It was only by arriving on the objective alone and covered in blood, he believed — no doubt supersensitively, — that he had been able to avoid being 'Returned to Unit', his chance of a commission lost. Now, as the sun sank in the Maghrib, another platoon wiped out — this time following an ill-judged and frantic attempt to make the Platoon in Attack work head-on, — on their way back to camp Horace and his men passed the immobilised truck, which may still rust in the desert air, a monument to the British Empire breathing its last.

There was just time for a swim in the Mediterranean. Horace filled a matchbox with sand and later gave it a place of honour among the objects of sentimental value included in his archive. CSM Wimper — who scorned him, accused him of incipient instability and boasted of his conquests in the married quarters — frolicked benevolently on the beach in surprising trunks which revealed bandy legs. Major Vale was himself again. Like many generally affable people Horace met in the army, he quickly became touchy under stress. Even CSM Pinch at Eaton Hall, whose exterior was ferocious, could panic like a recruit under pressure. Unlike Major Nettlefold, however, who had a Dennis Price confidence trickster look and once seemed furtive when met beside a newspaper placard on Oxford Street which announced an armed robbery in the area, Major Vale never pulled rank in an argument. Qualified by his years in the tropics, he guided Horace in the purchase of a souvenir Muslim prayer mat which, on later close inspection, was revealed to be a product of Birmingham.

The flight back, which Horace irritated his OC by being slow to join as he took last deep gulps of his sudden, new destiny, was longer even than the outward leg. The Beverley hung suspended in the sky at 130 knots and had to refuel in Marseilles before completing the journey to Abingdon in 14 interminable hours. It was another beautifully clear day and the take-off from the soil of France seemed to spread the whole of the Midi out beneath the eyes of the triumphantly returning warriors. Oxfordshire was an anti-climax, and a trainload of weary combatants — reaction setting in rapidly — plodded back to Barney.

Despite his fatigue, Horace was elated. The trip had been a complete, incredible success. He could fly. He could transplant his personality thousands of miles without risking its extinction. No one was going to bill him for the truck. Above all, the Arab world had entirely captivated him and settled his immediate future: there would be no reason to disturb the senior tutor with further inane, alternative study plans he himself found unconvincing. He had no doubt, indeed, that 47 hours in the land of an Arab monarch had irrevocably decided the direction his life would take. Arabic was his exciting way ahead and he couldn't wait to embark on it.

2

Teach Yourself Arabic (and Persian): Cambridge

Certain words are used with cardinals as classifiers. ... Among them are nafar (= person) used for persons. (nafar is also used for camels).

(A. K. S. Lambton)

Give me the haunch of a buck to eat, and to drink Madeira old, And a gentle wife to rest with, and in my arms to hold, An Arabic book to study...

(George Borrow)

Having learned of the connection between them, Horace finally arrived at Cambridge wanting to study Arabic with Spanish. He then weakly allowed himself to be persuaded that National Service would have made him too rusty to tackle a 'hard' language straight away. He had thus to waste a year going over ground already covered in his French and Spanish A levels — yet more Balzac and Galdós. He also had to accept the impossibility of doing his two chosen languages together thereafter, because, at the time, they belonged in different faculties. So he decided to combine Arabic with Persian, which turned out to be a rewarding pairing.

The summer before the change came into effect, Horace toured Jugoslavia with Mark (then answering to David) and John in Washbrook — a 1937 Austin they named after the favourite cricketer of two of them — and took Thatcher's famous Arabic grammar with him. (It got damaged in a storm when the Adriatic indulged in a bout of the 'black mischief' observed by Horace's poet namesake.) He was not stealing a march on his unknown future fellow students but unable to resist the anticipated challenges and titillations of Arabic, whose promise was triumphantly fulfilled.

When the new academic year began, it very quickly became clear that the staff charged with teaching Oriental Studies were not to be looked to for much in the way of tuition to match their feat in attracting to their subject a record enrolment of 12. (It is, of course, possible that students of greater superficial Orientalist promise than Horace received a better deal. His enthusiasm, in any case, remained undimmed, even if he did not go to the lengths of one of the group who turned his room into an imitation mosque, with no seating and no inch uncarpeted or undraped.)

Horace's Arabic studies were in the hands of two supervisors. Dr Bridgestone was language, but also lectured on early Islamic history. With each succeeding appearance in the faculty's unimpressive rooms near the station, his hearers became fewer. Horace stopped attending when he announced that the first Battle of Badr took place in AD 624 but that he had no further information on it. Once a week, no doubt awkwardly after decamping, Horace visited him in the front room of his small semi-detached house by the Grantchester road, next to the digs of his friend the future Olympic hurdler, to struggle through Thatcher's grammar with his one-to-one help and more morale-boosting: he began to hear it put about that, despite his own dissatisfaction with his progress, Dr Bridgestone had a high opinion of his ability. He formed no view of that of his supervisor. It was clear from his bookshelves that his interests went wider than the subjects he taught Horace and his friends. Prominent, for example, was *Teach Yourself Polish*. But it was not until his death, soon after he was reported as having lost his memory on a New England hill, that Horace had any inkling of the fact that Dr Bridgestone was one of the world's leading authorities on the fascinating Khazars who, from their homeland between the Black Sea and the Caspian, contributed so much to the creation of Hungary and about whom Arthur Koestler wrote so memorably in *The Thirteenth Tribe*. (Another supervisor was supposed to coordinate and put in context the instruction in Islamic history which Horace was in theory receiving from Dr Bridgestone and several other unconnected contributors. Only once in the two years when Horace went to see him, however, did he show how much insight he could have given if he had been bothered or if the system had obliged him to do so.)

In their first year, the 12 were not allowed contact with the professor of Arabic, the doyen of world Orientalists. There was only one, acutely embarrassing, sighting, at a public lecture. At it, Sir Mortimer Wheeler sought his concurrence in the view that Persepolis was an outstandingly interesting site. Although he published rather more on Persian than on Arabic, the professor admitted to never having been there. (They later learned that he had only visited the Middle East once, decades before, and, finding it uncomfortable, had not returned.) Now he took over from Dr Bridgestone.

Horace's group had been assigned a set text to read with him which seemed impossibly hard. The professor's method was to declaim passages of the work and then get them to translate in turn. They quailed at the thought that, one day, he might invite them to read the Arabic aloud, but he never did. The first canter through the work took only one term and benefited them little. Hoping that enlightenment would strike at a second reading, they were anxious to have another shot at the prescribed portion of Mas'udi's *'Uyun al Akhbar*. The great man had other ideas. 'Good luck with your exams,' he said, and disappeared from their lives for ever.

Persian was no better, though there was no doubt that their supervisor (the only one on the strength) was anxious to communicate his love of language and people to them. Unfortunately, Horace's determination to play his part as recipient did not survive Mr Dupois's impractical approach to the business. A certain eccentricity was manifest from the start. Offering coffee to those it had fallen to his lot to guide, he added sugar by hand to the cups of those who requested it. He fixed 9.00 p.m. as Horace's supervision time. Horace turned up then for six successive weeks but never got an audience. Mr Dupois was giving a cocktail party, he had people to dinner, he was in bed, he was too sad after a funeral. ... Horace finally gave it up as a bad job and, with a number of others, withheld his fees. On his return to Cambridge at the beginning of the following term, a card from Mr Dupois suggested that Mr Karam, the *lecteur*, might suit him better.

Mr Karam was a supersensitive Iranian poet. He did not rate Horace's coming a matter for rejoicing and was certainly not going to stoop to speak the language of Firdawsi, Hafiz and Sa'di with him. At one of their early meetings, Horace asked if the unit of currency in Iran were the riyal, as indeed it is. Mr Karam's reaction was to go into a huff from which Horace was unable to rouse him. On another occasion, in mid-supervision, he took up his pen to write a letter and became so immersed in the task that all Horace could do was to let himself out and hope that things would be better next time. Usually they were not. Mr Karam was often in a mood when his conviction that he was a candle burning at both ends was so overpowering as entirely to prohibit coherent conversation.

Cambridge Oriental Studies were so bad that their acquisition of their own smart Hayter centre only a few years later was a surprise. The following decade, Horace was interested to see in a leading Orientalist journal an attack on them by an Arab authority, a one-time Faculty visiting professor. His strictures were even more extreme, as well as more trenchant, than those of Horace and his contemporaries, and included the charge that the staff were unable to form the passive of Arabic verbs.

The obvious consequence of the lack of conscientiousness of his supervisors was that Horace virtually had to teach himself the two Eastern languages (one difficult, one easy) he had gone out of his way to tackle. In the first week of his studies, Dr Bridgestone gave him the titles of the Arabic dictionary and set text prescribed to go with Thatcher. Horace set about trying to master the tongue, writing proses for his supervisor which he could not translate back to himself and on which no very illuminating comment returned to him. It was not until the first Easter vac. that, after two terms which would have demoralised him if he had not been so determined to learn about the Middle East and its languages, literature and history, he felt that he was beginning to understand how Arabic worked — that, as he put it to Martin, his roommate, who pooh-poohed the claim, he had at last acquired the (Chomskian) key of the language. He had reached that stage much earlier with Persian.

From then on, progress came quickly. Horace's single-mindedness never lessened and not for an instant did he regret that he had seen the light in Tripoli. But the members of the group were never allowed to meet the Arabic *lecteur* lest their elementary standard offend him; and if there were any Arab students at Cambridge who might have afforded them oral practice, their paths failed to cross. The spoken Arabic Horace eventually

11

acquired is, consequently, an unhappy mixture of an updated version of the classical language (the one the group read in their set books) and the Iraqi dialect. It frequently attracts the comment, 'He speaks better Arabic than we do,' which merely proves that the form of language he employs is usually not the one best suited to the conversation in question.

3

Balkan Preamble: Ljubljana– Istanbul

The landlord asked where I was going: I said: 'Constantinople'.
(Patrick Leigh Fermor)

Hardly had he got in than he realised that the driver had no steering; the steering wheel was, indeed, held together with string. Horace instinctively adopted a procedure he was to need even more desperately in Lebanon. He talked all the time, in low tones, so that his companion — out of politeness unable to ignore his remarks in a tongue foreign to both of them — had to keep the engine's revolutions low enough to hear:

'Ich bin sehr glücklich mich in Jugoslavien zweiter zu finden.'

'So, dieser ist nicht die erste zeit?'

'Nein, ich habe besuchen Titos Reich im latste Jahr. Jugoslavien ist mein liebste Land.'

Horace had no Serbo-Croat. His German was so ungrammatical that, during their tour of Jugoslavia the previous year in Washbrook, only policemen had relished conversation with him in it. But he had indeed been impressed by the country. The little man, bald, bespectacled, endowed with no spirit of self-preservation and making continual alarming misjudgements, but luckily not driving fast, beamed:

'From what nation are you? (He pointed to the Union Jack on Horace's rucksack). British? Not really British? We must celebrate, comrade. How I admire the British. We must eat and drink. You will be my guest, we will drink toasts to Great Britain.'

They somehow reached Ljubljana without mishap. Tabriz

13

seemed a long way off. Horace, anxious to get on, could not but make the best of the delay as his new friend made a fierce stop at a café and began commanding large glasses of beer. How the very name of Great Britain tore at his heart strings! He drank to the Queen. Horace toasted Tito. He said he was the First Secretary of the Communist Party of Slovenia. A maudlin excitement came over Horace at this revelation that he was dining with the great — admittedly in a scruffy café with unwiped tables and the utensils none too clean, but the great nonetheless. But what would he say if, in the future, he were asked if he had ever associated with communists? The fact that the principal communist he had associated with, the self-proclaimed First Secretary of the CP of Slovenia, had now proposed the health of Great Britain so many times that he was drunk and sobbing uncontrollably (the bowls of salad brought up to take the edge off the liquid main course had had no effect), would not, he supposed, be viewed as mitigating the offence.

He was relieved that there could be no question of the lift resuming. He slipped away, leaving his host asleep, but still ecstatically murmuring, 'The Mother of Parliaments, the BBC World Service...'

South of Belgrade, where he saw Tito sweep past on the other side of the road, a promising car with Turkish plates appeared, but its lady driver was so startled by Horace's elaborate hitching routine, or by finding herself face to face, even at that distance and through glass, with a man, that instead of circumnavigating the roundabout beside which he stood — south led to Greece, east to Bulgaria and Turkey — she drove straight across it, jerking and wobbling as she regained contact with the orthodox driving surface on the far side. Her Mercedes roared into the distance in a cloud of nervous and affronted dust. Horace looked after her with scorn, surprised that she should have taken to Western means of transport before reconciling herself to more basic aspects of Twentieth Century living.

He didn't have long to ponder other imagined imperfections of the Orient. Ali and Ahmad, Iranians, arrived in their pair of (no doubt illegal) Mercedes and, the one sullenly, the other absent-mindedly, offered him passage to the unknown. They successfully negotiated the roundabout — and turned towards Bulgaria, for which Horace had no visa. As the border approached, Ali — making a display of another claimed characteristic of the East, unreliability — announced that they had to wait at the Jugoslav frontier post of Dimitrovgrad for a *Koffer* to appear by rail from Vienna. Horace volunteered to walk on to the border, try to obtain a transit visa and there await his new companions — whom he had known for less than two hours. After over a week of worrying, on the road from Calais to Trieste, about where his next lift was coming from, he was anxious not to lose one that promised to get him all the way to his destination, and on time.

He watched himself, suddenly disembodied, stow his rucksack in Ali's car. The chances of seeing it again seemed nil. Theirs was a likely story. He forced himself to undo his rash move to the extent — self-consciously, as though they were studying him and perhaps being hurt by his distrust — of retrieving his few vital essentials and, as he set off, memorising their car numbers.

He subsequently drove many times the road he walked that evening. The distance is a very long three miles. His apprehension at having to lift the Iron Curtain proper for the first time was partly soothed by the singing of a large body of male and female agricultural workers as they returned to the town from the border areas in the clear light just before nightfall. The sky above Bulgaria was bright but, as when he had first entered West Germany and Jugoslavia the previous year, he was unconvinced that a dark fate might not be lying in wait for him.

Though he secured his visa without difficulty, he learned at once that he was expected neither to retrace his steps in order to rejoin Ali and Ahmad, nor to remain where he was, but to proceed into Bulgaria. Hoping, now if ever, to be understood, he left hurried messages:

'*Wann meine Freunde kommen, sagen Sie ihre bitte das ich will ihr warten im Hotel Moskva in Sofia.*'

The hotel had been the idea of yet another Iranian, Amir, who, with friends, turned up in *his* Mercedes just as Horace was having his excess Jugoslav currency confiscated. Events had moved so fast that he had quite overlooked the need to spend, change or hide the 3,000 offending dinars. The operation was effected with gratifying formality.* He was diminished in wealth, however, as he found himself frogmarched across the no man's land dividing the two fraternal socialist countries by first a Jugoslav escort patrol and then a receiving Bulgarian one, a tin-helmeted soldier at either shoulder throughout. (What a comedown for a British National Service officer less than two years retired!)

Amir drove him the hour to Sofia and left him at the Moskva, where his declaration that he proposed to wait for Ali and Ahmad in the foyer provoked no positive objection. That established, he met up with Amir, as arranged, and consumed three plates of egg and chips and a bottle of beer before tiring of his over-inquisitive company. Returning to the hotel, in the heart of the city, through dark and muddy side streets full of puddles, he was surprised by the number of drunks reeling about or pouring liquor between their lips in the full glare of the few street lamps. Perhaps the local beer was strong. At any rate, the authorities made no attempt to hide the fact that, for some of its citizens at least, socialist Bulgaria was showing clear signs of falling some way short of the earthly paradise its propaganda pictured it to be.

He resumed his Moskva foyer vigil at 2.00 a.m. Anyone who has ever spent a night in a public part of a hotel when all the other guests are properly sleeping will know how embarrassing it is to be continually in the way of staff and cleaners who remain unconvinced by the reasons adduced for such strange, if legally sanctioned, behaviour. The management had agreed to levy no charge provided that he did not go to sleep. Horace — stuck alone in the middle of his first real communist country (not certain to help him, and probably with little interest in doing so) — was far too jumpy for sleep. His concern about his missing clothes and other possessions, anxiety at the dislocation of a phase of his journey which had bid fair to solve the whole problem of reaching Tabriz by the deadline, and consciousness of knowing no one except Amir and his friends (their prying usefulness had by now been vitiated by Horace's irritation at their conviction that he could achieve nothing without their aid) depressed and unnerved

---

* He kept the receipt and reclaimed the sum, less 100 dinars' commission, three years later.

him. A whole night is a long stretch to remain awake, though never longer than the one when his father died. But it was touch and go, and every time he threatened to nod off a hotel employee would shake him by the shoulder and, in one of the six languages that — luckily — all Bulgarians seemed to speak, say, 'If you sleep, you pay.' Now, you may ask, 'Why on earth didn't the chap cough up and have a better night?' One answer is, of course, that Horace only retained the clothes he sat up in, his camera and his wallet, the meagre contents of the last being all that he possessed to get him either on to Tabriz or back home in disarray. He could not afford to pay. More crucially, if it remained a possibility, he could not risk the loss of his lift.

Once the terrors of the night had been driven away by the breaking of a dull day, the Moskva's staff showed themselves to be marvellously kind. They rang the border twice for him without charge, attempting to discover if Ahmad and Ali had driven through. Both times the answer was 'No'. Horace sat in a square, asking about trains and feeling trapped. People came up to him and offered to buy camera, shoes, even trousers. Apprehensive and washed-out, he returned to the hotel, to receive a miraculous message which said that his friends would arrive at midday. How was that for the fellow feeling and trustworthiness of the East and the efficiency of the Jugoslav railway system? Elated, he had hardly time to bid the Moskva a fond goodbye before he saw them — half an hour ahead of schedule — driving into the square outside. The *Koffer*'s existence had been enigmatic; if a reality, it had seemed likely in any event to be subject to forwarding delays lasting weeks rather than days. But it had been held up, if at all, by at most five hours. Thus did Jugoslavs, Bulgarians and Iranians demonstrate the sort of qualities the British regard as unique to themselves.

They crossed Bulgaria. After the worry and lack of sleep of the last 20 hours, Horace made the transit in a mist of depersonalisation. His impression of the country was of one far more rural and colourless than it actually is. Plovdiv, in particular, he accused of mud-coloured, rain-soaked mediocrity. Ahmad and Ali considered stopping at one point in order to bathe in a dreary, reed-choked pond, but he could not have stood that in his neurotic state and managed to persuade them — Ahmad in Persian and Ali in German — that it would not be a good idea. He felt that it

17

would, indeed, be dangerous to him at least and that any attempt at immersion would risk stifling by the encircling leaden and oppressive air. He did no kind of justice to Bulgaria and only began to emerge from his dispirited condition when they had a cheery encounter on the Turkish border with a Lebanese. In lederhosen and goatee beard, looking like a troll or the denizen of a Tyrolean village, he invited Horace to look him up when, as planned, his travels took him and Mark to Beirut.

With the departure of the Lebanese, night fell, their watches had to be put forward two whole hours and they entered Turkey in the dark. If Bulgaria was depressing, Turkey seemed menacing. Edirne was a confusion of noise, and rain had left the town's broken paving stones slippery and half-submerged by puddles. Squeamishly, Horace followed his companions, who were perfectly at ease here, as they had been in the previous two countries and, no doubt, in West Germany too. They were contemporary versions of the Spanish picaresque hero who had no formal education, lived on his wits and always contrived to survive unscathed in all circumstances, no matter how dire. Being illiterate was not a necessary characteristic of the type, and certainly Ahmad and Ali were not that. Some years later, however, Horace knew in Baghdad a perfect exemplar of the genus who was.

Ahmad, the outgoing one of the pair (Ali was more philosophical, subtle and mercurial), plunged into a hole-in-the-wall eating establishment. He ordered the local fare without asking for sight of a menu (probably none was available) or seeming to indulge in any kind of preconditioning before tackling the traveller's cuisine of a new country. No doubt he was a regular customer. Horace considered that the recently and roughly killed chunks of meat, scarcely boiled potatoes, gravy by the pint and armfuls of stale bread were certainly lamentable and possibly lethal. Dogs snapped across thresholds, violent-looking characters jammed doorways and, beyond, the darkness threatened. Edirne, where Islam seems to arrive with a bump, was, and is, weird. To make matters worse, Ahmad had suddenly begun to fret about a service of which his Mercedes was in need, but luckily he could find none in the town. That he should have felt it worth seeking at eight in the evening was remarkable. Had he found it, Middle Eastern magic would have demonstrated again its capacity to

18

surprise. Persians are the most remarkable conjurors, but Ahmad was not of the fraternity.

Passing an enormous mosque which Horace took to be the Selimiye Cami,* the religious masterpiece of Sinan who had earlier built the walls of Jerusalem for Suleyman the Magnificent which still stand today, they drove on into the night, rarely seeing a light. Horace was convinced that only Alexander Kinglake's unfortunate companion, Methley, could have had a more uncomfortable journey to Istanbul, about 150 miles distant. There had just been a bloody coup. At intervals, soldiers in isolated sentry boxes demanded to peruse their papers. The road was mud-surfaced. Horace sensed diseased animals congregating beside it and wondered if the continual howling came from dogs or wolves. He reckoned it a reasonably safe bet that ten paces inland in either direction would produce, though rather quicker, the same result as Capt. Oates's last walk. When at last they stopped to spend the remaining hours of darkness à bord, he could at least be thankful for greater comfort than he had recently experienced during over-nights, earlier in the journey, beside the A2, in the middle of a French roundabout, under a hedge above Trieste or, indeed, in the Moskva.

Ali roused them at 4.30 and the drive continued through green and rolling country, smiling in invitation. The contrast with Horace's demeanour of yesterday could not have been more complete. A short and fitful sleep had sharpened the edge of his awareness and, coinciding with an idyllic day, suggested that his nocturnal imaginings had been exactly those. The Pathetic Fallacy, maintaining that nature sympathises with human moods, appeared the previous evening to have done Turkey, like Bulgaria, a grave disservice.

With the Sea of Marmara to the south shining like sunlight after rain, Ahmad announced that he could not possibly venture beyond Istanbul without having his car put right. Horace — his hopes of a lift the whole way shattered — agreed to stay with them long enough to share in a Turkish bath on the outskirts.

As they went down the ill-lit spiral staircase leading from a

---

* Turkish c is pronounced j.

perfectly ordinary frontage standing right on one of the main routes into the great city, Horace began to wish, not for the first time, that he had not set out on his expedition. Why had he allowed the siren East, where Freya Stark aptly said that 'the unexpected happens so punctually,' to take control of his destiny in this unnecessary — and soon to be alarming — way? Ali motioned him into a cubicle: '*Hier muss man auskleiden.*' (Why *would* he not speak a language they could actually communicate in, like his own?) He undressed, wrapped round his waist the grubby towel provided and followed his companions through a low, narrow door. Steam enveloped him. This was Aladdin's cave and the Wizard of Oz was going to roast him in a basin like a missionary.

The air cleared and they lay on a burning slab. He was self-consciously apprehensive in his vulnerable state of near nudity. Didn't Turks do unspeakable things to men? He remembered Lawrence of Arabia's ordeal at the hands of the Ottoman unit in Dera'a. An attendant — gap-toothed and with the build of the Turks who until not long before had been prominent among medal-winners at Olympic wrestling and weight-lifting — came and took each of them away. His aloneness unnerved him. Thoughts began to occur of premature endings to his travels, of crusaders in dungeons, Sultan 'Yıldırım' Beyazit encaged by Tamburlaine and the players of the Great Game in their pit in Bukhara. The man flung him onto a chair and — with what he took to be imprecations and threats in a language he had hardly begun to master and now found too gruff to be merely meaningless — began to twist his limbs and throw enormous scoops of water all over him. They slapped him like a choppy sea. The man started to pummel him. He twisted his neck this way and that and made it crack. His fingers dug into his nostrils and ears. It eventuated that this was no more than the standard treatment, and at the end of it Horace was free. The giant — probably with a heart of gold, like two of his fillings — beamed at him. He had expected to feel fresh and new with the sweat of 11 days washed from his pores, but — parting from his faithful, changeable friends — he merely noticed that the street was chilly.

Horace disliked Istanbul. His first impressions were similar to those of Beverley Nichols, who fled the 'cruel city'. He formed the impression that animals were not treated kindly. He found himself unwillingly giving an English lesson, he could see nothing for sale which he dared eat apart from chocolate, he grew irritated at passers-by all saying *elli kurush** and talking about cars. Santa Sofia was shut, which he gathered was normal. The Blue Mosque was superb, but not enough to allow Istanbul to charm him. It was probably not itself: it was only a matter of days since the former prime minister, Adnan Menderes, and two of his ministers had been hanged in the military takeover. He felt that an atmosphere redolent of the finality of death surrounded him.

He had decided that he lacked the courage to resume hitch-hiking. He had calculated that he would after all be able to afford a more secure method of travel. It was well dark as he boarded the train ferry. He marvelled that crossing a stretch of water as historic as the Bosphorus could leave his commuting fellow passengers so blasé. He struggled with his usual vertigo. There were the same noise and seething crowds at the Üsküdar pier as there had been in Istanbul. He realised that he was making his entry into Asia with a splitting head, which perhaps was not inappropriate in the place where Florence Nightingale's hospital still stood, but it was certainly anti-climactic in relation to the *tabula rasa* of his third continent. Just as the train was about to leave Haydarpaşa station without him, a little boy popped up. One of the indispensable, invaluable breed without whose services — whether freely offered, as now, or performed in expectation, sometimes disappointed, of payment — the foreigner's progress through the Middle East would on the whole be far less smooth than it is, with precocious, urchin interpretation skills, he obtained for him the National Union of Students' discount which bought Horace 800 miles of travel for TL 41, about £2.70. He forced his way on board and, in the crush and strangeness of it all, thought he would go mad when someone in the next compartment began to play the bagpipes.

---

* Fifty piastres, apparently the price of most things. (There were 100 in a Turkish Lira (TL) until inflation made them obsolete. Nothing can be bought for less than TL 100,000 today.)

4

Retreat from Iran: Turkey/Iran

.. perhaps, no country in the world less comes up to one's expectations than Persia..

(James Morier)

Themselves they consider in every way superior to everyone else in the world.

(Herodotus on the Persians)

Erzurum, the railhead, felt both like Central Asia and the 'extremus finis regionum Rumaeorum ab oriente' of Abu'l Feda'. Even at the end of June its air was crisp, as though the dramatic snows of Turkey had either only just receded or were announcing their imminent return. Conveyance from the station the short distance to the town was by *droshke*,* a taxi with wheels about to fall off drawn by a horse which would have been of interest to a Turkish RSPCA if there had been one. *Droshkecis* have not heard of mucking-out, so a ride with them — pitifully cheap — was nearly always an odoriferous experience.

Horace left his favourite walking stick behind when his driver deposited him at what he said was the best hotel. Utterly exhausted, and already starting to show the effects of his TL 1 per hour rail journey, he went to bed soon after 7.00 p.m. Next day, the Tahran Palas served the normal sticky Turkish breakfast of liquid cheese, watery honey and half-minute egg. Its services to residents extended to no other meals. Nor did it boast hot water.

---

* *Droshke* is a Persian word, taken from Russian; the Turkish commander of such a vehicle — now known in Turkish as a *fayton* and driven by a *faytoncu* — is called a *droshkeci*.

Horace set out in search of cash. He took *chay* with a hospitable bank manager who — to his surprise — spoke good English. With the other transit passengers from the train, marooned until the arrival of a connecting bus, he dined at a middling restaurant and returned to the hotel to spend the night with one ear cocked in case it appeared without warning.

Next day, the vigil continued. They could not stray far from the hotel lest the bus materialise and leave while their backs were momentarily turned. There was no timetable, and — even if they did not proclaim ignorance as to when it might please Allah to send it, like Gertrude Bell's steamer in *Persian Pictures* — company employees seemed to have no authority to hazard a guess as to when their transport could be expected. Resembling citizens expecting an air raid, the travellers rushed around the small town centre with their reflexes alert, too anxious to settle to anything. Like Robert Byron and Christopher Sykes in Afghanistan, they were the prey of rumour, the playthings of an invisible power which, Olympian, laughed at their mindless scurryings — and so arranged matters that even the one rumour which was true had them captive in a queue for an hour beyond the departure time which was finally announced.

Since there was little traffic to compete with buses for space on Middle Eastern roads, there was no logistical reason for services to be so unreliable. The causes could be spiritual (Allah had willed circumstances to be adverse), mechanical, or the character, inefficiency or lucklessness of humans. A bad start was guaranteed to any journey. Freya Stark said that 'There would be something eccentric about an oriental journey that made no false start to begin with.' If you arrive early, the driver has been unavoidably delayed — by a revolution, the death of his uncle, an untimetableable prayer — and there is wonderful scope for strife and shouting; if you are late, pressing business in the next town, the impatience of the passengers who have already arrived or the offer of a percentage on top of the fare will have caused him to depart before schedule, leaving you at 5.00 a.m. — when in theory buses always leave — with a ruined day before you. There is often a stop for lunch at 1.00 p.m., when the driver declares an hour's break before proceeding; you hardly have time to choose the components of your makeshift snack when at 1.15 the cry goes up, 'The bus is leaving. Be not among those left behind!'

Progress is always problematical. The driver may decide to take things leisurely, he may stop to converse with roadside friends and relations, a puncture is only to be expected. Perhaps he mistakes the way. Alternatively, he may drive like Jehu while the passengers — always fractious after their 4.00 a.m. awakening — pray out loud behind him and clouds of dust and diesel fumes envelop his bus. To crown it all, the inevitable wag, village idiot or truant schoolboy decides to take it out on the bewildered foreigner. When you possess a vocabulary of several thousand words — inevitably too different from the local dialect to be readily understood or, therefore, welcome, — 'You are try practise your Arabi,' he says.

The Middle East is perhaps most itself at the bus station. Tickets are available from guichets, but most intending travellers do not manage to obtain one. They have too many women and too much luggage, the former — according to an unkindly Gertrude Bell — virtually inextinguishable from the latter and of a shapelessness that enhances 'their personal disqualifications'. Elegant ladies do not travel by bus, where their less blessed sisters — in black, if not actually veiled, — are always getting in the way.

Finally the Persian bus swept out of Erzurum and ground its way purposefully to the east. The scenery grew increasingly fine, with larger and larger mountains beginning to dominate the middle view until Mount Ararat shouldered them out of the way and made them look puny. Dominating the whole of the corner where Turkey, Iran and Armenia meet, its regular sides, deep in snow for most of their length, seemed to cast a dazzling light over an area much larger than that dominated by many higher mountains set in less uncluttered landscapes.

The border is in the shadow of Ararat. The Turkish customs' arrangements there had for days provoked dread anticipation and fear in even the most carefree and experienced of Horace's fellow travellers. When the bus company told them the currency export rules, it was therefore with trepidation that Horace set about transgressing them. Only 99 liras could be taken out of the country. He hid 100 in an ashtray in the bus, and another 100 in his money belt, nonchalantly left lying on his seat. After the customs' officers had fully lived up to their reputation, taking six hours over their inspection and emptying onto the floor the contents of the suitcases of several passengers, most distressingly those of a woman from a country less developed than theirs, they were allowed to embus again. It was with considerable relief that Horace found that his hoard would, in addition to the legal TL 99 he had kept about his person, be available to him on the return journey after all. Even more important was his avoidance of a Turkish lock-up.

He had been impressed by most of the Iranians he had met and his expectations of their country were high. His first Persian hotel was right on the border. In it, life for in-transit residents was astonishingly free and easy. The permissiveness of which he did not approve seemed nonetheless to indicate social advancement to which — on the strength of his one Turkish Railways' journey — he considered in his precocious wisdom that Turkey had not seemed to aspire.

Four cups of black coffee and a dog barking combined to create a dreadful night. Daylight brought reality as the Mihantur pullman left for Tabriz at 7.00 a.m., instead of the rumoured 6.00.

With Ararat shrinking in the distance, they moved like a caterpillar through the rugged scenery of the first real desert he had seen. (In Libya, he had hardly penetrated the Sahara further than a batsman is from the pavilion.) Disappointingly, in view of his hope that Iran would be different and better (a hope that would likewise be dashed in the Sudan, years later), the villages they swept through, and the inhabitants who looked up without interest as their wake enveloped them, were as dirty as those of Turkey. When they eventually reached Tabriz, the object of his travels, it was so low in the ground, and of a pale brown colour so indistinguishable from the surroundings in which it occupied a shallow bowl, that he could not immediately believe that there was anything to disembark for. Gertrude Bell had felt similarly about Tehran. (Horace's initial — and abiding — response to Khartum was to be identical.) However, 'Tabriz, Tabriz,' they cried, turning round to him. 'Foreigner, this is the place you wanted. Out you get. Allah rewards the punctual. Husayn, help him out with his luggage, you idle object.' Unconvinced that his two-week journey should really be ending in this unlikely-looking spot, and fearing abandonment by the bus, he had to force himself to shoulder his rucksack and get off. 'Allah give you peace,' they chorused, and roared away.

25

An obliging Christian Iranian fellow passenger, also disembarking, indicated the way to the British Institute's combined office and residence. There, the Director appeared unmoved by the sight of a bearded and bedraggled addition to his assembling team and escorted him to the Metropole Hotel. He learned that he was to share a room with Passmark, the Tehran-based course leader grandly styled Director of Studies. He was relieved that the rucksack he deposited by his bed was in comparatively presentable condition. Suddenly joining up again with urbanity, in the shape of freshly laundered and generously funded officials in a country where the Shah required high standards of turnout, was a sharp contrast to the rough travelling and sleeping, and the unpretentious companions, of recent days.

He returned to the office for the staff briefing meeting which he could not have timed his arrival more finely to attend. Released, he walked through the narrow, boisterous lane of small shops which led from it and, at its end, turned left into the main street where Misafirkhane-ye Metropol stood in the midst of the traffic and associated noise and dirt. His room was locked. Suspecting that it was not unoccupied, he repeated his knock. A voice responded, 'I'm not prepared to share a room with a man with a beard.' Despite his complete lack of a fuse, he took the rejection well. This was a fine welcome to Tabriz, but it didn't seem worth making a scene about. Silent contempt fitted the bill better. (Years afterwards, Horace wondered if Passmark's objection had really been to having someone a generation younger, whether bearded or not, invading his privacy.*) He found alternative accommodation on the floor above, and when Passmark returned to Tehran after a couple of days, to reappear for the end-of-course certificate-distribution, was not well enough to move back even though his satisfaction at being the sole occupant of his new room had been destroyed by the late arrival of a course tutor drafted in from Bahrayn. Spinner, though anything but stuffy, was just as

---

* Horace has frequently told the story in the years since. He is no longer so certain, as once, that Anthony Powell's coincidences are implausible: more than 26 years later, at the opening of a Japanese festival in Washington New Town, he regaled a lady with it who turned out to be the niece of the villain of the anecdote.

irritating as Passmark might in a different way have been. Probably only in his thirties, Horace regarded him as being well into middle age (his Tabriz diary also referred to 'two elderly [46, 37] British nurses') and was repelled by his immature attempts to act younger. The only thing he liked about his roommate was Spinner's recognition of him as an Arabist when he observed him making a deletion with a right-to-left stroke.

Although known for epidemics of cholera and typhus, one interpretation of the name 'Tabriz' is 'fever-remover'. It is perhaps connected with Harun ar Rashid's favourite philanthropist wife who — during her husband's period as Caliph, when Baghdad reached the height of its fame as the capital of the Abbasid empire — inspired the construction of the eponymous Darb Zubaydah pilgrim route between Iraq and Mecca which Ibn Battutah travelled over 500 years later. Legend credits her with rebuilding Tabriz, which had fallen into ruin following the Arab conquest in the mid-seventh century, when she went there in the hope that a change of climate would lift a lingering temperature. It is not recorded that the hope was realised and, in Horace's case, 'fever-remover' certainly turned out to be a serious misnomer.

He had arrived exhausted. Acrid smoke from the lignite which fuelled Turkish locomotives had billowed into his carriage the whole way, and particularly after Ankara. He greeted Tabriz with a sore throat and took to his bed at teatime on his second day. On the third, he was coughing up blood. He fell under the care of an American doctor who interpreted an X-ray to mean that his heart was too big and feebly tried to lessen the shock of his tactless diagnosis by quipping that Horace therefore had 'more love to give'. Though Horace feigned insouciance, playing table tennis in defiance of instructions, this claim scared him and made a serious bid to ruin his expedition right at the start. He expected to drop dead at the next bout of exertion and couldn't imagine himself lasting nine months in Tabriz like Marco Polo.

He had begun his journey by hitchhiking from Lancaster to London. Poised to get far beyond the Channel next day, he had gone back to Cambridge so that his remarkably tolerant GP could assure him yet again that he was not suffering from cancer. The street on which the Metropole stood had a weighing machine every 50 metres. During his month's stay in Tabriz, a paradise for hypochondriacs, Horace imagined that he was undergoing a steady weight loss.

His condition and associated depression did little at first for the duties he had come so far to perform. The principal one was to be an 'assistant', a real-live English-speaker on whom the members of the summer school (which was for Iranian teachers of English) could model their pronunciation while gaining experience in the oral use of the language. Otherwise, he led readings of simplified texts, gave a talk on 'Life at a British University' and carried out various supporting tasks.

His purpose in travelling to Iran had been, at the suggestion of his supervisor, to obtain practice in speaking Persian. On his first morning he had an unpleasant shock. As he descended for the hotel breakfast, the staff responded to his *Subh bikhayr* with blank looks. He had to face the fact at once that the language of Tabriz was Turki, a Turkish dialect, and not Persian at all. His opinion of Mr Dupois did not rise. Luckily, however, most of the members of the summer school had come from other cities and Persian was their mother tongue.

Horace was glad to have reached his destination. He had done nothing before to prepare himself for the loneliness of a 4,000-mile journey unsupported — after Strasbourg, where in the youth hostel he had bumped into the college friend whose digs he had inherited in his first year — by anyone he knew. Language had not been a problem, but maintaining onward progress had been stressful — where would the next lift come from, where would he spend the night, would the unknown country beyond be safe? It was perhaps partly out of relief at having a context to fit into once more that he had fallen ill on arrival. But, as in Libya, his mood was one of triumph. Standing on the hotel balcony, he exulted in the cries of the bus conductors as they chanted their destinations. Two and a half thousand miles further than he had been before, he had surmounted all the perils of a long foray into unfamiliar territory, despite the strangeness of his surroundings he was spiritually very much on top of things, and above all he had reached a land whose language he was excitedly learning.

When his health improved, he discovered Tabriz to be full of character, like so many places far off the beaten track. It had become the chief commercial centre of the Middle East after the

Mongols destroyed Abbasid Baghdad in 1258. It was the founding capital of the Safavid dynasty which had made Shi'i Islam the state religion of Iran. But it felt like a backwater. Gertrude Bell would probably have bridled at the word: '... that which seems a backwater of life is the stagnant mid-ocean, after all — that is the first lesson which the East writes in her big wise book. ...' Undeniably, however, Tabriz had only recently been connected to the Iranian railway system. The city was far from recovered from the war when, by Soviet–British agreement, Iranian Azerbaijan was awarded to the USSR as a sphere of influence. It had certainly not forgotten the traumatic aftermath when, in 1946, it had had to fight to free itself from being yoked to Stalin as the capital of the Azerbaijan People's Republic.

Called the Heroic City because Alexander the Great could not take it, its 2000-year history had been studded with battles and earthquakes. The fragmentary state of its historic monuments — only two according to Robert Byron — well reflected the turbulent past of a place whose buildings (it has been claimed) set Isfahan and Versailles a standard they could not match when it was the capital of the Mongol Ilkhans and the Turcoman Ak Kuyunlus in the fourteenth and fifteenth/sixteenth centuries respectively. Now it had half a million people, half a million Mercedes taxis and a very large *bazar*, perhaps the largest in the Middle East though admittedly less colourful than at the time of Ibn Battutah's visit: the beautiful slaves had all gone, nor did Horace witness any riots.

Trips were organised for the directing staff to Yam and Rezayeh, the great salt lake to the south, but Horace was not well enough to join them. Closer at hand, however, were delightful, recuperative spots within his compass. One, five miles east of the city, was an irrigation reservoir of inviting though oily warm water, no larger than a cricket square, lying beneath tall, shady trees. He went there on the hottest day he had so far experienced. Richard, a fellow student of Arabic and Persian at Cambridge, sat on the bank above the pool looking, with his wispy beard and his towel coiled round his head, like an Indian fakir.

One afternoon, Horace went by taxi with the girls on the course to a more nostalgic place called Shah Guli, an island in a U-shaped lake connected to the mainland by a causeway and overlooked by a brooding eminence with steps running up it beside a falling

29

stream. The hilltop was likely to give an agoraphobic trouble, particularly on a lowering day. They went inland some way from the crest, but, to his relief and without him having to contrive anything, soon turned to view the lake immediately at their feet. Later, he discovered that a haunting song called 'Mustafa' was sweeping the Middle East. Now, as they skirted the ridge and tumbled back down the slope, the girls linked arms and, in an innocent chorus line, sang the Persian version, '*Dast-e man dar dast-e to*' (My hand in your hand).*

At times of real dejection about his health, Horace spent his afternoons in the Institute's garden, racing — though not at T. E. Lawrence pace — through volumes from the library which was three steps up from a small, shallow swimming pool beside which the air was always fresh. (An oddly mandatory cocktail party was held in the garden for Gen. Sir Dudley Ward, new C-in-C, Middle East Land Forces, at which Horace was the only guest without a suit.) Though poorly, he treasured these idyllic days, spent in the company of older people more experienced than himself — one, now prematurely dead, became a professor of English Language at Edinburgh University — as they in turn succumbed to bouts of sickness. None was so ill as an assistant at the Hamadan summer school the year before — this was the fellow student who turned his Cambridge room into a mosque, — who declined all inoculations and was rewarded with cholera.

Except when really indisposed, Horace taught every morning and enjoyed his role as *lecteur*, for which he was paid a useful amount. One class reported him for wearing sandals without socks. Though he certainly went dangerously far in calling a course member 'stupid and lazy', he found some of the participants and support staff ludicrously touchy. Once, when he opened a door, he was surprised when two ladies behind it — simple successors of the 'thinly-clad and shrouded forms' who 'stepped silently behind the shutters' in *Persian Pictures* — donned veils at high speed, making a swishing noise like startled cockroaches or vultures.

---

* Over 30 years later, he heard a Sri Lankan 'Caribbean' group perform the song in a hotel in Doha. Puzzled by the language of their version, he asked them to identify it and was amused when they said it was Arabic.

He was also in love. At least, this was in theory so. Devoted letters passed between London and Tabriz. But he was attracted by Aghdas, a nurse on the course from Shiraz, where — rather than Jerez — Persians claim sherry comes from. What was a nurse doing at the summer school? She attended some of his classes. They met at mealtimes when, chaperoned by two other girls, one the wife of her city's governor, she arrived for disagreeable iced soup and eggplant. She had been tense with a delightful unsophistication when they had done a reel at one of the summer school's socials. Otherwise, there were obstacles. They had to call off an after-dinner soft drink date because of local hostility to earlier innocent strolls by other participants. She invited him to a walk in the Gulistan, a civic park under construction whose beauty did not yet equal that of its name — Rose Garden, the title of a work by Sa'di — but Spinner gatecrashed it with a 'Patience'-like entourage while they drank Coca-Cola and ate sweetmeats. Then, astonishingly, she invited him to see her in Shiraz, which became added to his itinerary as a result.

At the end of the summer school, marked by a farewell staff dinner at Shah Guli at which he felt in physically wretched shape, neither could leave immediately. The chaperones had departed. They went alone together for a walk in the baking afternoon heat. It had to be short because of Shi'i susceptibilities and possible violent reactions. The Muharram festival, celebrating the most important event in Shi'i history, had taken place during his stay and the self-flagellations he had witnessed (and which had reminded him of the Seville *feria*) inspired caution. Aghdas had taken a risk in proposing, or agreeing to, their ambulatory tête-à-tête and was naturally nervous, like him, as they strolled gingerly along blistering, glaring streets at the siesta hour when the likelihood of observation was small. She said,

'What sort of life do you have in Britain?'

'It's not very exciting. I work hard, play games. I have travelled a lot since being at Cambridge.'

'Is travel not exciting? You have come such a long way from your home — to witness how poor our existence is here.'

'Yes, the journey has been a marvellous experience. But I came only to speak Persian and I haven't spoken much so far. I had no thought of meeting someone like you.'

'But are you not engaged?'

The day was dazzling — the sunglasses she wore against the fierce heat made her look even more attractive than he had so far seen her. But he had to let her make the running.

'No, I'm not. How could you have imagined so?'

'They said you were receiving letters from home.'

'Not engagement letters.'

'I am so glad that you will come to Shiraz. The Park Hotel is nice.'

'I'll be there eight days from today.'

That settled, there was no need to prolong their hazardous outing. They said *Khoda Hafiz* on a bridge over a dry riverbed. He felt strangely moved when she had gone, as though subconsciously knowing that he would never see her again.

He had accepted the offer of David, one of the directing staff, of a lift in his car at the end of the summer school to Tehran via the Caspian. Also invited were Richard, Horace's Cambridge contemporary, and one of the course members. They headed along dusty roads, first past Shah Guli in the direction of the capital, then via Ardebil, the cradle of the Safavids, towards the great inland sea. 30 miles from the port of Astara, their road began to run along the Iran–Soviet border at distances of between 100 yards and a quarter of a mile. On the Soviet side, there were watchtowers at regular, short intervals. The view Horace had formed of Iran — biased by the sweeping judgements of youth — was that it was devoid of anything worth coveting and he therefore could not conceive of what they were monitoring. It did not occur to him that they were perhaps on the lookout for their own citizens seeking greater freedom.

The restful tree-lined route — the least used of the roads to the Caspian — led in due course to the Astara promenade. The town was cut in two by the frontier. Horace contrived to stray across it and had to be hauled back. They turned east and drove parallel with the Caspian, but some way from it. Before it quickly became dark, he had the impression of a sea shining under a sun slanting acutely because of the absence of dunes, and of occasional wooden summer cottages, some on stilts and all colourful and rather Welsh, hidden in lush greenery on slopes facing the water. These surroundings, nearly 100 feet below sea level and condemned by the state of his inside as neither remarkable nor attractive, were at least a complete contrast to the arid stone and desert monotones of Azerbaijan. They camped by the road. Horace neglected to unpack his mosquito net and was badly bitten during the night, though protected from malaria by his Daraprim.

The road worsened next day. David was very sick until lunchtime, on account, he thought, of a contaminated tin. The dust-laden surface, imbued with oppressive blinding and choking qualities by oncoming heavy traffic, added to his distress. Richard was in a state of gloom, downcast by the news he had recently received that he had failed his prelims. He contributed to David's unhappiness by leaping into the Caspian on one of the few occasions when it came within half a mile of the shore and holding the progress of their uncomfortable caravan up while he indulged himself. Horace was feeling too anxious about his health to join in, and their Iranian friend also abstained. David made his displeasure at Richard's selfishness clear.

When they again rejoined the Caspian at Bandar Pahlavi, he authorised a swim. The sea was very warm. It tasted of the oil refineries of Baku. The coast, with its flat shoreline and continued absence of cliffs, remained unimpressive. Horace had still seen no scenery in Iran which demanded the adjective 'beautiful'. No one else seemed to be about. They parked the car on the beach at Rudsar, hired a hut and nailed their nets to its frame.

Next day, they left the Caspian at Chalus and executed an almost perpendicular climb to the tunnel pass through the Elburz Mountains. You go in from what becomes, with hindsight, the Spring-like coolness of the northern end and debouch into the disorienting glare and boiler-room heat of desertic Iran. It was suddenly as though they had never left Tabriz. They were boosted for the transition by a subterranean cave meal of kebabs and tomatoes which Horace thought Paradise would find it difficult to beat — even though the standard fare there would be Indian. In general, Horace rated the food in Iran about the world's worst for monotony and lack of taste, only to be outdone by Mexican, which had the additional feature of a mosquito bite with every mouthful. But the cave chef could have held down a job in the Savoy.

Emerging from the tunnel and passing the Karaj Dam, they entered Tehran by following one of the roads indicated by the signpost at its western edge which points both left and right to the capital. David dropped him off at his hosts' flat. Once installed, Horace had the opportunity to slake the craving for cornflakes which had gnawed at him for weeks and squandered it by drenching them by mistake in yoghurt, which — in the days before the fruit-flavoured kind had been invented — he could not stand. He tried to take his mind off his hypochondriasis by being active. He went more than once to the Embassy cinema, swam in its two pools — one shivering under trees and containing what Gertrude Bell thought 'the coldest of cold water' in the North Tehran compound of Gulhaq — and shopped for *Dast-e man* and Haim's massive English–Persian dictionary to help his studies when he got back. He wondered if he ever would. He went by bus to the historic site of Rayy, in South Tehran, where Harun ar Rashid was born and Reza Shah — Robert Byron's Marjoribanks, the founder of the Pahlavi dynasty overthrown by Ayatollah Khomeini — is buried. Conspicuous in the narrow streets, stared at by nesting storks, Horace was startled by an unexplained outbreak of shooting and hurriedly retraced his steps.

Though a large city, he found Tehran's centre simple to navigate on foot and, early in his stay, had worked out taxi and bus routes. The British Embassy, like the Soviet one, was on Khiaban-e Firdawsi, named after the epic poet whose statue stands at the top of it and whose verse history of Iran, the *Shahname* (*Book of Kings*), they were studying at University. He was in complete agreement with Gertrude Bell that Persian was 'extraordinarily easy'. His autodidactic year at Cambridge had equipped him with sufficient Farsi to be able to hold his own in shops and at a cocktail party to which his house guest status entitled him to accompany his hosts. They were Muriel, from the summer school directing staff, and Ted, the husband she had left behind in Tehran while she did her Tabriz stint. He looked like Captain Merrick and turned out, in an engagingly Anthony Powell way, to have been the joint head boy at Horace's first school whose briefcase he had competed to carry adoringly from the station on icy junior commuter mornings twelve or so years before.

The reunion was not entirely blissful. Under his friends' roof, he abandoned the short lifetime habit — when not taking a bath — of standing in the basin to wash. The Middle East found him out, his 13 stones were too great, the sink came away from the wall and the flat was under several inches of water and his watch ruined before Ted could quell the flood.

His valetudinarian summer approached its climax. At last arrived the morning of his journey to Shiraz, about which his real or imagined symptoms must have made him fatalistic. He got up at 3.50 a.m. Troubled by constipation throughout his travels — indeed, rivalling the author of 'The Ancient Mariner' for non-production, — he was delighted to receive normal signals before it was time to leave for the 5.00 a.m. bus. When his reward was a startling quantity of very red blood, he was paralysed with fear. Had he been right, his GP wrong? What could it be but cancer? He returned, shivering, to bed. The recommended doctor thought it was piles but offered an X-ray.

He spent the day washed out by worry and drained by disappointment. Leaving Aghdas to enquire vainly after him at the Park Hotel, it did not occur to him to make a second attempt to set out. He did not write until the following day — when also there were buses running — to tell her that the Shiraz diversion was off.

Perhaps it was a blessing that the character of his next visit to the toilet was — too late — as near normality as he had been striving to achieve all summer long. He had never considered what the results of his (now abandoned) journey might have been. If he had gone, what would they have done? It had been difficult enough to go out together at all — once, and that at siesta time — in a city 600 miles from her own. He was easily-led by his emotions, convinced by the French romantic poets his school had put before him too young that loving and being loved were the most important things in life. If he had been able to see enough of her to decide that love was the word to describe his feelings for Aghdas, would he have proposed to her? Would the rest of his grand tour have gone hang? What about Mark, soon to be waiting for him — or, knowing Mark, soon to be keeping him waiting — in Ankara? What about the girl who had written to him in Tabriz and whose letters had followed him to Tehran also? These were serious questions which he did not ask himself at the time. A letter Aghdas sent to Cambridge soon after the start of the following term, and which he did not answer, showed them to be realistic.

The day after, his urine turned blood-coloured, and remained so until he was well inside Turkey once more. In confusion, and turning his back on Shiraz, he left for the rendezvous with Mark. The Mihantur bus to Tabriz was timed to depart at 5.30 a.m. He did not think for a moment that it actually would leave then. At the bus station at 5.20, however, there it was — and he had left his camera behind. Urging a taxi up to the flat, he had to knock up his long-suffering hosts. He reappeared at six o'clock, in time to take advantage of an uniquely favourable late departure.

After a long and gruelling day, they approached Tabriz as the light was failing. They rounded a succession of tight bends, each poised precariously above a vertiginous drop. The passengers called upon Allah to protect them. He obliged, and Horace was able to keep his engagement to stay with the Director of the Institute and his wife, sleeping in a hammock on one of their verandas. Again Gertrude Bell was right: it was indeed 'rather refreshing to the spirit to lie in a hammock strung between the plane trees of a Persian garden.'

* * *

Back on the border, he tried to sleep in the bus to avoid hotel costs. The Turks were much too clever for him, producing a regulation which made it an offence not to make the contribution requested to their economy.

On their last lap on the bus, a rumour began to circulate that immediate transfer to a train would be possible. The authorities were too smart. When they reached Erzurum, their passports were taken away and the passengers saw the mail train depart without them. Hospitality that night was provided by the Aras [Ararat] Oteli. Rose Macaulay's habit was to favour hotels with *Palas* in their titles: they should have been given pause by its absence now. During the night they were devoured by creatures sharing their bedding. Horace was an unusually succulent target because for the first time he had acted on his conclusion that the best way to turn the unavailability of hot water to his advantage was to wash himself and his clothes without undressing. Everything is relative, so his note that, before that, they 'dined (no lunch) superbly in the Evropa [Europe] Oteli' may mean no more than that the fare was a banquet compared with the previous night's sardines à la Lawrence of Arabia, who used to hurl his empty tins into the rhododendrons at Clouds Hill.

On two of the three occasions when the bus had broken down between Tabriz and Erzurum, an irritating Iranian passenger, directing his attention towards the encircling, unbroken desert, said, 'Have you ever seen a country as fine as Iran?' He and like-minded companions, believing that they detected in Horace a luke-warmness of admiration for their scenery, made his night on the train to Ankara sadistically unpleasant. They seemed to feel no need for sleep, for themselves or him. The compartment door slammed regularly, conversation was conducted in daytime tones — which in the Middle East frequently involve shouting — and the light was never allowed to be put out. Horace's rest was badly affected by it, though in the rack he was, at least, more com-fortable than he had been on the wooden seats of a Spanish *rápido* the previous year.

One of his fellow passengers from Tabriz to Ankara was an effete Canadian called Hans. Nerve-fraying, if not repellent, he was the only other English-speaker making the journey. Their travelling companions, who included some aggressively busybody Turks, expected them to want to be often together. Hans had lost all his luggage and, unlike Horace, not found it again. Horace rated this feeble and only to be expected in one so feckless, whom he had no wish to get to know better; after a philosophical argument with him, he noted that 'he is an ignoramus and an RC.' Hans was on his way back to Vancouver with a view to embark-ing on a diplomatic career, an ambition Horace considered he had not the slightest hope of achieving — and certainly not in Vancouver. About a year later, Horace, and his wife, the author of the letters, took a furnished flat in a small block in Montreal. Not long after they had moved in, they came down the stairs one morning to see Hans at the bottom, using the public telephone. His plans had been subject to a 3,000-mile adjustment. Perhaps he was looking for Ottawa. He had not improved.

5
Gateway of the Wind:
Turkey/Syria

Now, I can talk a little Arabic and feel as if I had acquired a new personality, new virtues, new resources. There is no sensation more pleasing than the first steps into a new language.

(Sir Arnold Wilson)

... when I tested him further the cat was out of the bag, for na'am was the only word of Arabic he knew.

(Ibn Battutah)

S ince the Lebanese civil war at least, most road crossings of Syria from Turkey have begun with the climb through the charmingly named pass of Bab al Hawa' (Gateway of the Wind). Barbed wire demarcates the frontier separating Turkey's province of Hatay from the Syrian fatherland to which it was lost when — though the world has forgotten — France, the mandatory power, severed it in 1939. In ravines to left and right of the winding road through the defile, wrecked cars are piled deep. The gorge is dotted with the ruins of mysterious buildings — huts and palaces — which have no doubt been abandoned during strife along the border. The feeling of history is strong, a feeling contributed to by the ghosts of families which, on both sides of the wire, were divided by France's act of colonial highhandedness. The spot is beautiful, and its grandeur is enhanced by the clear, cool light of evening.

The clutter of the Syrian border post sits in prosaic contrast at the head of the valley. A large open area is littered with trucks and the air is full of their fumes and horn blasts. As if in protest against the workaday environment they have themselves created to be dispirited in, the Syrian officials always have a trick in store for the unwary, and for *habitués* too. Customs and immigration are separated by a distance which is uncomfortable for the pedestrian and irritating for the driver. People are dealt with in one place, cars in another. The question is — which, on any given occasion, is which? On the strength of your rebuff last time, you drive to what you now know to be the car section, only to find — surprise, surprise! — that everything has changed and you must master a new script. The only rule at Bab al Hawa' is that the traveller is always mistaken:

'Good day. God willing, everything's going well?'

(In English) 'Why you try speak Arabi?'

'No matter. Please, deal with these papers.'

'It is not Arabi that you are speak. Green card this side' (pointing).

'But, my brother, last time cars were here.'

(Dismissive click of the tongue).

While you are establishing the current arrangements, a dozen cars — or persons, as the case may be — are able to get into the queue ahead of you. Not that it deserves the title of 'queue':

'I shall be grateful for your generosity over these papers.'

'God willing'. (Putting your passport at the bottom of the pile).

(Owner of hand reaching across you) 'Your Excellency, I intercede with Allah for you. My uncle very sick.'

(Hand brandishes passport over your shoulder). 'May your life be long, sir. I rely on your sympathetic generosity.'

A diplomatic visa is of little help. Arabic only irritates when the officials — hard-pressed and worn out by wheedling threats, attempted bribes and lack of organisation — have lost control, which they do five minutes after coming on duty. They haven't invited you to share in their culture, you're probably a spy, the juxtaposition of your Arabic and your dress and features is in all likelihood ludicrous, foreigners can't possibly master Arabic anyway, the chances are that you're making fun of them... Your carnet descends ever further from the top of a cairn on which competing documentation descends like a blizzard, as hordes of travellers, disregarding the official's feeble protests, plump their papers down on top of yours. The only sure way to avoid being forgotten and ignored for eternity is to have with you a fair-haired child, who will be patted and caressed by everyone present and will soften the heart, and enliven the day, of even the most harassed and hostile Syrian immigration man.

* * *

It was appropriate that Horace's infinitely more sweet than bitter joust with Arabic should have begun in such a spot. As guide to the colloquial language, he possessed only the *Spoken Iraqi Arabic* of Van Ess, Gertrude Bell's wise friend, which seeks to teach the dialect of Basrah, 1,000 miles away and in the wrong country. From the start, Horace understood everything that was said to him and responded in accordance with the missionary's coaching. Van Ess does not go into great detail about the verb. Horace had not got very far in trying to understand its workings when, between Ankara and Antakya with Mark, he should have been devoting his leisure time to Turkish and, for the moment, had to make do with verbless sentences. At Bab al Hawa', his first Arab interlocutor, informing him that the tongue he was using was unrecognisable, was delighted to have the chance to show a foreigner up. (The Egyptian guard on the gate of Alexandria harbour was perhaps doing the same:

British Professor of Arabic: *As salamu alaykum. Atatafadh-dhalu an tukhbiruni 'ayna't tariq ila'l Qahirah.*

Egyptian official: *Pardonnez-moi, Monsieur, je ne parle pas français*).

Getting his own back, Horace exasperated him by breaking the ballpoint pen he had borrowed from him to demonstrate a point of grammar — the humiliating recourse of out-of-depth linguists.

There is a tremendous thrill in discovering that you can speak a language which you have only read before. It is intensified when its written and spoken versions, as in Arabic, are so different. The foreign student of the language, unlikely to attend an Arabic-medium school or live with an Arab family, has to travel in the Middle East to make the working acquaintance of the vernacular. Until come to terms with, it remains an object of awe. The Arabic script is mystery enough to the beginner and the grammar is full of terminology which — faithfully reproduced in Thatcher — gives it a fascinating yet forbidding aura. Its native speakers, who to a man believe that foreigners cannot master it and that those who try to are agents of some kind, do their utmost to reinforce the myth of the toughness of the language of God, given to them in the Qur'an, so that they alone should have true knowledge of it. The West has accepted their estimation of it. Many of those who teach it regard their students as presumptuous for attempting the task and then belittle them for making a hit-and-miss job of it.

Even if the border official did not rate very highly his efforts at handling his language, there was no doubt that in reality Horace was to some extent on his wavelength and communicating at least after a fashion. All his fears and apprehension, by-products of his anxiety to do well in a tongue which was of real importance to him, vanished at that moment in a haze of beginner's luck.

✳ ✳ ✳

Before a later transit of Bab al Hawa', during a short break from Ankara which took Horace and his wife as far as Aleppo, their Rover had entered one of its periodic phases when it would hardly go. There was no Rover agent in Aleppo. Though the garage recommended by their famous Armenian hotel, the Barun — in whose visitors' book were the names of Lawrence of Arabia and Agatha Christie, — warned them to drive the 520 miles back at a maximum speed of 50–55 m.p.h., they risked prolonging the journey — expecting the car to break down at any second — with a diversion on the edge of the area of north Syria which contains many famous dead cities, like Carchemish, where Lawrence spent a period as an "archaeologist" before the First World War. Their objective was Qal'at Simun where, like a petrified nesting bird, St Simeon Stylites lived for 30 years with a chain around his neck atop a 60-foot pillar. The stone of the surrounding village and the encircling hills was marmoreal like Palestine. The custodian of the site revealed that there was a category of visitor even more interested in St Simeon than them. A group of sightseers earlier in the week had gone off with a haul of *objets d'art* which, unlike the Elgin Marbles, had been kept until then in their proper context to the greater enlightenment of the tourist.

Bygone Heat

* * *

The last time they passed through Bab al Hawa', they had no child with them. In the rush to secure a reasonable place in the queue, they guessed wrong again. Horace was furious. Chancing his arm like Arthur Ransome on the Estonian–Soviet frontier, and unmindful of Freya Stark's maxim that 'the one thing that never pays in the East is to lose one's temper..,' he committed the only sin that, in Egypt, Lord Cromer would not pardon and flung his passport at the emigration officer who had rejected him. The official plunged into a sulk, would have nothing more to do with him and left his position, calling for his superior. Horace feared arrest. The result was far different. The supervisor looked him over reprovingly, processed their papers with unprecedented rapidity (his slighted colleague whining about his humiliation throughout) and wished them the company of Allah on their journey through Hatay. Horace's instinctively chosen tactic had worked but he made a mental note to be selective in repeating it.

6

Fertile Crescent: Syria/Jordan/Lebanon

Here is the East in its pristine
confusion.

(Robert Byron)

... what a different history might have
been written in Palestine if the
instinct of the (Zionists) ... had been
to share.

(Freya Stark)

Horace had been right to veto Mark's idea of meeting up in Aleppo. By the time he reached Ankara, his friend was already a day late — a day Horace spent worrying about the health condition he had brought with him from Iran, particularly the oversize heart.

When Mark finally arrived, they set off for Damascus by the central route. After Konya, Tarsus and Iskenderun, they reached Antioch, now Turkified as Antakya. Of it, little remains to bear witness to former greatness, but the fruit juices poured from containers strapped to the backs of its vendors there are unique in their quality. In Reyhanlı, shown on the map as being right on the border, they understood that it was too far to walk to it. They bribed their bus driver to take them the rest of the way. Imagine doing that at home! But the border area is uncongested and there was no one around to report him. They passed an identical bus overturned in a ditch and imagined that it had been the victim of too desperate a race back to legality.

The Turkish frontier post, emulating European standards of efficiency so as to contrast sharply with those of its Arab neighbour, passed them through in rapid time. All of the other few travellers had transport. They had to hitch a lift on a lorry through Bab al Hawa' and then take a taxi to Aleppo. The taxi ride was alarming. Syrian drivers turn off their lights until oncoming vehicles are behind them and thus pass each other in total darkness.

Aleppo, dominated by its magnificent citadel, was hot and vibrant, with superb smells and the first clean sheets since Ankara. The racket of its streets awoke them at 6.00 the next morning. Registration with Security was the initial task. Police at the first station at which they enquired drove them to the correct office at frightening, breakneck speed, with their siren helping them to force a passage — now overtaking on the left, now on the right — between trams. People were pleased to see them, and in no time they had been taken under the wing of three young men — members of the intelligentsia who did not go to the mosque — who gave them a conducted tour of their beautiful city by Volkswagen and took them for a splendid three-course meal based on kabab and arak.

Aleppo's welcome made Horace euphoric, and his Arabic studies felt magnificently worthwhile. Though Dora Altounyan believed that 'an old stick-in-the-mud like Aleppo will never do anything so exciting as revolt', the grey old capital of north Syria — like so many northern towns (Tripoli in Lebanon, Mosul, Edinburgh) — was out of step with the seat of national government. It was also, Horace thought, far in advance of any city he had seen in Turkey or Iran. He found it hard to imagine it, however, as the home town of the children of the classic Lake District stories of Arthur Ransome, who however found it 'a far finer city' than he had expected.

The bus to Homs via Hamah — famous for its great Roman water wheels and soon to be notorious for the government massacre of thousands of its political opponents — was immensely long and skilfully fast. They admired the beehive villages fringing a charming desert and separated from the road by broad and efficient-looking irrigation canals whose clean, strong waters seemed to race them. The landscape had a thrusting, fresh appearance.

In Homs they were again taken in hand by hospitable citizens, who drove them to Buhayrat Qatinah, the local lake, and fed and fêted them. They sat in a public park, sharing a *nargileh*, watching a Sputnik cross a sky which had not produced rain for four years and listening to confidences about Syria's racially tinged dis-satisfaction with the Egyptian-dominated United Arab Republic.

They made two memorable journeys from Homs. The first was to Krak des Chevaliers, one of the finest of the Crusader castles, which blends delightfully in with the surrounding black and rounded barren hillsides. (The visit was marred by battles with people they suspected of trying to dupe them over fares and who demanded too much, unasked, to guard their possessions.) The other was to Palmyra, to which a bumpy bus took them in four hours across the Syrian desert.

The Arab world has not produced its fair share of heroines. Apart from Shahrazad and the Queen of Sheba, who probably enjoyed no more than temporary immigrant status, few readily spring to mind. More should, notably the Prophet's favourite wife, A'ishah. The glittering Roman frontier city of Palmyra, however, is synonymous with another, Zenobia, its appealing and heroic queen. After the death of the husband to whom she was immemorially faithful, she took Asia Minor and Egypt from Rome in the name of her second son but was defeated in AD 272 and dragged there in chains behind the chariot of Aurelian, her conqueror. The columns of her city glinted in the last rays of the sun as they arrived. You round a bend and there is Palmyra occupying a vast plain far below. The pillars march in every direction and the visual effect is of an entirely golden panorama, homogenous yet — *pace* Robin Fedden — strange.

Palmyra has since sprouted hotels linked to international chains, but although the *Guide Bleu* then listed establishments to which it had awarded one star or even two, in Horace's memory the accommodation available consisted of a small, earth-surfaced enclosure bounded by chicken wire. Their bus was said to be returning to Homs at 10.00 the next morning. Taking no chances, they planned to be early. Horace claimed to be able to wake at any hour he chose and they were up at 5.00 without the benefit of alarm clock. Perhaps eating horribly, though cheaply, the night before, impelled them into early rising. It certainly upset their stomachs. They raced round the ruins, admiring particularly the Way of Columns, the Great Temple of Baal and the theatre and finding Zenobia's Palace still difficult to assail. Mark's internal *bouleversement* made locating one of her bathrooms a matter of urgency.

A boy spat at them as they waited to board the bus. Tourists from the West were infrequent visitors to sites like Krak and Palmyra, and their fair colouring, and the beards and shorts which betrayed their cultural naïveté, made them objects of suspicion and ridicule to desert dwellers. The bus left 40 minutes late. They were allotted seats right at the back. Their fellow passengers enjoyed the spectacle of their discomfort as they leaped and plunged all the way to Homs.

Gluttons for punishment, and delayed for half an hour by an inter-passenger squabble, they took an immediate connecting bus to the capital. Despite their states of health, making Horace rush for cover as soon as they reached the terminus in Damascus, they dined satisfactorily, as nearly always; though their hotel was the worst yet, they slept well on the roof.

Their fragile insides made their Damascus sightseeing even more perfunctory than their normal practice. They admired the Umayyad Mosque and marvelled to discover Saladin's tomb there. A boy deliberately rode his bicycle over Horace's foot in the Street Called Straight. Risking a fight in the *suq*, he hurled him to the ground. His assailant's inappropriate choice of venue was a harbinger of the put-up job which, religiously speaking, Jerusalem turned out to be.

* * *

He disliked Jordan from the first. Physically, the country was fine. How could he not have loved sites like Jerash, Petra, Mushattah and Araq al Amir and found the scenery predominantly 'nice'? The trouble was the people — or him. He and Mark thought the inhabitants they met puerile, ungrateful and too quick to criticise. There was, of course, something to be said in favour. There were several free taxi rides. When they were lost, people did not direct, but took, them to their destination. In some Arab countries, entry into mosques is forbidden, or difficult, for non-Muslim foreigners. In Jerusalem, Horace was ushered into the pulpit of Al Aqsa, one of Islam's oldest and holiest religious buildings, the 'furthest' mosque from Mecca.

His first entry into Jordan was dramatic. He and Mark had walked through Dera'a, the dusty and aromatic Syrian frontier town. They were picked up by a Volkswagen Beetle, whose driver had hardly welcomed them aboard when he was visibly disturbed by news on his car radio, which they did not understand. He dumped them at the Ramthah Rest House on the Jordanian border and made off to the north again as fast as he could go.

They gathered during the evening, when King Husayn's voice, addressing his people, repeatedly caressed the warm air surrounding them, that there had been trouble in Amman. This accounted for their chauffeur's eccentric behaviour. The rest house was inaccurately named: they found it impossible to sleep because of mosquitoes. They were in any case feeling isolated, and apprehensive about the situation which might await them in the morning.

To their surprise, the immigration officials made no move to delay their entry next day or to ask them to rethink their route. Their route was in any case, and as always, in the hands of the drivers they could persuade to stop for them. Two lifts, one by lorry, brought them to the capital through the sandiest country they had been in. Its deep brown hue was the perfect backcloth to the blood-red accoutrements of the guardians of the desert who examined their passports at frequent intervals. They visited the scene of the event that had unnerved the VW owner. An explosion, meant for the King, had blown away one wing of the Foreign Ministry building and killed ten people including the Prime Minister. It seemed extraordinary under the circumstances that they should have been able to set foot in the country without having to put up with any kind of inconvenience or restriction. If there was a curfew, they were not aware of it. Five days later they bumped into *Daily Mail* and *Daily Telegraph* men in a bookshop and — excited at the possibility of fame — told them all they knew.

In the interim, by a passenger service which soon ceased to feature in the timetable, they travelled by train from Amman to Ma'an on the most southerly Hijaz Railway stretch which Lawrence of Arabia had left operational. (20 years later Horace met at the Aqaba citadel an old man who claimed to have been in the reception party when Lawrence took the town 63 years previously.) They spent the eight-hour journey in the company mostly of peasants who, the further down the line they stopped, became increasingly negroid. They were hung about with rifles, bandoliers and silver daggers, and Horace and Mark felt that their first false move might be their last. But there is a sophistication about even the *fallahun* of Jordan that blocks the kind of unruly incident that is commonplace in Syria, which is nonetheless much the more genuine and hospitable country.

The Petra bus had broken down, but the engaging owner of the plushest taxi yet encountered — not difficult, since most Middle Eastern taxis are at any given time 20 years old — was anxious to drive them to Ma'an instead:

'You want go Ma'an? I take you. Best railway taxi. You pay me three *dananir** each person.'

'No, thank you. Too much. We're poor students. We walk.'

'Allah karim. Is too much kilometer. I take. You my guests here in Jordan. If you want give me anything, whatever you like.'

They accepted gratefully. In the Arab world, hitchhikers in principle pay for lifts, but more often than not friendly in-transit conversations soften the hearts of drivers who are initially demanding. The oral exchange has been payment enough. And if you are pro-Palestinian, as Mark and Horace were and are, you are lucky if you can proceed on your way without being delayed by pressing invitations to meals or weighed down with gifts.

The driver of the lorry which stopped for them early next day was not quite in this category. He demanded 500 *fils* each for the journey from Ma'an to Wadi Musa, the village gateway to Petra, but agreed to accept 100. As he pulled up regularly for local clients, Horace and Mark became jammed against the leading edge of the loading platform, above the driver's cab, a good observation point whence Horace was pleased to be able to understand the exchanges when the truck stopped to take on more passengers, if not the bargains being struck:

'Mark, he's only charged those people 20 *fils*.'

'What?! He must have seen us coming.'

'Shall we do something about it?'

'Do you think your Arabic's up to it?'

'I'm going to have a go. I object to being swindled.'

Indignant, on arrival they requested a part refund of their trivial fare. Protestations flew, a heated argument began, and the commander of an Arab Legion police post became involved. He occupied a position of vantage on an escarpment above the road where their lift had ended. Berating them for their lack of what he conceived of as true British spirit, he scornfully refused to help them settle on a compromise figure lower than 75 *fils* and they had to

---

*   Dinars, an example of the Arabic 'broken plural'.

make do with a 25 per cent refund. He then relieved them of their Petra entrance fee, drafted in a guide to conduct them round the ruins and — displaying none of the politeness Freya Stark had received from the Wadi Musa police — sent them on their way accompanied by expressions of contempt. As they descended the further side of the tell guarding the entry to Petra, 'Such behaviour not British' was the last phrase of his workmanlike English to reach their ears. They decided that he was typical of one kind of Jordanian.

The guide had perhaps been suborned by the policeman. Throughout, he displayed anxiety to conclude their joint business with all possible dispatch. He rushed them through the Siq, the narrow defile which leads into the heart of the pre-Muslim, Arabo–Roman troglodyte city, whose name is the same as that of Peter, the Rock. Horace was not permitted to linger to marvel as the Siq narrowed above their heads and then, without warning, confronted them round a bend, as in a frame, with the spectacular view of the *Khaznah* (treasury) to which chocolate boxes do no kind of justice. They had reached it in record time. Their exploration of nearby edifices, including the impressive theatre, was equally rapid and unsatisfactory.

At the residential area opposite the theatre, where money with menaces had been demanded of Layard, their escort tried to head them back the way they had come. It was only the chance passing of a British archaeologist, digging further along, that enabled them to locate the *Dayr* and other buildings at the western extremity of the site. Report had it that a cave near the restaurant there was the home of an American girl who during her tour of Petra had fallen in love at first sight with its owner.

It wasn't the guide who deprived the scene of impact. The condition of their stomachs had not yet reached a concentration-disturbing pitch. Petra is interesting and weird. But, even with its roseate complexion, it fails to outclass the columns of Palmyra or, indeed, of Jerash.

When they had clambered up to Wadi Musa again, they fell back into the clutches of their erstwhile police tormentor, who was keen to rejoin battle with them. It did not need their omission to tip their lacklustre guide to set him off again. Having allowed them to eat their usual improvised supper in the courtyard of his compound, he encouraged a cat to take a close interest in their meal as they sat cross-legged on the ground. It minced through it, sniffing, and returned with tongue and paw poised. No matter how much they urged it to go and pushed and, finally, shoved it out of the way, it would not desist. Eating being impossible under the circumstances, Horace grabbed it, opened a door which was within easy reach and placed — this is perhaps an understatement — the irritating creature inside.

'British supposed to be kind to animals,' he sneered. 'How can you be Britishs?'

'We would just like to eat our supper. Then we'll be as kind to the cat as you would wish. It doesn't look as if you can have fed it today.'

'Britishs say animals man's best friend. Seem not true the other way round. Love me, love my dog.'

'We don't love you much. Why should we love your cat? Anyway, the saying refers to dogs.'

'Why you different from other Britishs? I don't let people cruel to animals be in my compound. You free sleep outside.'

Relieved to escape his needling, they spent the night on the rounded shoulder of a precipitous slope, beneath the clearest imaginable sky. The stars were white and sharp and so close that they could almost bathe in them. Thanks to a sadistic Jordanian, they had a glorious sleep and a memorable awakening in the freshness of a mountain morning.

Heading for Jerusalem — now known as East Jerusalem — they caught a Mercedes, whose awful driver was going as far as Jericho. He named his price, they made their 'poor student' counter, he gave them lunch and would hear of no payment at all when he dropped them: 'You surely would not insult me with money?' At the lowest point on earth, with the Dead Sea visible to the south, they indulged between lifts in Petra cigarettes.

The Caliph Umar is to non-Muslims the most appealing of Muhammad's immediate successors. When he took Jerusalem for Islam in AD 637/8, he refused to pray in the Church of the Holy Sepulchre for fear of giving his warriors the pretext to convert it into a mosque. Though he was so tall that, in a crowd, he looked as if he were mounted, like Jesus he entered the city on the back of a donkey. When Allenby took Jerusalem from the Ottomans in the First World War, he made his entrance on foot. Horace and Mark arrived by lorry. The highway was broad, white and romantic. The countryside had the characteristic marble veneer of Palestine and Jordan, a scrubbed brightness — as if the municipal water cart had just been round — which should have been glaring, as in the Gulf, but in fact delighted the eye. As the road swept up to the skyline, they descried the minarets of Jerusalem, impossibly high above them as befitted the world's holiest spot. When Umar came, the approach view from their direction was of the churches of the Mount of Olives. Now that the area of Muslim control has been more than halved by the Israeli seizure of the city, the skyline is no doubt dominated by paramilitary blocks of flats. (Having reunited the whole of Palestine in 1967, the Israelis could, with magnanimity of spirit, have seized Freya Stark's 'great Jewish opportunity', prevented more than three decades of slaughter in the Middle East and made the tragedy of Lebanon unnecessary. Horace felt it a terrible day when East Jerusalem ceased to be Arab. He visited his cut-price furniture supplier in South London just as the news had begun to come through. 'Isn't it good to see them getting it in the neck?,' the storekeeper said, assuming — as people like him could still do with some confidence — that Horace would naturally agree with him or would not dare to demur. In fact, he made a suitable rejoinder and took his custom elsewhere.)

At the time of their visit, East Jerusalem belonged to Jordan, which had taken it when Britain abandoned its Palestine mandate in 1948. Horace, unconvinced about the significance of Christ, nonetheless felt that the Holy City was completely 'right' and one of the only two places which had come up to his expectations. (Granada was the other.) He agreed with Robert Byron that here, for once, was 'a capital whose appearance is worthy of its fame'. He and Mark were moved to be in so patently sacred a place. The fact that the Israelis were just over the border, only yards away beyond the Mandelbaum Gate and the barbed wire which partitioned the city to the north, added a culminating tension to the atmosphere. The apparently fake nature of most of the relics, notably Jesus's last footprint, did not mar their euphoria (as it had not Ronald Storrs's), though it was threatened by petty squabbling for authority among representatives of the various Christian sects whom they encountered. It did not approach the sort of violence witnessed by Layard, but officials of the Armenian Church locked them in the Holy Sepulchre during a lunch hour to mark their turn to be top.

Set amid its totally appropriate scenery, Jerusalem was easily able to shrug off commercialism. The Dome of the Rock could not have been finer. The *suq*s teemed as from time immemorial. It was hard to believe that the inhabitants of Christ's day had been significantly different from those they passed in the street as they gossiped, cleared their throats, spat, looked colourful and bargained. Horace bought a *nargileh* and immediately allowed it to slip from his grasp, shattering it in tiny pieces on the *suq* floor.

The onset of the Palmyra tummy which Horace and Mark had nursed for a number of days did not manage to spoil things. It was in Hebron that it gained the ascendancy. On arrival in the town, whose name in Arabic is Al Khalil,* they had been taken over by a student, who conducted them, much faster than they wished, round the striking Mosque of Abraham, whose tomb is — or was — its showpiece. The mosque is approached up an impressive staircase, steep and long like an outside Muslim pulpit, on which the local glass-blowers sell their fine produce. (Though absurdly low, their prices are undercut by their counterparts who operate off the Military Museum in Damascus and blow to order.) Horace and Mark resolved to return one day to view the mosque, one of the undoubted highlights of their journey, in a more leisurely and reverent manner than their escort was willing to permit them, and Horace did so twice in the next six years.

The lightning tour of the mosque completed, the problem of how to get rid of their student companion arose. They did not show themselves to be very adept at the task:

Student: 'Now I take you Ibrahim's oak.'
Mark (suffering badly): 'I'll just wait here till you get back.'
Student: 'Is only half kilometer, go and come.'
Horace: 'What is this oak?'
Student: 'Here Ibrahim sacrifice Ishaq (Isaac).'
Mark: 'All the more reason not to go when I'm feeling like this.'

---

* 'The friend of God', i.e. Ibrahim (Abraham).

Student: 'If not go, you will be sad always. My teacher, he
  tell me specially take you.'
Horace: 'Come on, Mark. Once in a lifetime.'
Mark: 'Deathtime, more like.'
Student: 'Ibrahim's oak, he make you feel all new. We go
  now.'

It was an enormous distance, and they trudged along with their
irrepressible guide fussing like a collie. Mark lasted out until, bad
tempered and cursing each other for weakly giving in to their
tormentor, they finally reached Abraham's blessed — and unmem-
orable — tree. Afterwards, relief emboldened them, and they lost
no time in driving their escort away. They felt bad about it when
he did not ask for payment for his services.

They hurried back to Bethlehem, which they had bypassed in the
morning. Sharing a bottle of beer in such a place seemed blasphe-
mous. They were rushed round the Church of the Nativity, where
the sects vie for supremacy in an even more undignified fashion
than in Jerusalem, and unsurprised to find their tour ending in a
souvenir shop. They hastened on, having decided to head for home.

One of their first lifts towards the Jordan next day was with a
driver who, as he accelerated, began the usual litany:

'Are you German?'

'No, we're poor British students.'

'The British poor?' (Quickly coming to a stop). 'Find someone
else to take you.' (Pulling the door sharply shut behind them.)

They did not greatly relish his attitude, but a few years later they
were able to appreciate that the wrong note struck with someone
who — as perhaps was the case with him as well as the policeman
at Wadi Musa — might have lost his land, home, possessions and
loved ones thanks to Balfour would certainly merit such a response. They had not known then that more than half of Jordan's
population was Palestinian, the majority uprooted as a direct
consequence of his evil Declaration. Horace later knew in Amman
many people whom Balfour had made refugees thrice over. Nonetheless, it remained typical that some of the Jordanians they came
across should have taken it out on people like them who were
clearly far too young to bear any responsibility for their plight,
whose parents had not even met when the Declaration was pro-

nounced. This was in marked contrast to Syria, which — admittedly less directly affected by the existence of Israel at that point — had shown them nothing but courtesy and open warmth.

When in due course they re-emerged from Jordan, a Beetle counterpart of the one in which they had entered the country dropped them right at the Dera'a customs, obviating the need for them to walk past the border toilets, as redolently representative of the Middle East as the Baghdad Saray and, indeed, the metallic humidity of the Gulf when the aircraft's doors open. They ended up in their least dignified means of transport, a lorry with no springs which had not been cleaned since its last, sheep-carrying run. They travelled in the back, in burning heat, all the way to Damascus, bumped and jolted until their gratitude at only being charged 1.25 Syrian Liras each turned into contempt. On the rebound, they selected for recuperation the most expensive hotel of their journey. Their mood included an element of anxiety to be home now that they had called a halt to the Grand Tour. They left early the next day for Beirut and the boat back.

They found that they had three days to wait for a boat. The Lebanese capital had already been the site of a civil war, a practice for the one of unimaginable barbarism which was to set in in the mid-1970s. To them, newcomers, violence seemed to hang in the air.

The pre-embarkation period passed actively, partly to counter the effects of staying on the ninth floor, where Horace could not sleep, of a hot and humid hotel boasting no lift. Hitchhiking back out of Beirut on one of the days, and aiming for Baalbek, they became apprehensive about the deferential attitude of one of their chauffeurs; gathering that their elaborate roadside gesticulating had called up a meterless, 'unofficial taxi', they requested an immediate stop and scrambled out. He was understanding about their error, levied no fee and waved encouragingly as he drove away, his sympathetic approach contrasting with the Lebanese reputation, in general justified, for money-grabbing.

Appropriately enough in a place called, in antiquity, Heliopolis, the City of the Sun, it was enormously hot in Baalbek. Though not feeling that it outdid Palmyra, the location of which is far superior, they were impressed by the remains there of the Temples of Bacchus and Jupiter, made up of the tallest columns and largest stone blocks found in Roman building; compared with the Little Temple, the Parthenon — visited when their ship stopped at Piraeus — was to seem small. They little suspected the dreadful fate which would befall Baalbek, so soon to be a civil war battleground for Lebanon, Syria, Israel and Iran.

The thuggery which only just failed to wreck Lebanon later was well demonstrated on their return journey to Beirut. One of their drivers — even worse than the Slovene Communist Party Secretary — overtook on blind bends down the racetrack to the capital. He pointed out the spot where he had written off another car the previous week. Their kamikaze drove at maniacal speed. Horace was only able to restrain him by addressing him non-stop. The rules of Eastern hospitality compelled him to lessen the fury of his acceleration in an attempt to make out what was being said, in deliberately low tones and in the Van Ess dialect, which was even less applicable in Lebanon than it had been in Syria. They parted from him with barely concealed scorn.

On their final full day in the Levant they went to Byblos, 'the oldest continually populated town in the world', whose name has given us both 'book' and 'Bible'. Less interested now in history than in blatant tourism, they spent the time swimming just off the charmingly reconstructed Roman theatre which stands at the point of high tide. Horace noted that they ate grandly for once.

✻ ✻ ✻

During a winter journey to Jerusalem three years later, Horace and his wife ran out of petrol a mile before Rutbah, about halfway between Baghdad and Amman. It was cold when they finally reached the H4 Rest House. Their room, reminding him of skiing accommodation, and with two outside walls overlooking the Syrian Desert, had only a small electric fire for heating. It was connected to a socket whose three holes were activated by a two-pin plug and a twig. A tap which would produce no water in the evening flooded the bathroom during the night. They had a freezing start in the morning.

In Jerusalem, they stayed in the American Colony Hotel, right on the border where there had been bad firing earlier in the year. 'Israel — horrible, 30 yards away,' Horace's diary said. It had become ever more poignant to visit the West Bank, which he did once more before its seizure, and to stay amid the emotive Palestinian landscape and unmatchable air in which the inevitability of an eventual Israeli takeover could be clearly felt. They noticed the Hashimite Hotel where Horace had stayed with Mark. Their waiters said life had been better under the British. A Damascus University student of philosophy showed them round Al Aqsa. They saw another last footprint of Christ's during a tour of the Mount of Olives and Gethsemane. They revisited Bethlehem and Hebron and, seeing how far they could get towards the Israeli border, turned back when the villagers of Yatta proved hostile. A similar atmosphere greeted them in Nablus, in the northern and more vengeful part of the West Bank. They crossed the old Nablus and Haifa Railway several times. The inhabitants had plenty to be vengeful about, in Horace's view. Their resentment at their fate was in many cases exacerbated by the sight of their family homes just over the border being lived in by usurpers. The narrow neck of land which separated them from the clearly visible Mediterranean and which — though it was only a few kilometres wide — the Arab world's armies had been unable to cut in 1948, must daily have taunted their impotence.

At the Dead Sea Horace tried to reach Qumran, where the scrolls were found. A general's jockey showed them the way and got them stuck in the sand; they had to be towed out by other tourists and then return the jockey — suffering from severe loss of face — to his starting point.

On their way back to Baghdad, they visited Old Jericho (Tell as Sultan) and had a long and friendly talk with two young refugees who, 'like everyone else this time', blamed no one but the British government for their situation. Their car overheating, they drove through wonderful Alpine country to Jerash and Amman, where they lunched in the old colonial Philadelphia Hotel. They arrived at teatime to stay with people they had known in Baghdad — the husband an admirer of Horace's wife — and hoped in vain that there would be something for supper. There was, however, lunch next day, before they resumed their drive, and Horace's main course included a piece of glass.

7

To the Garden of Justice:* Cambridge–Baghdad

A signpost pointing up an empty road said 'Baghdad'.

(Jonathan Raban)

Horace believed that Fowell, the senior tutor, had admitted him to the college for knowing the French for 'bagpipes'. Subsequently, he had frequently seen him hobbling on his stick round the main quad. But not counting a 'long vac' Russian course, which taught him only to say *Ya nye govoryu po-Ruski* with great conviction before he pulled out early to face the stress of getting married, it was not until his last night in Cambridge that, for the first time for five years, he met Fowell again. He had done much better in his finals than he or anyone else had forecast and, as a result, found himself seated on the senior tutor's left at the graduation dinner top table.

They did not exchange a word until it came to the fruit. Horace began to peel an apple and was dismayed to see a piece of skin fly from his knife and hit Fowell on the cheek. The senior tutor's piercing blue eyes swung round to gaze at him:

'Have you considered what you will do if the balloon goes up?'

It was as memorable an opening gambit as the first remark

---

* This is the meaning of Baghdad if — as Margoliouth and Freya Stark agree — its name is derived from Persian. If it is Arabic, it embodies a heavy hint that the inhabitants of the city swagger and strut about. (According to Abd al Aziz ad Duri, the Andalusi poet Ibn Jubayr accused them of arrogance in 1185.) The Persian derivation is preferred by contemporary Iraqis.

addressed to him, three months later, by the director of the Canadian postgraduate institution to which he went on from Cambridge. Then, he discovered the great man sitting at a large desk with his head bowed above a pen which appeared to be in the throes of creativity. He gave every impression of being oblivious to the presence of the new student for whom he had worked hard to find financial support, but Horace was not convinced by the display. The wait irritated him as he looked about the room. Five minutes after he had been admitted, the director looked up. 'I see that you are contemplating the lacunae in my bookshelves,' he said.

Horace had heard the Fowell question before, when his friend, the future international hurdler, had told him that it had been posed to him. It had to do with spying.

'Only in general terms. I've formulated no definite plan.'

'Come and see me before you leave Cambridge.'

Horace had no reason to anticipate that enrolling in the Canadian university — against doing a PhD in which the Cambridge supervisor who had sent him to Tabriz had advised, correctly as it turned out — would decide his life's work as distinct from its theme. He therefore accepted Fowell's invitation. Once he had done so, their outbreak of conversation ceased and the senior tutor levered his shoulders back in the direction whence they had swivelled to so surprising an effect. While eager to investigate any possibility of a job, Horace was astonished that one had arisen on the basis of little knowledge and less talk. His self-esteem nonetheless soared.

All packed, after breakfast next morning he crossed the main quad, wet with dew even in June, and ascended Fowell's staircase. He knocked on the inner door. There was a scampering inside worthy of Rabbit in *Winnie the Pooh* or Dr Grantly and Ripton Thompson hurriedly hiding forbidden literature, before the door opened a crack and a myopic stare assessed him:

'Come in young man, quick.'

Like a soldier unconvinced that it is safest to stand still when flares are fired, he threw the door wide, pulling Horace inside, and then slammed and locked it. Indicating an upright chair, he collapsed behind a desk weighed down with portentous-looking volumes:

'Thank you for coming. What time are you departing?'

58

'I'm hoping to catch the 10.41.'

'Straight to the point, then. Are you embarking on a career?'

'I'm starting postgraduate work abroad in September but I don't know whether or not it will lead to a career.'

'Have you ever thought of the Foreign Office?'

'Yes, I would have gone in for it if academic things had not come up first.'

'Willing to discuss it? There's a man in London it might interest you to meet.'

Fowell reached for the phone.

'Ben, it's Jon. Got a chap here you should see ... Tension ... What's your first name? ... Horace Tension ... Leaving Cambridge today but doing a long vac. course... What in? ... Russian... 17th at 11.00 suit you?'

* * *

Passing the building where, the plaque said, De Gaulle had organised the rebirth of France, Horace found his way to the block containing Stanier. The entrance was round the side and the door was screened by a sort of greenhouse. Stanier was pleasantly urbane, and Horace was not surprised, years later, when his name became known, if only fleetingly, as that of a writer of spy stories. They had lunch in his club and the vaguest kind of proposals were put before him. He was unsure of exactly what was being suggested and was glad to have the excuse of Canada so as to be able to prevaricate without discourtesy. After the meal, he was relieved to be back once more in a world of which, for the time being at least, he was still in control.

A year later, after Canada had indeed disappointed him, the route to his alternative first choice of career seemed uncertain. Horace took up Stanier's standing invitation to more smoked salmon. Although he was as unwilling as before to commit himself to something which remained so unclear, he was happy, *faute de mieux*, to fall in with Stanier's suggestion of employment on the fringes of the Foreign Office. Six months afterwards, this led to an offer of a posting to Baghdad. Anxious to go overland, he was required to leave ten days earlier than he wanted so as not to miss vital briefing in Beirut.

59

Bygone Heat

*   *   *

The normal characterfulness of Jugoslavia was readily apparent. In Slavonski Brod, the hotel orchestra played 'Tipperary' (twice) and 'Auld Lang Syne' in their honour. They slept in the bridal suite in the Hotel Moskva in Belgrade, met a man with an axe in Kragujevac and, soon after narrowly avoiding driving at full speed over a 12-inch high 'sleeping policeman' on the autoput, ran out of petrol on the outskirts of Skopje. With its roads clogged by horse and cart traffic squelching in the rain through rutted, muddy streets, the city had — his diary said — 'all the depressing marks of the Middle East' and none of the uplifting ones. They spent a night there and a downpour and high winds caused Horace to voice doubts about the stability of the Makedonija Hotel where they ate supper. Next day, there was a two-and-three-quarter-hour wait south of Skopje when the autoput was blocked by a lorry. Uncomfortable nights in Greece, where they were surprised to encounter no bandits on the road to Kavalla, and Turkey — where soldiers stopped them to offer cigarettes, their car's performance was badly affected by steep inclines on the road to Ankara and they saw in Adana the John F. Kennedy Body Work and Paint Shop — made them wish that they had not chosen to travel by road.

They contrived to get onto the wrong carriageway of the Beirut autoroute in the dark. He knew from three years before that, even on the correct side of the road, driving in Lebanon was stressful enough. He thought of the story about Egypt in which the foreigner disembarks from his ship in Alexandria, gets his car unloaded with the usual difficulty and, unused to Eastern ways, seeks guidance from a port official at the harbour exit gate:

'I say, which side of the road do you drive on in this country?

Official (trained in handling tourists): 'Drive any side you like, sir.'

He was to be in the Sudan when it changed the rule of the road from left to right overnight without mishap. It couldn't have been done in Lebanon without immense carnage.

Though they extricated themselves from their alarming situation with surprising ease, they counted themselves lucky to have saved their skins. Then they could not find a hotel room. They reconciled themselves to sleeping in the car, parked on the Beirut Corniche.* Horace settled down behind the steering wheel, which on the Washbrook trip he had decided was the most conducive position for sleeping. Sleep did not come. He was still wide awake when a melon moving behind the back window and down the side of the car made his blood run cold before the police motorcyclist drew himself up to his full height and pushed his helmet back:

'It is forbidden to sleep in cars. You must go to hotel.'

'Officer, we have searched most carefully. There are no rooms free.'

'You must go. I give you name of hotel with place.'

'The night is half over. It is too late. I am British diplomat. There are no rooms.'

'You cannot stay. Hotel Excelsior have rooms. You must be go now.'

In truth, they had not tried the Excelsior. It was by no means certain that their subsistence was designed to cope with the bills of such an upmarket establishment.

In more combative spirit, Horace reported to the Embassy next morning. The man he had curtailed his summer at home for was away and nothing had been prepared for him. Once they had got over a Lebanon tummy probably caused by a fruit drink on the Syrian border, they hung around pleasantly enough for over a week at the expense of the taxpayer. Horace was cheered when a Beirut postcard seller told him, 'You speak Arabi very nice.' He grew familiar with some ungenerous FO attitudes. A journalist invited to meet him at an Embassy house was labelled in a file which came into his hands the next day as a heavy drinker, prejudiced and ill-informed.

Philby had just defected from Beirut, which thought it was still in its heyday despite the warning sounded in 1957 to those willing to hear. Though Freya Stark had thought it 'horrid', the local British were sure that there was nowhere in the Arab world, or anywhere, to touch it and looked with pity on people who, like them, were proposing to go over the horizon to places which, they

---

* The word is transliterated in the Gulf as Cornish, making trans-Tamar expatriates feel at home.

were confident, their gin and tonic civilisation had never penetrated. Though an encounter with the Mutasarrif of Kirkuk, allowed out of Iraq for the first time in five years, whetted his appetite, these expatriates depressed Horace and made Baghdad (which they had probably never seen but to which his love of Arab history deeply attracted him) sound so frightful that — still bereft of briefing — they postponed their departure for five days, unwilling to lose contact with a meretricious but comprehensible base.

Ten days after their Skopje supper, they heard on the BBC World Service that the Makedonija had been toppled in an earthquake. Had it not been for their enforced early departure from London, they would have been there, caught up in it.

* * *

It was a long drive from Beirut to Baghdad. They decided to make a teatime start, getting the Syrian border post at Chtawra* under their belts and spending a night in Damascus. At Mafraq in Jordan, where a signpost indicates that it is 948 kilometres to Baghdad, they left behind the route Horace had travelled three years before with Mark. The Jordan–Iraq border was a line of empty petrol barrels. They drove round them and handed their passports through the car window to a magisterial old *bedu* in voluminous robes who had a dagger at his waist and a falcon on his wrist. He looked at their documents upside down, inscribed noteworthy passport details on the back of a cigarette packet, pointed at Horace's passenger, asked in English, 'This its wife?' and said, 'Welcome, glad to see you.' They felt that they had arrived and were thrilled at the prospect of a new Arab country that had made such a charming beginning. They entered Iraq in their handsome grey and red Vauxhall on a marvellously clear evening, the desert light on the tells beside the road seeming to tame the day's fierce heat. Glowing with self-exaltation, they drove on to H3, a pumping-station on the oil pipeline to Haifa which had carried

---

* The name of this small town should be written Shtawrah in English, but the method of transliterating used by the French in the Arab countries they colonised or where they were the mandatory (Algeria, Lebanon, Morocco, Syria and Tunisia) continues to be uncritically reproduced by the British.

water since the 1947 war for Palestine, and Rutbah, where Iraq proper commences and the real entry formalities — sullen and hostile — took place. Finally, however, they got clear and were rewarded by being allocated the Rest House's European Bedroom no. 1. For supper, they were served fried egg, chips and tomato ketchup, followed by that great Middle East invention, crème caramel.

Next day, the telegraph wires were thick with rollers and, for long stretches, every kilometre post seemed to be an eagle's perch. (In Jugoslavia then they were occupied by crashed vehicles resting on their roofs, now no doubt by disabled tanks.) The road is really the road to India and Australia. During the next three years they were frequently to meet intercontinental travellers broken down on it who, after their current repair, were making for Tehran 'next stop' in unroadworthy vehicles.

The scenery is of endless and vast, but friendly, desert, which gives way to the sown at Ramadi. There a barrage separates Lake Habbaniyyah — known to Britons because of the Second World War RAF base on its shore — from the Euphrates' crossing at Fallujah. The river has coursed to this point through Anatolia and past Aleppo, the sites of innumerable ancient and mysterious civilisations, and — its habitually depressed role as the border between Syria and Iraq abandoned — Hit, a place of many legends where the bitumen was acquired to make Noah's Ark watertight and, according to Herodotus, for the construction of the walls of Babylon. Xenophon and the Ten Thousand marched down its east bank.

The river goes on to pass to the east of the holy cities of Najaf and Karbala where the split in Islam between the Sunnah and the Shi'ah occurred in the second half of the seventh century AD. According to perceptive Arab observers, Iraq's David and Goliath mentality— so pronounced a feature of the response of Saddam Husayn's government to the threats of Desert Storm, Desert Fox, &c. — was born of the pitiful rout of Muhammad's grandson Husayn at the latter spot in AD 680.

Just short of Ramadi, while they were in the first flush of an intoxicating involvement with the beginnings of history, Horace's wife, at the wheel, espied an old lady setting out on a tentative traverse of the highway that stretched, otherwise empty, through the desert ahead. The old lady hesitated and his wife hesitated, beckoning and sending each other back for half a mile until they met head-on and the black-parcelled pedestrian fell over in the road. Horace had to jump out and apologise.

The journey for the rest of the way was to the last degree desolate. In Baghdad, their tyres skidded on liquid tarmac as they followed unilingual signs to the city centre. It was 1 August and the temperature was 120. One of the few people they saw out in the crushing heat directed them to the Embassy. The Chancery Guard informed Horace that if he was in by 9.00 the next day he would be able to attend prayers. He was surprised to gather that religious observance was institutionalised in British missions.

8

Features of the Garden: Baghdad

We sat in the garden after dinner for the first time, with Baghdad lanterns
hanging in the trees and they thought it a half acre cut out of Paradise.

(Gertrude Bell)

They had a wonderful garden. When they felt like an orange
— skin light yellow in colour, taste uniquely sweet, — they
snapped it off one of their trees. The lawn was big enough
for cricket practice. It really came into its own in the evening,
when the fierceness of the heat of the day had abated, the hooded
crows quietened in the coolness of dusk and guests could stand or
sit in exotically scented comfort. Their open-air film shows were
popular, and not the least appealing programmes were the archaeological and historical productions of the Iraq Petroleum Company and other oil companies which gave sensitive and romantic
accounts of the past of one of the world's most interesting
countries — cleverly made features rendering seemingly ridiculous
any unspoken thought that black gold, with Balfour, had been
responsible for most of the Middle East's problems. Even in the
second half of November, just before wood fires and Aladdin
stoves had to be lit for the first time and the rains began, they
could sit in the garden all afternoon. Their plants flourished better
when the gardener did not lend a hand. At his dismissal, the noble,
strange-eyed figure drew himself up guardsman straight, saluted,
said to Horace, 'Thank you, sir, and thank you Britain' and
shuffled off without complaint or backward glance.

A preoccupation of life in Baghdad was organising the animal world. In a country where rabies was widespread, a dog was the only real burglar-deterrent. At a very early date they had abducted Zora from a hedge at the Embassy. When her adventurousness, combined with a total lack of traffic sense, quickly led her to death under the wheels of a car passing in the main road outside, their Bulgarian neighbours immediately brought round the gift of a substitute, Ursie, so-called because she closely resembled a small bear. She rapidly grew into a big one and became an incredible barker, very difficult to persuade to honour the theoretically silent night hours. Ronald Storrs might have had her in mind when noting how the din made by Baghdad's dogs brought conversation to a stop. They once returned from a function to see with alarm that all their house lights were on, only to discover that their Embassy neighbour had been driven by their guard dog's interminable noise to force an entry in an attempt to restrain it. Ursie was, of course, completely reliable protection for the Top Secret documents Horace brought illegally from the Embassy to work on at home. She was borrowed by neighbours when they sensed on returning from a function that a burglar was on their premises.

Cats were always seeking adoption. Charlie Sue's names reflected the fact that, on acceptance, though not later, it seemed to be female. Perhaps as a result of getting in the way of one of Horace's firmer forcing shots, it developed an obsession with the top of people's heads. It ran up their fronts to squint at them in an insane manner which could induce panic in a victim and create embarrassment during functions at home. It, like Zora, met an untimely end. Horace returned to lunch from the Embassy one day in a furious temper, a not unusual condition. Charlie Sue was sitting in its accustomed spot on the driveway. He backed in more roughly than usual and was surprised to feel his rear wheels bounce over an obstacle. The possibility that it was the cat occurred to a corner of his mind but a winter log dropped on delivery seemed more likely. When he got out, he discovered Charlie Sue looking regal and covered in blood. Their cook, Abbas, running out to perform the duty of shutting the front gates, had seen the backing manoeuvre and accused Horace of deliberately killing the cat. Horace could not bring himself to speed an end to its pain. Abbas — adherent of a religion which is alleged to think dogs unclean — had earlier taken Zora to the vet after she was run over, buried her when she died there and prevented Ursie from killing Charlie Sue. Now he delivered the mercy blow and interred the cat before coming in to serve lunch.

The tales spread about the uninvited animal life of Iraq by expatriates in Beirut, who delighted in scaring the inexperienced in transit, had some basis in truth. Post reports were full of advice and warnings about Woolly Bear, which was supposed so to revel in the contents of British wardrobes as to be entirely responsible for the length of a tour of duty being exactly that of the interval between the major London sales. Horace never came across one of them. On the other hand, a snake was once found slithering into the Embassy pool. Two scorpions were encountered. One hitched a lift from Beirut in a Spinney's duty-free drink consignment, the other was dug up to be killed for their delectation by urchins beside the glorious ziggurat in Samarra* on top of which his wife once posed while, cowering, he photographed her from the ground.

There were two famous rats. The Embassy card, who persuaded Horace's second ambassador to entrust the Residence to his care while he was on leave, seized the chance — like the stoats and weasels in Toad Hall — to host a series of grand dinner parties to which he invited his chums. At one of them, considering the room a little warm, he switched on the desert cooler (air-conditioning had not quite arrived), whose first revolutions — normally designed only to direct indoors a wonderfully refreshing shower of moisture — now propelled a rat into the middle of the silverware on the plenipotentiary dining table; Horace was not present and cannot remember whether it was reported as being dead or alive. Even more alarming must have been the rat which surfaced one day in a secretary's lavatory bowl. Almost as shocking, though less dramatic, was the discovery by the wife of the air attaché, rounding off an elegant Alwiyah Club dinner, of something velvety at the bottom of her Turkish coffee cup which, on being inspected under the light, revealed itself as a cockroach, presumably dead. She shrieked for the manager:

'There's a cockroach in my coffee.'

---

* The Abbasid capital during the short period when the caliphs could no longer control their over-mighty Turkish generals in Baghdad itself. The name means, 'He rejoices who sees it'.

'It's never mind, madam, I bring you fresh cup.'

Horace's most traumatic personal animal episode involved a cat, befriended outside the General Motors' garage when it was taking longer than expected to complete a job. As he played with her and her kittens, she licked him — and he remembered that rabies, which they often saw tormenting unfortunate creatures lying in the dust while ragamuffin children mocked them — needs no more than that. Dr Terzi, their favourite Embassy-appointed GP, counselled him to have the prescribed injections if in doubt. Sensing his cowardice, born of hearing lurid tales of the agony caused by needles being plunged for weeks into the same holes above the stomach, he cheered him by stating that his number would not be up unless the cat died within ten days. Horace determined upon surveillance. 'Make sure it's the same cat,' Dr Terzi advised. Ludicrously tracking an animal which lived miles from the centre of town and had given the impression of enjoying radiant good health, Horace located her, alive and well outside the garage, for four successive days. On the fifth, she was nowhere to be seen. His temperature rose and his glands swelled but he still remained too squeamish to face the treatment. Only when, surviving repeated imagined convulsions, he reached Jerusalem for Christmas was he convinced that his time had not yet come.

Mosquitoes, though not malarial, were a constant nuisance, but at least you could see them. Dr Terzi had once, however, to deal with a very high fever produced in Horace by the invisible sandfly. Cockroaches, repulsive, were ubiquitous. Their septic tank was home to a colony of albino ones, sight of whose translucent bodies — fortunately not often necessary — was liable to induce queasiness. On one return from a home leave, they entered their sitting room, whose curtains had been closed during their summer absence, to find the furniture and books deep in layers of the standard variety. As the cockroaches fled towards the kitchen, rustling like a flock of miniature crows, Horace leapt on as many as he could.

* * *

He consecutively had two superb Vauxhalls in Baghdad. Each of them drove on several occasions to and from Britain and to and from Jordan, and one circumnavigated Iran. The official Vauxhall agent was not up to much. Horace naïvely objected to corresponding with the USA about his problems when he thought it was a British car he had bought. A colleague recommended a small garage to do his servicing which was so jammed with customers' vehicles that manoeuvring in or out was a test of advanced driving. Karim, styled Haji because he had done the pilgrimage to Mecca, had no real equipment and relied solely on a set of basic tools and his not inconsiderable mechanical skills. He was once under the bonnet of Horace's car, making a preliminary assessment of a problem. Turning to his boy assistant, his mind made up as to the course of action to be tried, he said, '*Jibli ispanir wa darnafis*,' spoken Iraqi borrowing nouns from both English and French to deal with the Arabic for Special Purposes' situation.

Horace persuaded himself for six months that a dead battery only needed cosseting and frequent long runs. The car had to be push-started the whole time. He should have been mortified when the headmaster of the British School lent a shoulder, even more when Diamond, the Embassy Counsellor (Oriental) — in a downpour after an official event at his house — convivially volunteered a push in his own driveway, already an inch deep in casual water. Horace was only finally convinced that it was useless to go on when the battery was as flat as ever six days after they had returned from their three-week tour of Iran.

Though car insurance was not certain to bring compensation, negotiations over it could be protracted. When the details of Horace's had been worked out, the representative of the company — whose female staff had all been Jews since a post-coup nationalisation which had caught 30 firms unawares, including the local branches of such British concerns as Barclays Bank — found that he had no change. This presented him with a problem which was rapidly solved by the addition of Horace's wife to the schedule even though she then had no licence or plan to drive.

The traffic was uninhibited. The taxi driver who ran into Horace on Rashid Street knew a fool when he saw one. He promised to return to the same spot next day in order to discuss a settlement but of course was never seen again. Iraqis did not use trafficators, claiming that they were invisible in the blinding glare. When Horace's wife eventually committed herself to a course of lessons and approached the task of handling the car in western fashion, her instructor grew increasingly irritated at her attitude to the business and finally exploded, 'Why you look in mirror? Just put arm out and go.'

* * *

It was amusing in mid-summer to think what a nice sinecure the Iraqi television weatherman enjoyed. The temperature reached 120 on 1 May and did not descend from that level until the Soviet National Day in November. For all those months, there was never a cloud and the sky was an uninterrupted deep blue. Steering wheels had to be fitted with special non-heat-absorbing covers if cars were to be driveable. They were not air-conditioned and invariably overheated on a long run.

Outside the hot half of the year, the weather was interestingly varied. It had never been known to snow in Baghdad, but it did so in Rutbah during their first winter, which was the coldest for ten years. Cars seized up and taps refused to pour. Life would have been impossible without wood fires and heaters. It sometimes rained in a rather British way, which was always particularly depressing in a desert city. A combination of rain, dust and wind occasionally produced an unpleasant, long-lasting sandstorm. In the middle of the day, the sky was blotted out and replaced by an orange mist, car headlights had to be used, trees bent double, a power cut would necessitate lunch by candlelight and shots would be heard coming from the direction of the Presidential Palace.

9

The Team: Baghdad

But with it all, the dust, the heat and the violence, there is hardly any Englishman [sic] who has been associated with Iraq, who has not come to feel a real affection for the warm-hearted Iraqi people.

(Sir Humphrey Trevelyan)

I have for months slept in my office within six feet of the telephone and within fifty feet of the telegraph office.

(Sir Arnold Wilson)

Baghdad seemed a magnificent spot, worth every mile of the journey. The fact that Horace had never before gone to the Arab world's eastern fringe, where the frontiers between Arab and Kurd, Arab and Persian, Arab and Turk and Sunni and Shi'i ran through Iraq, made it all the more exciting. Though it was not the *Arabian Nights* of eleven and a half centuries before and its remains are disappointing because it has been so regularly fought over, Baghdad felt exactly right, and quite different from Damascus, Amman, Beirut or Alexandria, which he had seen already. A breeze from the east, full of challenge and promise, distinguished it from Aleppo and Jerusalem.

The author of the *Nights* would not have scorned it. The ancient and characterful *suq*, historic Rashid Street — named for Harun, the most familiar of the Abbasid caliphs — and the anthill suburb of Karkh remained. Some quaint, historic thoroughfares had survived. Until the British drove them out in 1917, converting a geographical expression into a country, the Ottoman Turks ruled Iraq from the Saray area of downtown Baghdad whose lanes the centuries had neither widened nor rendered less insanitary.

By virtue of a mandate awarded after the First World War, the British stayed on until 1932. (The Iraqis say that it was not until 1958 that they actually left.) The rulers of independent Iraq exercised control in a capital with main streets *durbar*-wide. Architectural style was restrained. There were very few tall structures. Contemporary living and working accommodation was washed uniform desert white in contrast to the brown of the Turkish houses overhanging the noble, palm-lined Tigris which surged its deep and powerful way through the centre of the city. A large number of bridges overhung it — one rail, the rest road, some old, one elegantly state of the art — and had to be renamed after every revolution. The characterful, emotional, friendly and generous Iraqi people were unspoiled by political change. Shoppers discovering bargains in the *suq* but carrying insufficient cash are pressed to take the object of their desire away and to 'come back and pay me next time you are passing'.

Horace replaced two people in the Embassy, both successors of Freya Stark. One was remembered for dancing in a grass skirt at the least provocation and — subscribing to the Starkian principles of paper-handling described in *Dust in the Lion's Paw* — for burying official letters unopened beneath his office carpet; some 800 were only discovered there after his departure. The other was a great-great-grandson of Charles Dickens.

Of the colleagues who were remaining, the ambassador was away when Horace joined up. Acting for him as chargé d'affaires was the political counsellor — the Counsellor (Oriental) — to whom Horace had written from Beirut to announce the date on which he expected to report for duty. Not realising his exalted status, he had addressed him insubordinately as unvarnished 'Dear Diamond'. A languid, cigar-smoking individual, he had a charming American wife with whom he spoke on the 'phone in Chinese until one day a secret police tapper told them to change to a language with which he was conversant. He had written a book before the war and had a drawl and a tone of voice which seemed to convey sarcasm. He hated the heat and the allegedly unsophisticated natives — who were sophisticated enough to negotiate with him in his own language. To Horace, new, keen and deeply committed to Arab civilisation, this was discouraging, though not disillusioning. He was to have many rows with Diamond, inwardly scorning his attitudes and once riskily slamming his door. He was not the only one. He was the embarrassed spectator of a scene between Diamond and the British Council representative, with the latter shouting at him across the impressive Embassy patio. On one subject Diamond and Horace did agree, however: both— for Horace had deteriorated once more — were afraid of flying and had to find excuses to avoid it, as when 'Cat's Eyes' Cunningham brought a demonstration Trident to seek orders, successfully, from the Iraqis and the Embassy was invited to sample it. Whereas Horace's chosen mode of substitute transport was his overworked private car, Diamond's was the taxi. He once travelled that way from Baghdad to Beirut. The conversation between him — aloof and disapproving — and his Iraqi chauffeur across 800 miles of the Syrian Desert was not likely to have been memorable.

Another colleague who shirked the air was the second of Horace's secretaries. When she left Baghdad, the first stage of her journey home was by the Nairn Bus, which offered luxury transport from Baghdad to several other Arab capitals with minimal use of asphalted roads. Her car was to reach Beirut in the charge of an Embassy driver. The bus left a day late on account of air-conditioning problems and passed her car travelling on tow in the wrong direction.

The ambassador, like the vast majority of his kind, finally arrived after the high season for coups was over. A knight, Sir Reginald dressed incongruously in the most expensive Bond Street suits. Dapper, and with boyish features, he appeared to have sprung from the pages of J. M. Barrie. He, too, evinced no sympathy for his country of posting or its people. He was perhaps prejudiced by the treatment accorded one of his predecessors — who like him knew no word of Arabic — when the July 1958 revolution overthrew the monarchy and its British patrons. With his residence burning behind him, Sir Michael Wright and his staff had been made to stand all day in broiling sun on the Embassy lawn, and no doubt were threatened with worse. Temperamentally far above the dust and sweat of Iraq, the ambassador could not but have appeared remote to any of the country's inhabitants he met and he must have been lonely in his unappealing situation. When he was making his farewell calls, he had to ask the whereabouts of one of the more prominent ministries.

As a new member of the diplomatic team, Horace had expected to be summoned to be looked over by the ambassador. The call never came, giving him the strong impression that the team captain had no care for his staff. When one of Horace's locally recruited translators died, he accordingly did not bother to tell HE — and was winded by his wrath when he found out. When the ambassador was posted to another unsuitable Arab capital and Horace asked him for a reference, he stressed that a request for one should not delay above six months or he would have forgotten Baghdad and him as well. Although it did not occur to him at the time, the ambassador — like Diamond — was old enough to be his (rather elderly) father and perhaps found his fresh-faced enthusiasm and irrepressibility wearing.

The ambassador died in his next place of posting, not during his term of office there, but when revisiting it on the sort of tour of inspection which people in London inflict on colleagues working well in the field.

The man whom Horace had rushed out to Beirut to see had told him to regard the ambassador as God. God only once stooped in a human way to show what he could have been like. Horace was visiting the hairdresser, a downmarket establishment in a shabby kiosk near his house. The barber who was taking care of him had to pause periodically to spit blood into the sink in which he regularly washed customers' hair. As Horace felt ashamed to be found in such a place, the ambassador strolled past with Lady J., put his head through the doorway and waved and nodded at Horace in the friendliest possible manner just as a crimson jet took off.

Third in the Embassy hierarchy was a colleague whom having a much younger wife had perhaps impelled to buy a smart sports car. With her pregnant beside him, he established the record Baghdad to London journey time of two and three-quarter days in it. (Horace, flat out, took seven.) He fell off his roof at home during a leave, possibly similarly provoked. His superiors tolerated in him what appeared to be an extraordinary level of naïveté. He was the biggest scaremonger where coups, and the floods to which Baghdad had been prone since the beginning of time, were concerned. Once he announced at 'prayers' that two groups intent on a putsch, stumbling upon one another the previous night, had decided to call it off and return to bed. No one pooh-poohed this absurd tale. He cultivated an air of mystery and was frequently seen to be conversing in lowered tones with the Embassy spies. He was a frequent target of the secret police, who several times drove into the back of his car. He was the appointed Embassy expert on the Kurds, which — though there was no suggestion that he knew Kurdish — perhaps excused him for bringing up the rear in a triumvirate at the top who were unfamiliar with the principal language of the country. He once took Horace with him to the Ministry of Foreign Affairs to complain about the Iraqi lack of reciprocity in some area or another and kept on saying in English to an official, 'We must have reciprocity, we must have reciprocity,' of which four words his interlocutor was only familiar with two. He was one of the two people who considered themselves Horace's boss.

He remained when a new ambassador, bringing with him his own no. 2 (no mere counsellor, but a minister, the first since 1958), arrived. This ambassador, another knight, was godlike, tall, blonde, genial, democratic and, at last, Arabic-speaking. He had had an earlier posting in Iraq and loved the place and its culture. He would ring Horace up — a very recently promoted second secretary — and announce himself as Dick Clough. He once held a small official lunch at which Horace found himself alone with three other ambassadors and the Minister of Finance. It did not undermine Horace's admiration for him that he kept unaltered the time-wasting arrangements for 'prayers', the ambassador's daily briefing meeting which involved the whole of the diplomatic staff on Fridays but only Horace and three others — the political heart of the Embassy (the chancery) — for the rest of the week. They often lasted until 11.00 a.m., leaving only two hours for any real work to be done. Horace had to come to them ready to give the participants a part-summary of the contents of the press; he could not always take it for granted that they had even managed the one English-language daily, the *Baghdad News*, for themselves.

Like a very high proportion of Horace's diplomatic colleagues, the minister afterwards became an ambassador. He wrote minutes to Horace on the proper use of pins ('Sir Humphrey Trevelyan once pierced his index finger with a pin whose point had not been correctly tucked in') and on the rules for using paper clips:

'These papers came to me attached to [*sic*] a paper clip. All papers should be kept together with Indian tags as paper clips are dangerous and normally forbidden.'

In a prominent position in the porch of his house was a coffee table volume on Eton, a school he had not attended.

The high-flier of Horace's years, who had, also asserted the rights of a superior over him. A classicist and Roman Catholic like many leading British diplomats, he was skilled at taking all the credit for himself. He and his wife were suspected of sitting up half the night composing and typing minutes to be on the ambassador's desk when he arrived in the morning. His junior, the Third Secretary (Oriental), also a classicist, had been an exact contemporary of Horace's at his Cambridge college. They had only once exchanged a word, however, when Derek appeared in the quad one day with a broken arm. Now, two years later, they found themselves flung together beside the Tigris in the room next to the one in which — according to Philby père — Arnold Wilson had successfully asked him for his job and where Gertrude Bell's noisy negotiating had so irritated Wilson after he became Sir Percy Cox's stand-in. They were stimulated as Storrs had been by working by a great river, though their office was heavily polluted by the pipe Horace smoked from alarm clock until lights out. Since Derek never complained, he had perhaps, like Gertrude Bell — a chain-smoking enthusiast — mastered the art of indulging his habit without giving offence.

Derek was obviously capable of going far. He had the great gift of being one of the boys one moment, idolised by all of them, and, effortlessly, the undisputed boss the next. He was a linguistic product of MECAS, the British school of Arabic which was set up after 1945 in the hills above Beirut and when the Lebanese civil war broke out became peripatetic (to Tunis and Beaconsfield among other ill-assorted places) before finally expiring. A monument to the Islamic reluctance to allow foreigners to share in Muslim culture (this almost completely precludes the possibility of British students of Arabic or Persian living with Middle Eastern families), it was jokingly said to teach its graduates an Arabic which only other MECAS alumni could understand. Horace's own grounding in Arabic had been shockingly unsatisfactory, but he dropped his inhibitions about his own inadequacy when he heard some of them try to get their tongues round it. Arab suspicions about

MECAS were shared by *The Daily Telegraph*. When a diplomat known later by Horace in Beirut and Abu Dhabi became head of MI6, the paper made the connection between his graduation from it and spying which had already been drawn by the Arabs who nicknamed it '*madrasat al jawasis*' — the school for spies.

When Horace had presented himself to the Civil Service Commission, he had in vain requested exemption from the Arabic oral examination, the purpose of which was to assess his ability one day to earn the language allowance he was already drawing. When he underwent it, it was an occasion of deep embarrassment because his professor examiner could not speak the language anything like as well as he could.

Derek and Horace divided up Gertrude Bell's one-time daily job of reading the press before prayers, for which about an hour was available. Derek was responsible for the news, Horace for the editorials. The first was much the larger task and it accordingly threw a heavy burden on Horace when Derek, who was burgled with monotonous regularity, was unable to do his share after driving straight across a roundabout after an excellent evening out or arising to find that his car had sprung a puncture. It was particularly irritating when his incapacity only became known ten minutes before the beginning of prayers, which were timed to the second. (Horace was slightly late for them one day. Accusing him of thereby offering an 'insult to the ambassador', Diamond charged in with him only to be asked to wait outside for a moment.)

When Derek left Baghdad, his desk in the shared room was taken by a young man who possessed the golden spoon of destiny and could, of course, do no wrong in the eyes of the minister, the Old Etonian manqué, who regarded criticism by Horace of him as in principle unacceptable.

An older colleague, Shanks, the First Secretary (Commercial), was connected by one of his Christian names with the elder Philby. Horace's first ambassador, not in the habit of making jokes, once quipped that, wherever he was on tour in the Middle East, he could not but help thinking of him. Shanks was one day asked to move from the ground floor of the magnificent Embassy building, originally the Residence of the Ottoman Vali of Baghdad, to the one above. He calculated that it now took him 14 seconds to reach the Registry, the womb of the operation, and — seeing his freedom to meddle with the contents of his colleagues' in-trays gravely threatened — wrote a minute of protest to the ambassador. During at least one coup he was discovered riding on the back of a tank. He doctored his bouts of Baghdad Tummy by self-administering, as single doses, whole bottles of Enterovioform. His deeds were heroic, and subject to unmalicious sniggering.

One of them, after Horace's time, earned Shanks an OBE for setting up a hot drink stall. Following the Six Day War of 1967 in which the Arabs lost Jerusalem, the West Bank and the Jawlan (Golan) Heights to Israel, the Iraqi government decided to cut diplomatic relations with Britain. The Embassy staff were prohibited from leaving the capital until the arrangements for their expulsion were complete. Shanks disregarded the instructions and twice made his way to the border with Iran, following the route which the evacuees would take. On the other side of it he conducted successful negotiations with authorities, suppliers and shopkeepers which in due course enabled the tired, and probably frightened, Embassy deportees, together with other British refugees, to refresh themselves before advancing further.

Shanks opened the bowling for the Embassy cricket team and was therefore more of an all-rounder than an eccentric. One leave, Horace met him in Piccadilly wearing a bowler hat, perhaps symbolic of a wish to be seen, in Whitehall at any rate, not to be one.

Going by the principle, attributed to Bismarck and quoted by Grey of Fallodon, that 'the most certain way in diplomacy to deceive people is to tell them the truth', the Embassy spies, two at any one time, made no secret of their function, being as open about it with Iraqis as with the tiny British community. This was so excellent a cover that when Damascus Radio once broadcast the names of the agents in the Embassy, neither of them was mentioned. Horace, however, appeared in second place on the list, which was vastly more lengthy than the facts justified. No sounder justification for this slur would have been needed by the compilers than his knowledge of their language and his responsibility for relations with the media — vital weapons of dictators and of those bidding to replace them.

When Winston Churchill died, few Iraqis naturally chose to take the dangerous risk of attracting the attention of their rulers by coming in to put their names in the condolence book. Their government, of course, saw him as the arch British imperialist who had used Glubb Pasha as his instrument to overthrow an Iraqi administration little more than twenty years before. Horace was told to scour the highways and byways of Baghdad and assemble a decent crowd of mourners who were prepared to sign up. Because he felt that it would have destroyed his press relations, he declined to circulate a rumour that a prominent member of the government had done so, earning a severe rebuke for failing to undertake this undignified task.

Horace revelled in the ex-officio pageantry of his job. Its major manifestation was the Queen's Birthday Party. This was a very grand affair, a moving expression of what Glubb himself characterised as 'the tragedy of British–Iraqi relations', the collision of two peoples whom history had brought together but denied consistent friendship. After the 1958 revolution, it was decided that the ambassador would be safer living outside the Embassy than over the shop. A fine house on the banks of the Tigris was rented for him from the Iraq Petroleum Company (a transaction which the Iraqis probably felt proved one of their suspicions correct) and the QBP was held there. Some 2,500 guests were invited and had the run of both the public rooms and the large garden. These were the days of residual imperial pomp and circumstance. The number of Britons present suggested that inspiration from the motherland arrived only in trickles now. The other guests seemed to sense the British decline. Before dismissing it with 'Colonel Bogey', the Iraqi Army band captured the mood by playing 'God Save the Queen' with tears rolling down their cheeks. The existence in Baghdad of a Commonwealth War Graves' Commission cemetery holding the bodies of significant numbers of soldiers from Horace's unit — the Lancaster Regiment, held at the Diyala River in 1917 'against overwhelming odds' — seemed appropriate at that moment.

When he had an appointment on the other bank of the fast-flowing, muddy but manageably wide Tigris, on the far side of which were all the newspaper offices and most ministries, Horace would summon up the ambassadorial launch if it was available and picture to himself Gertrude Bell doing the same early in the century. (While the ambassador had a boat, the Air Attaché held a third of a share in a 'plane, which was used for gentle aerial surveillance and occasionally for flying Sir Reginald and his lady to regional conferences.) Like Layard's travel by Embassy caique when an unpaid attaché in Istanbul, this superficially grand manner of going about one's business — with the boatman at the tiller and the ambassadorial pennant flying at the masthead — was extremely good for the ego of someone scarcely adult (despite two years as a National Service officer), even if deeper consideration of it led to distaste at its possible Raj-like nature.

The level of the dealings of a mere Third Secretary in the Embassy (as he was at first) was absurdly high. He called on under secretaries and directors of broadcasting, he debated BBC versus Baghdad Radio with Iraq's new ambassador to the UN, he looked after the visiting Malaysian Attorney-General. At least some Iraqi officials must have resented the presence of such a whipper-snapper. How could the ordinary Iraqi spectator, however, imagine that that haughty personage in the stern of the launch was not the real thing? These were turbulent and strange times: in mid-stream, with the boatman reversing his craft in a stately manoeuvre, Horace felt the perfect target for a sniper; failing one, a water buffalo.

The cocktail round was of course a central feature of the diplo-matic life. Even though he spent a lot of time attending farewell parties for people he had never met, or greeting others he would never see again, it was one Horace approved of because it allowed a great variety of business to be conducted rapidly. A husband and wife Iraqi Ministry of Foreign Affairs' couple, both more British than the British, were regular attenders. Horace could never work out whether, with their intimate knowledge of the latest position on all things held dear at home and their unlikely enthusiasm for imperialist pursuits like cricket, they were *agents provocateurs* or genuinely pro-British; if the latter, how they got away with it under so anti-British a regime.

The frequency of such functions, with the same people regularly attending, encouraged tragic cultural mismatches between Briton and Iraqi, Christian and Muslim, to occur. They were illustrated by a mixed marriage of whose course Horace was a relatively close observer. When he was first preparing to go out to Baghdad, the wife-to-be, who had seemed to hold him in particular regard, had been a self-important official in his part of the Foreign Office. He was surprised to find her in Iraq at all, let alone beating him to it. What she was up to was unclear, but it soon became apparent that she was spending a lot of time with an Iraqi from the professional classes. She rapidly married him. He was an Embassy favourite who prided himself on being westernised, partly as a result of the two-way contact between him and British diplomats. Unfortunately, in many cases the westernisation is rather superficial, particularly among the intelligentsia. Stories began to circulate that he was showing signs of active jealousy and, before long, he was threatening her with the pistol it was now revealed that he kept under his pillow. The irreversible collapse of another marriage planned in two uncoordinated heavens quickly followed. In fear, the wife fled the matrimonial home and threw herself upon the protection of the Embassy. Unlike other British wives of Iraqis whom, under similar circumstances, Horace had seen driven away weeping without having got past the Chancery Guardhouse at the front entrance, she in due course was repatriated into a new life as a family planning counsellor.

On the whole, British cocktail parties were boycotted by the Iraqi government, which left the field to diplomats representing countries with which it did not enjoy cordial relations. The Iranian ambassador was a regular invitee. A personality, enjoying considerable standing at home as a former governor of the heartland province of Fars, whose capital is Isfahan (called by the Iranians *nesf-e jehan* — half the world), he reckoned that the existence of a Shi'i majority among Iraq's Arabs allowed him to throw his weight around with impunity in Baghdad. In the short term, he was possibly right. He had close relations with the British Embassy and certainly expected his friends in it to applaud him, as they did, when he recounted the story of yet another exchange of shouted insults in the Presidential Palace. Even if he did not relish his anti-Iraqi exploits, it was perfectly possible for Horace to be on socially pleasant terms with him. He was very kind to a junior couple like Horace and his wife, an object of his admiration, and particularly helpful over a journey they made to his country. They were invited to his residence a great deal. At one lunch, the ambassador went out of his way to pay warm tribute to 'those two great British public schools, Eton and Harrods'. After a dinner there, he introduced one of his staff, a remarkable conjuror whose skill Sir Humphrey Trevelyan had witnessed and who now aroused the incredulity of the spectators. For his most memorable trick, he swallowed mouthfuls of coloured drink and washed them down with cotton wool and razor blades. The liquid was a different colour each time: first Coca-Cola, next orange Fanta, then lemon 7-Up, &c. When he had consumed the requisite amount, he began to haul the various ingredients back out once more, this time, however, as a symmetrical chain of connected coloured strips and blades.

The rest of the Baghdad diplomatic corps was hugely character-ful. Unusually, there was an ambassador for Afghanistan. As befitted the representative of a country which had discomfited Britain more than once in the previous century, this old warrior, who would have looked more at home behind a rock above the Khyber Pass, teased them unstoppably — with outrageous winks — about the catalogue of ceaseless military failure which, he maintained, had been the fate of their country in its interventions in his.

Similarly playful was the skittish Romanian chargé d'affaires, who — after the Embassy had given the necessary permission — quickly enlisted Horace's wife to improve his English and, like the Persian ambassador, tried, for whatever reason, to turn himself into a friend of the family. He had a press attaché whom Horace liked and with whom conversation had to be in Arabic. After an occasion at the Baghdad Hotel, the only one in the capital which was then of anything like international standard, the Romanian invited them for a drink at his residence. They entered his Iron Curtain-type limousine and found themselves being driven off at high speed in the wrong direction. The chargé sat submissive beside the driver, who appeared to be controlling matters and to be talking down to his supposed boss. Eventually, the lift ended tamely, but for a time Horace had been convinced that they were being kidnapped.

There was quite a fuss when, in his turn, the Soviet Military Attaché asked if Horace's wife could do something about his

English too and they agreed to the suggestion without consulting higher authority. When the minister discovered what had occurred he was indignant because of the possible security implications, but did not press his opposition to the point of forbidding the lessons to continue.

Once, with a well-timed, lofted on drive, Horace scattered the non-diplomatic Bulgarians next door as they sat at lunch. They had been friendly from the start. His wife gave the wife English lessons. They went to tea, consisting only of brandy and cigarettes. Sofia perhaps thought that relations were too close, for Horace returned from a leave to find that their neighbours had disappeared without trace.

The Indian Embassy raised a cricket team which took part in Baghdad competitions and contributed members to the Baghdad side against the Iraq Petroleum Company in Kirkuk and the Iraq XI against Kuwait. Its captain and wicketkeeper was a Third Secretary of whom Horace was fond. When he came with his wife to lunch on their first Christmas Day in Baghdad, however, his Indian friend embarked on an attack on British imperialism. Horace was a lively critic of that phenomenon and nearly ejected him from the house when he found the term being applied to him too. The flare-up having been damped down, however, Hamid went away with a borrowed *Wisden* under his arm.

* * *

The Embassy junior staff, as the non-diplomats were called, were the clerks, secretaries, wireless operators, registry team and chancery guards. The sterling work they did received little recognition from Horace's Olympian colleagues. They only attracted attention when they attempted to murder their wives and were sent home on the next 'plane.

The locally engaged staff of the Embassy were full of character and interest like their masters, but came from much more colourful backgrounds. For Horace, it was stressful enough being a representative of the host government's least favoured country, who in a certain kind of coup could expect no better treatment than his predecessors had suffered so recently. As Freya Stark noted during the siege of the Embassy in 1941, the position of

Iraqi nationals who worked with the British was potentially much worse. In a melting-pot of a state, Iraqis could be Sunni, Shi'i, Yazidi, Catholic, Greek Orthodox or Jew; racially, they were Arabs, Kurds, Persians, Armenians, Assyrians, Chaldeans, Turcomans or Anglo-Indians, like those the British imported in wartime to run Iraq's railways. (They taught native Iraqis of the servant class to address Western males as *sahib* and made Baghdad a 'zone of Indian influence, the land of tiffin for lunch, of curries and so on'.) Racially, the Arabs were a controlling majority. From the religious angle, on the other hand, all Iraqis belonged to a minority, with the Shi'is the largest one. The British had always chosen their military allies from the Kurds and lesser minority groups, especially the Christian ones. As the civilian successors of the Armenian, Assyrian, Chaldean and Kurdish soldiers who had unwisely agreed to fight for the occupying power during Britain's mandate, most of the local staff of the Embassy would have been unhappily placed if the regime's suspicions about them had taken an active turn or (which to Horace's knowledge never happened) information about the Embassy's activities been wanted. The government guard on the gate at the beginning of the Embassy's shady driveway did everything short of manhandling to dissuade Iraqis from coming to call, but no alarming action was taken either against Iraqi local staff or visitors during Horace's three years.

Tuma, his head translator, not very good at his job, was an unhealthily squat Chaldean, a member of an Aramaic-speaking race. Michael, another, was the staff member who died in harness. Horace replaced him with a beautiful Sunni Muslim girl whose husband would not let her out of his sight during the recruitment interview. Films were the preserve of Joseph, an Armenian. In charge of the Information Section's bicycle and of the delivery of its publicity material was Abbas, a nondescript little Shi'i who never raised his voice but, it came out, was at the beginning of a career as a minor union leader. He had, on political grounds, already seen the inside of one of his country's prisons. Salim, a Sunni Arab, faced the prospect after being arrested and questioned by a military court two days before the first anniversary of the November revolution. Wagner, a Christian, avoided a similar ordeal by allowing himself to be called up.

The Team: Baghdad

Five months after his arrival, Horace's staff surprised him, as the Embassy began its Christmas holiday, by suggesting a seasonal Section lunch. This was well intended but, though the shish kebab came wrapped in one of the local newspapers with which Horace had good relations, it put him to bed for several days with a severe bout of Baghdad Tummy which required the intervention of Dr Terzi, a characterful Jew. In a way they came to enjoy, he jokingly considered cholera and typhoid before deciding that this was not the terminal malady.

At the beginning of each day at the office, Horace was received by Jasim, the Section messenger. He was old, toothless, tall, straight-backed, spare as a whippet, and illiterate. His peaked cap pointed at too elevated an angle to the sky. Like all his colleagues, his devotion to the British — who, indulging one of their least attractive national habits, had so interfered in his country — was his reason for living. Compared with his allegiance to them, his endorsement of Iraq's rulers, Sunni Arabs like himself, came nowhere. He presented Horace, at the beginning, with an extraordinary reference, which described his profession as that of *syce* and among other points recommended him as 'good for secret thing'. When Horace left Baghdad, he had a letter composed which, 'after compliments', asked him

> ... kindly [to] convey my best wishes to your respectable parents and to all the members of your honourable family. PS. It would be great help to me if you would kindly recommend me to your successor, should you happen to see him in the FO. Also a few words from your charitable hands in the form of certificate will be highly appreciated. Thanks.

Jasim certainly performed services for Horace. As he began his daily hour with the Iraqi press, the smell of the Aladdin heaters cheering him in winter, Jasim would wrest from him the pipe he had first lit an hour before and pour rusty water from the Section's tap at maximum pressure into the bowl. Later in the morning, he would provide Horace's guests with drinks. On the whole, they could not order them until they were settled, so Horace could often not avoid taking part in a ridiculous, security-related ritual which involved him in immediately having to ask

85

newly-welcomed visitors to leave his office, which they had just entered, while he concluded refreshment arrangements with Jasim, who obviously was not allowed into the inner sanctum where Horace functioned.

Jasim was at his most serene when there was a cocktail party. He had two responsibilities. The first, vital one was to collect the ice. Five minutes before the first guests were due, with the host and hostess becoming more nervous by the minute at the prospect of drinks having to be distributed uncooled, Jasim would appear, chauffeur-driven in a horse and trap, looking like Don Quijote in decline but with blocks of ice on the back seat. As he alighted, one usually slid into the gutter. After completing his crucial delivery, it was his task to stand on guard at the gate and throw a ramrod salute at the arriving company until satisfied that all were accounted for. Only then would he unbend and sit, erect and dignified as ever, outside the kitchen. Holding court within they had, like Gertrude Bell, an expert Iranian cook, Abbas 'the Persian', who was 30 but looked 20 years older. Supervising operations from his chair and smoking heavily, he stole a drink from every tray sent out to circulate.

The kitchen became on these occasions the working environment of the whole of Horace's office staff, readily transformed into their secondary incarnations as barmen and waiters. In both roles, their performance was unmarred by their mixture of races and tongues or sectarian inhibition. The rest were ashamed when Abbas, who did not figure in their Section lives inside the Embassy, let the side down by overindulging. There was a celebrated occasion when Horace, aghast, had to pull him, unshaven, away from Sir Reginald whom, in intolerably familiar fashion, he was treating like an old pal and leaning on as against a lamppost. One of the spies once borrowed Abbas and — to Horace's indignation — said that he found him too loud and objectionable to think of hiring him again.

Despite the excellence of Abbas's cigarette-flavoured cooking, they suffered at home from Baghdad Tummy more often than they should have done, particularly after receptions. Once, to their chagrin, a diplomatic service inspector was slightly poisoned by Abbas at a buffet supper they ingratiatingly gave in his honour. Horace, whom he had just promoted *in situ*, was also afflicted.

Abbas died soon after their three-year term was over, perhaps killed by too much drinking and smoking and too little eating. A little more love from Horace would not have come amiss. In their third year, Abbas decided that he should look for a new employer. The crisis was precipitated by a tyre giving out on the bike he rode many miles to their house and for their shopping. He asked Horace to replace it as an approved extra and Horace refused. Abbas went missing. His brother, Ali, reported him as saying that he could no longer stand his inhuman workload; he was being treated like a donkey. Although they paid him the leading Embassy rate, with which their colleagues accused them of selling the pass, 27 Dinars (about £30) a month seemed in reality far too little for a man with a wife and 11 children to support. He made no complaint about the money, though. In due course, he returned, having failed to find his fortune in the south of the country. They had missed him a great deal. He used to sit with them to have coffee. Like the Iranian ambassador, he had an attractive line in English. Deeming something to be of no value, he would advise them to 'put it to the New Zealand (museum)'.

Ali, Abbas's much smarter brother (Derek's cook), was also unlettered and yet had a productive line in the irregular importation of vehicles — like Ahmad and Ali on the road to Tabriz, as well perhaps as Freya Stark. He could effortlessly make his way from Iraq to West Germany, purchase a Mercedes and steer it back to the Garden of Justice without being able to read a map or a signpost. An enviable and vital skill he did have, however, was — to complement the plausibility of the *picaro* — his ability, like Ahmad and Ali, to speak something of all the languages required along his route.

* * *

Horace had been in Baghdad for only a short time when, rather than inflict on his contacts the lingua franca form of Arabic which is proper to the radio, the press and formal speeches — the modern Classical Arabic, understood throughout the Arab world — he decided to get down to the serious study of the spoken language of Iraq which he had not had the opportunity to use before in the country where it applied as distinct from to guides and the like in the Levant, where it didn't. That the dialect contained a large amount of Persian made him all the keener to master it as the natural climax to the process which began when he took up Oriental Studies at university. He bought grammars of the colloquial more modern than Van Ess. One taught him sentences like, 'He entered in under the table.' Another, the work of one Van Waggoner, an American, was excellent. Horace put an advertisement for a teacher in the *Baghdad News*. Only one reply came, but it was of unanticipated quality. In faultless English, Ziyad informed him that he was prepared to give him the lessons he was seeking. Horace lost no time in engaging him. Ziyad turned out to be a handsome, moustachioed IPC employee with an aristocratic air, a legal background and a snappy line in tailored cream suits. He rather resembled Lord Lloyd. The lessons went well and Horace made rapid progress with the help of his new books and a sound, if uninspired, tutor. He did not need help with monitoring Baghdad Radio's broadcasts for hours at a time in periods of instability or advising on the contents of letters the Embassy received in Arabic — as, on one Christmas Day, when the British removed Shaykh Shakhbut of Abu Dhabi. For his talks with editors and for interpretation duties during such visits as that of the Manchester Chamber of Commerce, however, the conversation classes boosted his confidence greatly. It was not dented when, behind his back, a Ministry of Foreign Affairs' official who wished to be addressed in English complained about him communicating with him in Arabic, 'the language I use with my cook'.

The lessons perhaps gained Ziyad entrée into the Embassy. After they ceased, he married a secretary from the typing pool who quickly presented him with their first offspring. Then, taking part in a mild bout of Russian roulette, he fell out with the regime and was exiled to Arbil, in southeast Kurdistan. When last heard of, he had become a millionaire restaurateur in London. But this was long after Horace had lost touch with him, for after leaving Baghdad he was careful not to do anything to compromise the friends of a happy period, as he was unwittingly to do in the case of the leading journalist of the day.

10

Nanny Johnson's Television: Baghdad

... men know best about everything, except what women know better.
(Celia Brooke, in *Middlemarch*)

'Lady Johnson needs a new television set. I'd like you to accompany her and guide her selection.'
'Of course, sir. Shall I liaise with Lady Johnson about where to meet, timings and so on?'

He was to drive her from the Embassy into town once she'd arrived from the Residence:

'Would you care to wait for me at the main entrance while I bring the car round, ambassadress? It's parked at the side.'

That was where he'd always left it. To reach her, he had to negotiate an electricity pylon which jutted out from a right-angled bend in the waiting room's outer wall. He had cleared it without thought or effort on hundreds of earlier occasions. On this one, the prospect of escorting Lady Johnson had provoked a quite irrational state of nerves which seriously flustered him at the wheel. As he hit the pylon, a loud bang preceded his junction with the ambassadress 15 yards further on. The owner of a vehicle now dented to an extent he could only guess at and pray about, he imagined her looking at him with surprise and alarm. As she was handed in by the head *farrash* through a door which had at least retained the ability to open, he tried to act — like a batsman who knows himself plumb lbw — as if the noise of the impact had had nothing to do with him, or with the nonchalance of one to whom such happenings occurred so regularly that he had given up noticing them:

Bygone Heat

'Would you like me to adjust your seat, ambassadress?'

'No, thank you. I think this is right for this humid weather.'

'I thought we'd go through Tahrir Square and avoid the congestion of the bridge.'

They reached the television shop in historic Rashid Street without further mishap. Nanny Johnson, who looked after the ambassadress's children and whose real surname, if it was known, no one ever used, was waiting for them after having had the foresight to travel to the rendezvous in the ambassadorial Rolls. Horace gave her and Lady Johnson the benefit of his totally uninformed advice before, in accordance with the agreed plan, leaving their chauffeur to convey them back to the Residence.

He had earlier been incautious in the house of the headmaster of the British School, who lived next door to him:

'How are things in the Embassy then, Horace?'

'Still pretty stressful, I'm afraid.'

'What's the problem?'

'The whole place is so no-can-do, somehow.'

'I can imagine that your high-flier chap must be pretty awful to work with.'

'Yes he's rather a strain. Of course, the ambassador's not interested in his staff.'

'Nanny Johnson's looking at us. Isn't she one of his spies?'

'She could have heard every word.'

When it was revealed that the television was for her and not for the ambassadress at all, Horace wondered if, in the shape of Nanny Johnson's revenge, he had been in receipt of poetic justice.

Lady Johnson must have thought him, at the least, an accident-prone driver. One weekend, the Embassy mounted an expedition to Hit, the isolated town on the Euphrates of which Gertrude Bell ungenerously said that she hoped she would never see 'a more malodorous little dirty spot'. Its inhabitants have the reputation of being suspicious of outsiders. They also boast a number of small and still operational Roman water wheels. After the party had picnicked and admired them, Horace found that he had locked his car keys inside the Vauxhall. It was Lady Johnson who came to the rescue, forcing her walking stick through one of the quarter lights, breaking it in the process. Horace recalled that, according to one theory, Job's home had been in Hit.

90

One way and another, Lady Johnson was the chief automotive hazard Horace encountered in Iraq.

11

Iran Revisited

Journeys are a trial.

(Kai Ka'us Ibn Iskandar)

Horace's second visit to Iran, five years after the first, involved a circular drive from Baghdad via Hamadan, Tehran, Isfahan, Shiraz and Basrah. The Persian ambassador rang before they left to advise them to take 'too much' warm clothing because the temperature in Tehran had suddenly dropped to two degrees centigrade.

The antagonism existing between Sunni Iraq and Shi'i Iran since the beginning of the sixteenth century, and entering one of its periodic crescendo phases as they set out, kept cross-border movements down to a trickle. Though Britain had contributed much to the conspiracy theories subscribed to by Iranians in the twentieth century, however, Horace and his wife were delighted to find themselves treated like VIPs by the Shah's immigration and customs' officials. They called on the new Iraqi consul in Kermanshah, a ginger-haired friend, and found him depressed after a week's experience of his thankless task. Although it was April, snow and ice began soon after their exit from Iraq and conditions remained decidedly wintry as far as Hamadan. There they visited the Mausoleum of Ibn Sina (Avicenna), the eleventh-century medical pioneer and philosopher after whom streets throughout the Middle East are named. Although Horace had already had two winters in Baghdad, when seven boiling months became a memory as oil fires were brought out in offices and wood smoke made the houses smell like Scotland, the towns in the foothills of the Zagros Mountains felt miserable and looked anachronistic in the chill and dampness of late Spring. 'Nothing is colder than the East when she chooses,' as Kipling noted.

They did not realise it at the time, but an assassination attempt was made on the life of the Shah on their first day in Tehran. In part escorted by his Civil Adjutant, met by chance, they visited those few sights which were open. Since the crown jewels, the peacock throne, the Sepahsalar Majlis, the Archaeological Museum and the Zurkhana were not, Horace had ample opportunity to confirm the belief, formed in Tabriz, that Persian food was in general anything but to his taste.

They passed through Qum, second only to Mashhad as a Shi'i shrine. It became a place of pilgrimage when Fatimah, the daughter of the seventh Imam, was buried there, and it was to be the planning office of Ayatollah Khomeini's revolution. In time-honoured, elegant Isfahan, they ate in a hotel run by a Briton whose idea of an annual break was to drive to Aberdeen and back every summer. Their ambassador friend had alerted former colleagues of his to keep an eye on them at their various stopping-places. This did not deprive them, in Isfahan itself, of a novel accommodation experience. They had already, in Belgium, come across a motel bedroom with an unscreened lavatory in it. Now, their Isfahan hotel featured an unique sliding scale price-structure for its bedrooms. Taken up to vet one for the night, they discovered that it had no curtains:

'Why are there no curtains in this room, *Agha-ye man*?'

'Curtains extra, Sahib.'

'Do you mean to say that there is a two-tier charging system for hotels in Isfahan?'

'Isfahan *nesf-e jehan*, sir. Two prices for hotel room.'

At Horace's insistence, he proceeded to pin across the windows lengths of unpromising green baize material which, in the event, served effectively if crudely.

Continuing their journey south, they paused at the tomb of Cyrus the Great in Pasargadae. Alexander had done the same. A slight diversion took them to Nakhsh-e Rustam, where Darius I and some of his successors are entombed in the rock. At Persepolis, 250 miles further on, Alexander had led a brawl during which the magnificent platform site was burned. The nearest Horace came to emulating his performance was when a window he was closing after dinner in their hotel there fell out of its frame into the room they had needed a note from the ambassador to secure.

It was at the Park Hotel in Shiraz that Horace should have met up with Aghdas five years before. Later, he found it incredible that he made no attempt to contact her now. In his diary, he noted in Arabic his sadness at not seeing her and — rushing ahead in Aquarian fashion — speculated that life might have been better if he had married her.

When they arrived at the Park, lunch was in full swing. Two elderly British ladies were anticipating the production of their main course. A volcanic sneeze from the kitchen almost tore the serving door from its hinges. Seconds later, their rice and lard were placed in front of them. Conspiratorial winks were exchanged by their two tables.

Not a single signpost or kilometre stone marked their 395-mile journey to Ahwaz next day. It took them down to the shore of the Gulf, which Horace found menacing under a dead and overcast sky but had no premonitions about. It ended dramatically when, on the outskirts of the capital of Khuzistan, their road ended without notice on the edge of a drop. They put up in a caravanserai-type hotel. The bedrooms were arrayed behind flimsy curtains around a hollow square which acted as the lounge. Sleep was scarce. There was much for the Ahwazis to talk about. It was not every day that cars with Baghdad number plates came through their province, called Arabistan by the Iraqis who have a half-hearted claim to it. (When Saddam Husayn entered it in 1980 to start the Gulf War with Iran, the inhabitants — who had wept that Horace and his wife could return so effortlessly to their heart's desire, Iraq, an impossibility for them — did not rise up to support him.)

After inspecting the spot where they had narrowly missed cartwheeling into a ditch the night before, and finding their way out of Ahwaz only with great difficulty, they crossed back into Iraq. They coincided at the entry post with a group of Iranians travelling in the opposite direction. The official was fat and idle, and much too sleepy to welcome having to deal with them. But he'd had lots of practice at scorning his neighbours:

'Going or coming?'

'Going.'

(Contemptuous amazement.) 'Going? Where on earth to?'

The one direction of which he approved brought Horace rapidly to the river-cooled palm groves of Basrah, where the waters of the fast-flowing Shatt al Arab, the combined Tigris and Euphrates, sweep past the colonial-style corniche and playfully bounce the light river craft up and down at their moorings. They quickly came to the Airport Hotel, an oasis of civilisation after their arid drive from Tehran. They started with lentil soup. The waiter, conscious of their parched and exhausted condition, left the tureen beside them, encouraging them to give vent to their self-indulgence. They were glad once more to be where they felt at home. It rained in torrents in the night.

On their way back to Baghdad, they passed Qurnah, where the Tigris and Euphrates meet. The spot is marked by a notice which proclaims it to be the site of the biblical Garden of Eden.

12

The Opposition: Baghdad

Esmé Dobbs and I agreed at lunch that much funnier things happen in Baghdad than in London.
                    (Gertrude Bell)

Of course the British Embassy was blamed: it always is in Iraq, for everything.
                    (Freya Stark)

T he only unpleasant feature of life in Baghdad, detracting from its perfection but adding to its romance, was the political tension. It was palpable. Their house had a quaint, triangular mezzanine bathroom. Shaving there every morning, Horace could immediately tell from the sounds of the city heard through the window whether or not trouble was to be expected. It very often was.

They had been there for no more than three and a half months when a split occurred in the Ba'th government which had been in power since the violent overthrow of the regime of the terminator of the monarchy, Abd al Karim Qasim. Horace was about to leave his office for 'prayers' when he heard his secretary say, 'Oh no, not again.' She had been in Baghdad when Qasim met his end and had his corpse displayed on Baghdad Television. He heard the sharp crack of machine-gun fire far above them. An Iraqi air force Hawker Hunter flashed silver across the sky and returned to make another attack. This was repeated a couple of times, provoking no answering fire, before quiet returned and the city held its breath. A curfew came down and he and his colleagues had to remain in the Embassy until the middle of the evening until, with typical optimism, the government announced that the affair was over and life had returned to normal. The staff stowed away the camp beds they had been expecting to spend the night on.

Though Baghdad Radio only days afterwards fecklessly put on a

play featuring the capture of a radio station in a coup, the matter
was not closed. Before breakfast each morning during the following week, the voice of Baghdad boded ill, the prophecies of the
Embassy Jonah grew more insistent, reports of troop movements
were received with alarming regularity and their Iraqi friends became
increasingly nervous. Mercifully, it was not until Friday, 18 November, when all but the British Embassy had their one day off —
the Embassy anachronistically took Sunday, — that the universally
anticipated climax was reached. They awoke to the staccato thud
of directed automatic fire. How apt Freya Stark's comment had
been when she spoke of 'something quite indescribable in the slow
approach of this noise, so full of fate, so full of all the unknown.'

Their house was a block away from the west bank of the Tigris
and the action was obviously on the opposite one. Throughout the
day, unable to reach the Embassy to lend the duty officer a hand
but in contact by telephone, Horace watched films on the television replacing the normal schedule of the glorious, quasi-martial
Egyptian music which President Nasser — who, unlike President
Huwari Bumadyan of Algeria, never came to Baghdad himself —
had exported to Iraq along with a prominent and ugly feature of
the times, generous doses of political interference, now apparently
achieving the desired result. As someone who already loved Iraq
and was deeply concerned that the outcome of the events he was
monitoring should he beneficial to the country, Horace with some
euphoria viewed a succession of the male idols of the Egyptian
cinema, supported by Sabah, Shadiah, Najat as Saghirah, Faydah
Kamil and Wardah al Jaza'iriyyah (the most beautiful of the Arab
world's female vocalists), thrilling their audience — not least him
— with such stirring pan-Arab songs as 'Watani al Akbar', played
initially at the wrong speed. (It was ironic, and no doubt a
reflection of the shortage of suitable indigenous compositions, that
the same numbers were used during anti-Nasser coups, mounted to
block the influence in Iraq's affairs of the adherents of the
President of Egypt, the 'Nasserites'.)

Horace followed on the radio, which tried to keep up with
events, the progress of Abd ar Rahman, the soldier brother of Abd
as Salam Arif who was trying, by means of a counter-coup, to
break free of the Ba'th domination he had helped Qasim to impose
and subduing in the process the Ba'thist *Haras al La-Qawmi* —

the 'un-National Guard'. By the end of the day he had done so and the people could smile with relief. A chorus of thousands of dogs barked in the night to acclaim the feat. Horace, who was, after all, only a young idealist, rejoiced at Abd as Salam's victory and hoped that his hero could pull the country together. They were nonetheless depressed at the thought of the lives lost in the cause, which the Embassy local staff put at 1,500.

They were soon to be shocked by revelations about the inhumanity of the Ba'th, whose favourite method of punishing those who incurred its displeasure was to tie them to ceiling fans and turn the power full on. The walls of many government offices were found to be covered in blood. For a few days, it was dangerous to use a car with diplomatic plates, like Horace's, lest its number be misread as that of a member of the Syrian wing of the Ba'th which would be most irate at the outcome of the coup. British journalists swarmed in and got around by bicycle. The radio station bristled with tanks. British Centurions were dug in around the Palace. Horace called on an official whose walls were riddled with bullet holes. The curfew was not lifted for over four months but the first mention of British imperialism on television was made only 20 days after the dénouement.

When they spent Christmas in Jerusalem, Horace was delighted to discover that the majority view there was that things would be better in Iraq under Arif, a good and religious man. Unfortunately, however, the reign of the elegant Abd as Salam was brief. Inevitable trouble first manifested itself while he was in Casablanca on an official mission and his brother had to foil an attempted pro-Nasser coup by Arif Abd ar Razzaq, the commander of the air force (an arm of the Iraqi services which played a disproportionate part in the instability of the period), who had been prime minister for ten days and now had to flee. Long before the days of President Aun of Lebanon, it seemed odd if not unique for a premier to carry out a coup against his own authority and to make such a mess of it.

It was in reaction to conciliatory moves towards the Kurds by the new prime minister, Abd ar Rahman al Bazzaz, that the resilient Abd ar Razzaq mounted the most violent coup attempt of Horace's time. The first sign that anything was amiss only showed itself after lunch — timing which was in contravention of the spirit governing the rules of conduct for Iraqi *coups d'état*. They were relaxing with their coffee when a 'plane went over, unusually fast and low. Horace knew immediately that they were in for another period of stress. And indeed, before he had a chance to think about official action to be taken, cannonades began to be launched from the skies directly above them. Again it was a story of a single 'plane, with no support and no answering volleys from the ground. He imagined the overweight officers of the Iraqi army sluggishly abandoning their siestas to deal with the emergency. Unlike the last solo aerial revolutionary, this one treated Baghdad to an extended aerobatic display. As he dived, crossed the flat city at rooftop height, fired his salvos and climbed again, they sought refuge under their stone stairs. (They had no reason to think them less than solid, but the fact is that — corroborating Gerald de Gaury's observation that Baghdad houses were 'unstable, being made of mud brick' — their two-storey residence fell down soon after they vacated it.) According to a canard, 'Said Mr H. T., young British Embassy official: "I could hardly follow the Test match commentary — the air raids were so fascinating to watch from the garden".' In reality, a number of nasty moments were spent under the stairs that afternoon until, suddenly, the world became silent once more and the chatter of their neighbours reasserted itself. The respite could not last. In due course more firing was heard, now from a formation of 'planes which, in their turn, proceeded to bomb Baghdad with abandon before flying across the Tigris and heading north to Mosul.

Dashing, handsome Arif Abd ar Razzaq, closely resembling Wing Commander Jimmy Edwards in appearance, did not deserve to get away with his disregard for the conventions. Abd as Salam announced that he was returning home to put down the Egyptian plot. Before he had time to get back, however, Abd ar Rahman had brought things under control for him. The split in the air force, which had led to two unopposed assaults on the city during the course of one afternoon, was, however, a signpost to the future. Baghdad was all smashed-up, buildings had disappeared, lamp-posts leaned at drunken angles. It was a signpost no one bothered to read because Iraq was in such a condition of instability that the final act, emanating from whatever source, was probably unavoidable and unlikely to be long delayed. Meanwhile, Al Bazzaz, the first civilian prime minister since the monarchy, announced with naïve optimism that tanks on Baghdad's streets were a thing of the past. Abd ar Razzaq had to flee again but was soon pardoned. Less than ten months later he rebelled once more.

The *coup de grâce* occurred when Abd as Salam made a tour of inspection by helicopter, a time-honoured Iraqi instrument of high-level assassination. His death as it crashed saddened Horace, who had been beguiled by the normality of his appearance — as with Hafidh al Asad and Gorbachev — and disillusioned by the Embassy's rejection of any idea of him as the saviour and steers-man of Iraq — a view which contrasted with that of Sam Falle (a charismatic British diplomat who left Baghdad just before Horace arrived) who regarded him as 'Iraq's last best hope'. The Embassy never credited any Iraqi leader with being more than a figurehead.

Horace had not heard the news when he set out to walk to work one morning. He went to the office on foot only twice in his three years and on both occasions a distressing death had occurred. The first was that of John F. Kennedy. Like most people, Horace has no doubt of where he was when he heard the news of it. Five days after the 18 November coup, when private cars had not yet been allowed back onto the streets, he was making his way along the main road which starts at the Presidential Palace and ends at Jum-huriyyah Bridge. He passed a man in tears. Inwardly concerned for him in his private grief, he pressed on. He met another, and another. The same personal tragedy could not have struck them all. He asked the last one what the matter was and received the reply, 'Haven't you heard? Kennedy's dead.' Seeming land of con-trasts, for the Iraqis were sincere when they said that they put blame not on peoples but on leaders. Kennedy was a rare excep-tion. Abd as Salam ordered a day of mourning, which he did not do for Churchill. China and its allies refused to half-mast their flags.

The other death was that of Abd as Salam himself. The faces of the tank crew always on guard outside the Parliament Building — there was no parliament and the Foreign Minister used it as his office — were wreathed in gleeful smiles. As demonstrated by Yasir Arafat's support of Saddam Husayn in the Gulf War, the Arabs never learn:

'*Ya sayyidi*,' he asked, 'what has happened? Has there been a joyous event for you to seem so happy this morning?'

'Brother, there's wonderful news. Abd as Salam is dead, *'l hamdu li'llah*. Indeed, now at last Iraq can progress.'

'Allah willing.'

A moving and impressive funeral ceremony was held, headed by Abd ar Rahman, now his brother's successor. *Khairi khalaf li khairi salaf* — a good successor to a good predecessor, — loyalist Iraqis said. Troop carriers, named 14 Ramadhan and 18 Tashrin after the Muslim calendar dates of the two coups Abd as Salam had led, escorted a procession by dignitaries, to Chopin's 'Marche Funèbre', down the whole length of Karradat Maryam. Since he lived there (it is now an out-of-bounds government enclave), Horace obtained a ringside seat. The Iranian Ambassador, no doubt footsore by the time he slow marched past, but incorrigible as ever, risked losing the step to give him an outrageous wink which meant, 'You know all those rows I had with Arif in his palace? Well, look who won!' Another victor was the Ba'th, which was soon to reach the pinnacle of its fearsome and impregnable power under Saddam Husayn.

* * *

Abd as Salam, handsome and smart in his photographs, was probably actually a roughneck. Baghdad was amused when he took a last minute decision to make a surprise public appearance at a girls' school, arriving at the wheel of a Volkswagen Beetle. He somehow contrived to manoeuvre it on to the assembly hall stage. It was not amused when at some point in his address there was whispering and the President silenced it with a gross colloquialism for 'Shut up.'

Tahir Yahya, who came from Tikrit like Saladin and the majority of Iraq's modern rulers, was prime minister during most of Arif's period. Horace thought him 'the only one who seemed interested in the people'. With a figure like a junior Cyril Smith, he was the butt of affectionately cruel stories. According to one, every year he telephoned his tailor — perhaps the Chic Tailleur in Rashid Street from whom Horace received better service than Ronald Storrs had enjoyed in Baghdad — to order a further supply of suits: 'Same as last time only with larger pockets.' Another described him and Abd as Salam bidding farewell at Baghdad Airport to Khrushchev and Bulganin:

Bulganin: 'Well, I think we'd better get on board now.'
(Making to consult his watch)
Arif: 'Give him it back at once, Tahir.'

Incongruity and comedy were frequently encountered in Baghdad. Only a little over five years after the overthrow of the monarchy and the murder of the young King Faysal II, the regent and Nuri as Sa'id — the prime minister who had been a comrade of Lawrence of Arabia, — Horace went to the Presidential Palace to sign the book on the Prophet's Birthday and accept the tea and cigarettes which were offered on such occasions. The tea came in glasses stamped with an F and a crown.

Islamic Fundamentalism had not been heard of but alcohol was already subject to disapproval. Anticipating sterner times, one restaurant had begun the practice of serving Special Coca-Cola in a teapot to customers requiring beer.

The delight of the Iraqi character in the ridiculous was catching. The Embassy, which derided administrative incompetence on the part of the Iraqis, instructed its staff to put their heads out of the window in the event of a break-in or other emergency at home outside office hours and to summon help with a whistle provided. The theory was that a response would be forthcoming from one of the nightwatchmen who patrolled the streets of the city. They maintained touch with each other, keeping their courage up (Baghdad was alarming enough in the daylight but infinitely worse during the hours of darkness), and the citizenry awake, by their own regular whistling from block to block over the rooftops. It was penetrating enough to be heard above the barking of the packs of wild pi-dogs, many of them rabid, whose din made sustained conversation impossible, as during Storrs's visit. The difficulty about the instruction was that the windows of Embassy houses were fitted with fixed anti-mosquito netting which effectively vetoed its implementation.

It is true that the Iraqis kept their ends up well. A colleague once asked the Embassy's local contract handyman to put a bathroom cabinet up in his house and showed him exactly where he wanted it to be positioned. He came home from the office to find it secured not centrally and symmetrically above the shelf where he laid his soap and razor but grotesquely off to one side. Summoned so that his incomprehensible performance could be enquired into, the operative said, 'But, sahib, no possible fix place you showing me. Bottle of Dettol in way.'

The Embassy received marvellously eccentric letters, from both the British community and Iraqis. One memorable day, the post brought an airmail envelope from Francis Bedros Kurukchi and addressed to Queen Elizabeth, British Embassy, Baghdad, with copies to the House of Commons and the Archbishop of Westminster. On the first of three colourful pages, he wrote:

'Onwards, Allah's soldiers, forwards to Palestine! The homeland of Christ, Mohammed and mine! In your ranks and files Allah's armies will fight, And thrust the Python Jews out of Palestine with might!'

The Soviets built a factory which, after the grand opening, was found to be capable of manufacturing shoes for the left foot only. They introduced Russian classes at their centre on the street on the east bank of the Tigris named after the dissolute poet, Abu Nu'as. Iraqis enrolling were arrested as they left the building after the lesson.

Horace once had to meet a delegation of visiting British MPs at the airport. One of them, appearing at the top of the 'plane steps, yelled, 'Show me your prisons.' It was hard for Horace to forgive this attitude to a country he had quickly come to regard as special, but it was not the spirit of Iraq which was to blame. Another kind had found a Welsh MP an easy victim.

Horace was also indignant about a sour-faced and sinister member of the Foreign Ministry Protocol Department who, one day when he arrived for an appointment, rang up the official he had come to see and said, 'There's a person just about identifiable as human (*shakhs*) here who claims you're expecting him.'*

Against the background of the British–Iraqi love/hate relationship, bringing his government's policies daily mauling in the media, Horace was astonished at how much he was able to achieve. The short-term needs of the press and television for material from whatever source, even the most tainted, outweighed their ideological inhibitions.

Horace positively relished his calls on the half-private, half-

---

* In Islamabad many years later, Horace telephoned the British High Commission. In passing him on to a colleague, a clerk referred to him as 'a bloke', which is rather similar in tone. But this was ignorance rather than malice.

official, press. Most of the papers were produced in cave-like rooms beside the Tigris. Temporarily free of the tense atmosphere of the Embassy, he delighted in making his way there, in scorching heat, along Mutanabby Street, past Mackenzie's Bookshop (the book-shops of Baghdad were the best he ever came across in the Middle East) and the marvellously named Orozdi Bak department store, where you could buy a cricket bat, and through the narrow, wind-ing lanes of the old Saray, with open sewage channels of an unmis-takably Middle Eastern character. His tasks were to attempt to deflect editors from an anti-British line and to persuade them to publish the pro-British written and photographic material he could supply. He had to be careful in his choice of photographic subjects in a country where it was forbidden to point a camera at many things:

PHOTOGRAPHY IS FORBIDDEN

10. Dunghills and places of garbage
13. All scenes of slaughtering and skinning sheep by untechnical methods outside slaughter houses
27. Hand-operated civilian drying places run by primitive methods and all their annexes
31. Places where bones are burnt for extracting oil behind the eastern bund
32. Intestines factories in Shaikh Omar.

For tourists as distinct from Embassy officials, there was, how-ever, nearly always a way round the law, especially if requests were made politely. With the possible exception of Kadhimayn in Baghdad itself, the holiest religious sites (mostly Shi'i) usually had a member of staff on hand to act as escort to a photographic vantage point. At the city boundary of Najaf, there is a sign which says in English, LADY, VEIL YOUR BODY, and, although the pro-genitor of the Shi'ah is buried there, entry to the Imam Ali mosque, which Gertrude Bell was unable to approach, was free. On the other hand, to the Sunni one in Samarra, perhaps deemed in part a tourist attraction, it cost 300 *fils*.*

---

* There are 100 *fils* (plural *flus*) in an Iraqi dinar.

When, at first, Horace was not confident enough in his spoken Iraqi Arabic to discuss current issues and historical skeletons unaided, he asked Tuma to accompany him on a trial run. This went so well that, blossoming linguistically with the help of Ziyad, he dispensed with his assistant thereafter, sparing him the embarrassment his risky frankness would have caused him. The fact was that most of the British policies Horace was charged to present in a favourable light were deeply repugnant to the Iraqis. They thought, correctly, that the creation of Israel on Arab land was a largely British responsibility. It was undeniable that Britain was impeding their links with their younger brothers in the Gulf, whither — a slap in Arabism's face — they needed a visa from the Embassy to travel; the reluctance with which one was granted was, they felt, an indication that the British were up to no good in the easternmost part of the Arab world. Any British initiative Horace straight-facedly raised before confiding his personal view on it was, therefore, so unlikely to be welcomed by his Iraqi contacts as to make the idea laughable that the editors of Baghdad newspapers interested in preserving a connection between torso and head would consider for a second speaking well of it. Following the example of Sam Falle, whom the Iraqis knew was 'as far as it was possible for an imperialist official ... on their side', Horace did not attempt to make them. (In the belief that only thus would she be believed, Gertrude Bell had — unbeknown to him — done the same; Layard had campaigned in the Istanbul press against his government's Turkey policy.) Equally, if any of the journalists with whom he was so open had given him away for behaviour resembling that indulged in by Glubb while pacifying recalcitrant Euphrates tribes, the penalty would have been severe. A headline reading 'British Diplomat Attacks Imperialist British Policies' would not have endeared him to the Embassy. He observed with interest the fate of a British ambassador to another Arab country. He was notorious for his blanket refusal to receive official visitors from Britain on his weekly day off — which is the same day as they invariably insist on arriving — and for urging the Foreign Office, in telegrams copied to Baghdad, to be even-handed as between the Arabs and Israel. After several repetitions of this call, he appeared to be removed from his post, which led in due course to his departure from the Foreign Office. These were certainly times when it was unacceptable for British diplomats to be overtly pro-Arab. The Embassy's delight at the formation of the first post-revolutionary civilian administration in Baghdad would not have been of much benefit to Horace if *Al Watan* had revealed that it had passed his opinions on Britain and the Arabs on to Dr Al Bazzaz. The principal effect of his candour was, however, the forging of personal links between him and his journalist friends which, he considered, were far more useful to Britain than unvarnished accounts of the party line could ever have been.

Though Freya Stark had spoken of 'the iniquity of oriental journalism', Horace much enjoyed fencing with the press, whether with the friendly but uninfluential *Al Alam al Araby* (The Arab World), the middle-of-the-road and coyly intellectual *Al Watan* (The Nation) or the stern maintainers of the ideological status quo, *Ath Thawrah* (The Revolution), *Sawt ash Sha'b* (Voice of the People) and *Sawt al Jamahir* (Voice of the Masses). But he quickly found that some newspapers were more receptive to him than others. *The Baghdad News*, by far the least important of his targets, was written in English by Iraqis for the foreign community. This made it a much more genuine product than the English-language papers, or the English-language radio and television programmes, of Jordan or the Gulf which are crudely got up by amateur expatriates to keep other expatriates happy and have neither anything useful to say about the local culture nor any message to convey from rulers to guests. It also led it to carry splendid headlines, like one on the Belgian National Day: 'President greets King Bedouin.' Its editor and staff, who had never seen the game, urged its readers to support Horace's attempts to revive cricket in the capital and themselves came to the matches. At one point Horace had a team with sons of five former Iraqi prime ministers in it. (The best cricketers in Baghdad were an Australian and a Southern Rhodesian, both aged 59. One of the people who stood as umpire had no-balled Wes Hall.)

The paper attracted uniquely arresting advertising:

ANNOUNCING
Winter Season opening
OF
Hamouraby Gardens

The Opposition: Baghdad

It was eager to take most of Horace's material, but this was no great victory for him since it was hardly seen by Iraqi eyes. *Al Alam al Araby* was more worthwhile from this angle. Its editor was, to all appearances, genuinely friendly towards Horace. He was the first Iraqi journalist to summon up the considerable bravery required to call on him at the Embassy and he entered with gusto into the spirit of his cocktail parties. With a group of like-minded media men he used to organise entertainment of his own. He came to the cricket and, like one of his competitors, published photographs of Test Match action. Horace offered him a game in aid of a fund for the family of a popular journalist who died untimely. For Big Brother reasons, the Iraq News Agency withheld from the editor monitoring reports of radio stations broadcasting from outside the country. Horace was able to supply them. The editor's use of Horace's material was dangerous for him unless counterbalanced by periodic savage attacks on Britain which Horace, like Storrs before him, did his best not to take to heart and which had caused Freya Stark's fulminations against the Arab press.

In conversation with editors of papers like *Al Alam al Araby*, Horace would joke about the British imperialism every Iraqi had a perfect right to abhor, especially in relation to Palestine. While he could occasionally use his relationship with them to shame them into abandoning or toning down an attack, British policies had been so malevolent, and were still so antagonistic to Iraq and the Arabs, that he could not win in the long run. The Embassy applauded when *Sawt ash Sha'b* attacked China and Indonesia in an editorial, but Britain was seen as hostile power no. 1 and nothing Horace could say would alter the fact. While unhappily characterising an Ulbricht visit to Cairo as the thin end of a Communist wedge being inserted into the Middle East, it was ideologically impossible for the editor of *Al Alam al Araby* to

107

avoid parading for a Jugoslav press delegation in preference to meeting a *Financial Times* man in Horace's charge. 'Why could the British not have made themselves better liked?', he asked.

With newspapers closer to the government or under its control — and mostly new, for papers could become submerged for long periods after a coup, if not suppressed completely, — "imperialism" was a deadly serious obsession. Because their futures were so precarious, their anti-British activity had to be regular and fierce. Horace made very little headway with them, though with impunity taking a chance of being selectively indiscreet with some.

The less fanatical journalists would invite Horace to their houses, which does not happen in every Arab country. The editor who attacked your national policies in the morning would welcome you with smiles at night, happy to be providing for both of you the opportunity to pretend that the future could be more positive. The editor of *Al Alam al Araby* dined with him in London.

Horace ignored the news-sheets which, like desert flowers after rain, suddenly sprang up in the wake of a coup, sold ten copies on the first day and collected three annual subscriptions before quietly expiring.

The only adverse reaction to his press dealings surfaced after he had left Baghdad. Two months back in London, he heard that the editor of *Ath Thawrah* had published a typical Arab tabloid account of an imaginary conversation he and Horace were alleged to have had:

'Mr Tension, the former Press Attaché at the British Embassy, once asked me, 'Do you know why *that* paper attacks Britain and does not attack the USA?'

'No'. He added, 'We have definite information that it receives certain allowances from the USA.'

I asked, 'What about you? Whom do you pay?'

He feigned innocence, saying, 'We don't pay a single person.'

Laughing, I asked him, 'Am I to understand then that everybody receives something from your government?' Pretending astonishment, he gazed at me, saying, 'Never, we don't pay anything to anybody.' But did I believe him?'

This was followed up by *An Nur* (Light), which suddenly accused the President of the Journalists' Union, Mr Filan Muhammad, himself the editor of one of the papers, of having been in

The Opposition: Baghdad

Horace's pay. It published the text of a letter 'addressed to him from Mr H. Tension, former Press Attaché at the British Embassy, Baghdad. In this letter, Mr Tension thanks him for his co-operation in publishing news sent by HBM Embassy.'

Commenting on the letter, which predated Horace's departure from Iraq by 17 months, the paper continued, 'Congratulations, Mr President, on this excellent testimonial.' Though Horace had found the President pleasant and straightforward, he had never written a letter of any sort to him — the reference must have been to an 'id card, sent routinely on the occasion of one of the two most important Muslim festivals — or paid him a *fils*. (He made no payments to anyone during his quarter century in the Middle East.) Later, in a statement published by the paper,

'Mr Filan Muhammad gives his reasons for not offering himself as a candidate for the Presidency of the Journalists' Association in the forthcoming elections, which are to take place next Friday. His reasons are (1) because of what has been said of a meeting between King Sa'ud and myself that I have received a sum which certain slanderers put at 20,000 dinars, (2) the story of the so-called historic, significant letter sent — by a Press Attaché who was in Baghdad and who seemed to be 'the Napoleon of his age' — to my paper because it publishes what the Embassy prepares about the government and people of Her Majesty!

'From where did this letter come? And when? Why it was not published until now I am at a loss to understand.

'I swear by God that I did not receive that letter nor do I know the occasion of it...

'I do not know in what Embassy it was printed. However, I would like to ask every honest journalist whether he does or does not receive such letters...

'Is it a letter written by me and stating my commitment to serve any side other than my country? Have those who published the letter forgotten that agents follow a different method, and that those who use them are keen to keep their relations with them secret? ...

'If I had been co-operating with the British Embassy, the Embassy would have tried to protect me rather than send a

109

letter that might fall into the hands of anyone and be used as evidence against me. ...

'I would also like to know whether my paper has really ever published anything to deserve so much as a routine expression of gratitude from the British Embassy.'

Although contact with all the media was Horace's job, he was selective in his dealings with the official radio and television. Baghdad Radio was unremittingly political, the Embassy only listened to it during putsches and its studios were not comfortable places to be caught in when the first coup shots were fired. The last consideration also weighed with him in the case of the government-run television service. He did not attempt to sway its editorial policies and prejudices, which were most unlikely to be susceptible to foreign influence, but set himself the limited aim of getting it to screen light propaganda films — *Aberdeen Angus*, *Letter from London* and *London Transport* were representative — from his library or on loan from the Central Office of Information. His efforts were satisfyingly successful.

He was the informal agent of the BBC, whose tendency to file unhelpful reports with irritating frequency didn't appear to have changed much since Freya Stark's day. Although Baghdad Television and he did not understand why it could not actually buy an early *English by Television* series which mainly seemed to owe its popularity to the charms of Connie, the female lead, he succeeded in persuading it to accept a rental arrangement. The BBC man who brought the films out to Baghdad was hard work. He first left his luggage in a taxi and then failed to confirm his onward flight to Kuwait. Horace asked BOAC if he could sit beside the pilot and was surprised when permission was granted.

The rest of the British media also had a point of contact in him. Horace went out of his way to develop cordial relations with the British correspondent of an international news agency until the newsman complained about him to Horace's visiting Beirut boss and then was found, incapable through drink, beneath a car parked in the street. A similar type was a tabloid journalist in transit who invited himself to lunch and, in interludes between helping himself to their gin, thought he was impressing them with his tales about the mistress allegedly waiting for him in St Tropez.

1. Aya Sofia, Istanbul

2. Mark at the Way of Columns, Palmyra

3. ABOVE. The Mosque of Ibrahim, Hebron

4. BELOW. The Temple of Bacchus, Baalbek

5. Shuhada' Bridge, Baghdad

6. The British Embassy, Baghdad

7. Horace and his team
8. Cricket at Baghdad College

9. Khwaju Bridge, Isfahan

10. Fallen colossal statue, Persepolis

11. Ctesiphon, the world's largest unsupported arch
12. Spectators of Black September on Horace's garden wall

13. Batin, on the west side of Abu Dhabi island

14. Commuters on the Dubai Creek

15. Old and New Jerash
16. Fuwayrit, Qatar

The Opposition: Baghdad

Iraq was not on the main line as far as most British newspapers were concerned. Early in Horace's stay, however, the Middle East correspondent of one of the quality Sundays, an acknowledged expert on the area, called at the Embassy and confessed to Horace that he had no story in mind. Horace suggested to him as a theme the British lack of interest in improving British–Iraqi relations as evidenced by the Embassy's failure to request a British minister, then touring the region, to include Iraq in his itinerary. The journalist adopted the plan and promised not to give Horace away. When the piece came out, his colleagues were unable to understand the motivation of an attack on them from someone they considered 'tame'.

Horace was on their side when, a little later, the BBC quoted the same minister as telling the UK–Israel Association that Britain was not neutral on the Israeli question, i.e., that it was pro-Israel and anti-Arab. This was a patently erroneous report, as a Foreign Office telegram confirmed. Horace, despondent at 'this blow', released the true text of the speech to four friendly Baghdad papers in an attempt to limit the damage it threatened to cause.

* * *

He went out of the capital when he could to talk to the press in the provinces and to deliver printed and visual publicity material and films to places not reached since the 1958 Revolution. There was an old-fashioned imperialist idea at one point of sending a cinema van on tour to show propaganda films up and down the country, but nothing came of it. Sillier proposals were current. It was recommended in Aden, where the empire was collapsing fast, that tribesmen should, as a parting colonial gift, be issued with radio sets capable only of receiving the BBC Arabic Service. While that branch of the BBC was unlikely to broadcast the kind of gaffe which was so common a feature of English-language transmissions, it was not difficult to imagine what would be thought of the new toys when it was discovered that they could not pick up Cairo, Beirut, Damascus, Baghdad.., and what would be the fate of the mementoes so generously presented by Her Majesty's Government.

In press terms, the provinces meant Basrah and Mosul. Horace's first visit to Basrah was as escort to his second ambassador on a

111

tour of the south. They stayed in the British Consulate-General right by the Shatt al Arab, on which the Consul-General had his own launch; he took them in it to Sindbad Island. Next day, Horace and Sir Dick drove through the desert to inspect the new Iraqi port of Umm Qasr. The British diplomat's Bible, by Sir Marcus Cheake, laid it down that ambassadors travelling by car had to have an unimpeded view forward from the back seat. Horace therefore rode behind the driver, on Sir Dick's left. (Once, in London, accompanying an Arab ambassador, he was invited to occupy the wrong seat, probably for reasons of hospitality, and felt very exposed to the possible attentions of assassins.)

On their way to Umm Qasr, they passed through the village of Zubayr. A school of Arab literary thought, led by a respected critic who acted as the Civil Service Commission's local Arabic oral examiner, claimed that the author of *The Merchant of Venice* was an Iraqi and that the proof was that his name was a corruption of his true title of 'Shaykh az Zubayr'. The harbour works at Umm Qasr much impressed them by their newness and efficiency, but these could not disguise the fact that the seaward outlook was almost completely blotted-out by Kuwaiti islands barring the route into the Gulf. Much of the strife between Iraq and Iran over the Shatt al Arab, where the great Sir Percy Cox drew a boundary line on a scrap of paper which was unfair to the former, has of course been caused by Iraq's almost total lack of a coastline. This, together with the Arab character of both shores at the northern end of the Shatt, where Khuzistan faces Kuwait and part of Saudi Arabia, goes some way to explain the Arab insistence — which would otherwise seem childish — that the Gulf should be called Arab, not Persian.

Before visiting an IPC installation on their return journey, they strayed over the unmarked border into Kuwait. Saddam Husayn was later to find it no less easy to do. The final result of his campaign was, of course, to lose his country even more of its coast when the UN, with extraordinary injustice and shortsightedness, awarded part of Umm Qasr to Kuwait after the Gulf War.

✤ ✤ ✤

The IPC was British in practice. In one of his early stints as

Embassy duty officer, a telegram arrived for it whose contents Horace tried to communicate to the head of the company over the 'phone. He was surprised to learn that he had committed a serious *faux pas*, the kind that led Iran to believe in 1971 that British oil companies were government organisations.

The IPC had its main centre of operations in Kirkuk, parallel with Mosul and, like it, a racial frontier post. (Alive to their petroleum possibilities, Britain, on the initiative of Arnold Wilson, had taken both from the Turks after the First World War cease-fire had come into force.) The Baghdad XI went up to play the dull Kirkuk oilmen. Horace not only hit the first delivery of the match for six — if the old wives' tales had been true, it would have been perilous for a fielder to retrieve the ball for fear of encircling Kurdish rebels — but also recorded his highest ever score. A quarter of a century later, Derek reminisced when they met in Doha about a partnership between them there which had not actually taken place.

From as early as 1914, the West's need for oil was exerting what Freya Stark rightly calls its 'baleful and magnetic influence in international affairs'. Great harm has been done to the Middle East thereby. Its peoples and governments have been systematic-ally exploited by the companies, many of whose concessions were awarded before their host countries had achieved their indepen-dence and been in a position to bargain free of pressure from their colonial overlords. The western determination to retain control over actual and potential oil-producing areas played a significant part in the creation of Israel. British governments — receiving oil at prices which, even after the huge increases imposed by the producer countries in the 1970s, are puny — have never recog-nised the contribution the huge taxes they add on to them have made to the exchequer. The Middle East, lucky of course to possess such a source of revenue beneath its sand, has not done well, in the Stark phrase, out of 'the fire and brimstone of Middle Eastern oil'. Properly paid, many Abu Dhabis could have been built by now, not just one.

Mosul, where you stay in the Railway Hotel and are kept awake at night by a surprising number of trains, is on the edge of Kurdi-stan and just across the road from Nineveh and Nimrud, among the most historic sites in one of the cradles of civilisation. From the city, it is easy to imagine that you can hear on the wind the hooves of the Assyrian coming down like a wolf on the fold. Or, one can imagine Hulagu's galloping hordes as they approached to overthrow the Abbasids, whose 500-year rule over the Arab empire from Baghdad and Samarra, which began in AD 750, ended in mounds of piled skulls.

Throughout Horace's stay in Iraq, a Kurdish rebellion was in progress except during a three-week period when a peace of sorts held. While the lull lasted, they deliberated about possible visits to places further north than they had ever been able to go and decided that they would wait until a more convenient time. War broke out again before one arrived and deprived them of a second chance. The nearest they got to Kurdistan was when, on a short drive out of Mosul, they persuaded the guards on the 'border' to allow them through on a short lead. This favour was only possible because they agreed to deposit their passports, guaranteeing an early return after a short drive of no consequence between rolling upland meadows. On the way back to the capital, they stopped off at the black tent inhabited by the niece of the Astronomer Royal, Sir Bernard Lovell, and her husband, an Iraqi prince of the desert.

* * *

The off-duty atmosphere of Iraq was well captured by a trip to Diwaniyyah, a town on a tributary of the Euphrates to the south of the capital. The first night passed off uneventfully as the members of the expedition registered and got to know each other. The next day set the tone of incongruity from the outset, when the rest house, which had started to call itself 'hotel', offered at breakfast what it declared to be white wine, which emerged from the bottle purple. (It was vodka with which Sir Roger Stevens was once served in Iran.) Unimpaired, they drove off into the desert, intent — except for Horace himself, who hated its unending openness and lack of feature — on the form of amateur archaeology which is called 'telling' after the Arabic word for hill or mound. The sites of the south of Iraq were built of mud and all lie in ruins. Technological developments are far from reaching the point where proper archaeologists can, politics permitting, examine more than the most accessible of them. Telling enthusiasts — trusted even by a revolutionary government to surrender finds of possible historical importance or value — had the run of the non-Kurdish countryside.

One couple had had to leave their Jaguar behind to be serviced in Baghdad. The party met it miles from the capital, tearing through the desert on a 'test run' and billowing clouds of sand, with two mechanics aboard hysterical at their daring. Another pair were driven by Eva, a plain German girl in a Beetle who — perhaps irritated because her sticking choke had made her lose face at the start — kept on trying to pass Horace and then hooted her way through, which seemed an antisocial approach to a group outing along uncertain, difficult tracks. Though an ordeal for Horace, the telling proved rewarding for the enthusiasts. Eva hadn't wanted to call it a day as early as the rest of the party, who were anxious not to leave a return dangerously late. Thwarted again on the way back, she cut in front of Horace as they were navigating towards the irrigation canal which was their most crucial reference point. Approaching Diwaniyyah once more, Horace waved Richard, the organiser, through so that he could lead them back to the rest house; he prevented Eva from coming past again in his wake. Richard pulled in to the kerb and proceeded to make a scene on the pavement:

'Horace, your behaviour has been most uncivil today.'

'Richard, have you not seen how rude she has been to me, without cause, from first thing this morning? You are wrong to put the blame on me.'

'She is a foreigner, a guest and a lady. This will not help her poor opinion of the British Embassy. I demand that you apologise.'

Eva having driven off to Baghdad in a huff, they returned to the rest house to learn that another couple had paid a bill for them to stay for a second night, which had never been the plan and which, indeed, they did not do.

It is not recorded whether or not Eva, with her strong views on the Embassy, attended QBPs. Horace, however, who had been ludicrously miscast as Othello in readings staged at Richard's British Council premises, changed his mind about being in his next production, *Widowers' Houses*.

13

Wolson: Beirut

Back at Oran. NO LETTERS. NO
TELEGRAMS! *This correspondence is
getting one-sided to a degree.*
(Mark Sykes to his wife)

*During my long absence I had only
three times received letters.. ...
Although there was this British
Mission in Meshed I did not receive
a single message from them.*
(Lieutenant-Colonel F. M. Bailey)

Wolson was a legendary figure whose deeds were familiar
even to those members of the organisation who had
never met him. When their ship entered Beirut port, the
legend it was that greeted them. He had news, no less depressing
for being expected. They had crossed the Channel to BBC bulletins
on the car radio that Jordan — the object of their journey — was
aflame with the civil war of Black September:

'You'll have heard the reports. London has told me to hold you
here until the position clarifies.'

'We feared as much. What a way to begin a new posting.'

'I'm sorry. Muhammad will go with you to the Mayflower
Hotel. I've made an open-ended reservation for you there. Come
and dine tonight. Bring your little boy.'

During their enforced stay in Beirut, a place they found dispirit-
ing enough even without the likely loss of a dream job and
certainty about their future, Wolson was not very well. He could
not walk far and seemed apprehensive about going out. He relied
very much on his supportive driver, a former Lebanon international footballer. He treated them like a true godfather. It
wasn't dinner only tonight. It was dinner every night, often lunch
as well and, occasionally, breakfast. Had it not been for Wolson's

116

confirmed bachelordom, Horace might sometimes have suspected him of making up to his wife.

At the office, where things were found for Horace to do — notably representing Wolson at occasions of a kind that his age and bad leg made an ordeal — he tried to keep himself occupied, covering for the absence of a lady with a fearsome reputation for aggressive dourness. She returned unexpectedly from leave. Killing time among the library's periodicals, he found his path blocked by an unfamiliar female burrowing there:

'Can I be of any help to you?'

'I know my way around perfectly well.

'What is your business?'

'I only work here.'

'So do I. You're preventing me getting on.'

Wolson used to reach the office late and, as his first daily task, write up his personal diary of the previous day before leaving it on public show. Increasingly, Horace featured in its pages: 'Distressing quarrel between Horace and Giblitz over his subsistence,' 'Words exchanged by Annie and Horace about her visits' programme,' 'Had to check Horace for pointing the sole of his shoe at a visitor,' &c.

Horace grew increasingly irritable and dejected as the weeks passed and nothing came from London, which did its utmost to enforce the financial book of rules against them as though their position were not exceptional. A higher-ranking colleague passed through, heading for Jordan as stopgap replacement for the man whose deputy Horace was to have been. Horace was certain that he would bear news of their fate. Wolson bade them all to dinner. As the meal progressed, Horace grew more and more furious that their plight was not being mentioned and eventually gave full rein to his bitterness:

'Have you no message for us, Mr Double-Turner?'

'What message were you expecting me to be carrying?'

'Surely you must know that we've been stuck here for over two months now waiting for news.'

'I'm afraid that I've heard nothing about your situation.'

'We were posted to Jordan but Black September stopped us getting there. We made sure that you would have something to tell us.'

'As I've said, I have no information.'

'What kind of employer have I got? London know perfectly well the anguish we've been in all this time and yet they let you come out here with no word for us. If you can go to Jordan, why on earth can't we?'

'Well, you certainly cooked the Jordan goose,' his wife said.

In the end they did move on, but to Khartum. Wolson, who had been so attentive, did not come to see them depart. Further glimpses of his past and rumours of his later exploits reached them. They learned that he had set the organisation's record length of stay in one post, Cairo, where he remained from 1939 until finally forced out by Suez. He appeared to have spent most of his time there acting as a piano accompanist in the local musical theatres. It was perhaps this which had influenced his dress. Adorned with a single earring long before such accessories became familiar if repulsive on males, he looked like a pirate gone to seed, mellowed yet still dangerous to know. His waistline was extensive and one imagined him with a parrot on one shoulder and an eyepatch half obscured by a foulard. Wolson invariably indulged in a siesta. He would retire garbed in nothing but a towel hung from his waist. He liked to show guests what sort of figure that apparel made him cut. When he went on from Lebanon to Kuwait, his father, who lived with two maiden sisters and must have been a great age, came out from home for a holiday and died under Wolson's roof one lunchtime. Wolson rang the approved undertakers and departed for his nap, clothed in his usual fashion. He was a deep sleeper. In his gruff, grating voice, he used to recount with glee how he was awakened by his head hitting one step after another of his stone stairs as he was dragged out to their vehicle by the professionals he had summoned. The dialogue that ensued between the old artist of the Egyptian music hall and the unskilled operatives — no doubt Baluchis, speaking neither Arabic nor English — would have delighted his admirers. An encounter between Wolson and the ambassador Horace was to encounter when he finally got to Jordan, many years later, would have been one to treasure had it been conceivable for the two to represent Britain in the same country and era.

118

14

Gloom in Khartum

Khartoum looks like a mere village ...
(Alaric Jacob)

*... a provinciality, a Khartum
atmosphere, a lack of the feeling
of a capital.*

(Ronald Storrs)

They were marooned for three depressing months in the hotel in Beirut, whose repetitive menus and muzak drove its captive guests quickly to distraction. Being stuck in Lebanon had one advantage, however: the unexpected opportunity to reassess some of the country's attractions. Horace naturally wanted to visit Byblos again. Sidon was new. They admired its picturesque harbour, with fishermen sitting near it mending their nets, and crossed the causeway to the photogenic crusader castle. Anjar, an impressive site to which Muhammad took them, was not only new but also unknown, not featuring in any of the guidebooks,

The violent character of Lebanon — 'a country of brigands and thugs', he called it in his diary — was always on display. The anarchic traffic on the coastal road to the north caused his wife to weep with apprehension. They saw their hotelier, aided by his sinister barman, drag a taxi driver in off the street and — for what reason they failed to discover — beat him up at the back of the establishment, graced at the time by Ted Dexter on his way to a cricket event in Kuwait.

On the death of President Nasser, Beirut exploded in a practice for the greater civil war which was soon to engulf it, an orgy of both grief and joy fuelled by a general lack of self-control. Bursts of live ammunition were fired down the streets, their nerves suffered severely because of the noise and worry about their three-year-old, and for a week they were afraid to go out lest the spent cartridge they found on their veranda were followed up by one with a little more stamina. On official advice, they placed a photograph of the dead President under a windscreen wiper — with some trepidation lest anti-Nasserites take exception to it.

When all hope of going to Jordan had vanished, on the day before their departure for Khartum and its own journey by land, sea and rail to meet up with them in the Sudan, Horace found that someone had run a nail right round the boot of their car. The hotel manager had told them who had been the author of an earlier mystery bump and this looked like revenge for the revelation.

Muhammad, chauffeuring them to the airport, was as sentimental as most Arabs are about fair-headed children, and Andrew accordingly climbed the steps of the Sudan Airways' Comet clutching an unexpected warplane.

* * *

On arrival in Khartum, they spent a demoralised night in what passed for a hotel, a Greek establishment where, two decades later, a British family unit like theirs was wiped out by terrorists. The worst caterwauling ever heard, from creatures which must have been twice the normal size, gave their hours of sleep a ghastly wakefulness.

Khartum means 'elephant's trunk', perhaps after the shape of the confluence of the Blue and White Niles when they join at Omdurman to set off together for Egypt. The romance of the name was at once dissipated when their first day revealed the city in all its lifeless dinginess. What a contrast with bright, vibrant Baghdad! His boss, Ariel, drove them round Khartum itself, Khartum North and Omdurman, the three towns which make up the capital. Although this was the cool season, they were so deserted that Horace wondered if the population could produce enough work to justify their journey of several thousand miles. They were taken to a mediocre buffet lunch at the Sudan Club. A dismal failure in its imitativeness, the Club was drab and felt neglected, no doubt partly because membership was not, despite its title, open to the people of the country. Later, Horace's motion seeking to get the name changed was voted down. The only one carried authorised the construction of a bar to complement the two the club already possessed.

Their departing colleague had a thing about being single. He had been burgled an enormous number of times. 'I've been asked to show you your accommodation,' he said. He drove them through the dead, tree-lined streets of the city, across roundabout after roundabout with children's play equipment in the middle but not much in the way of children. The whole place had a pre-Gorbachev East European feel about it. He parked his ancient vehicle outside a house that was to turn out to be only identifiable by the colour (blue) of its gate — imperfectly, because one taxi-driver would think that blue meant green, another red; in Sudanese Arabic, yellow of course was black and purple orange. A path ran to the front door between patches of grass which looked as though they had not recovered from a severe drought. They entered. The house was all faded blues and greens and deep in dust. In the oven were the remains of the last meal cooked on the premises, it was later confirmed, by the office's 'fixer' and one of his lady friends. After Baghdad, it was enough to break your heart. They moved on. Addressing them with the sort of formality which may confront the just on nearing the Pearly Gates, 'This is your sitting-room,' their guide announced. With a flourish, he flung open the door, setting it bowling into the middle of the frayed carpet, where it collapsed with a crash of doom. Their Sudanese cup was overflowing. The television they were surprised to find supplied blew up the first time they switched it on and never subsequently functioned. His wife's shock expressed itself in tears next day. 'Lack of adaptability,' said the boss's spouse, with all the sympathy of which she seemed capable. Her husband, Ariel, agreed to loan them the office Land Rover for Christmas. It had to be push-started and then was declared to be unserviceable.

They had been in Khartum less than a week — and had already dismissed the first of the many cooks they were to engage — when they were invited to a buffet supper at which a senior diplomat in the low-grade British Embassy, Sledge, opened a conversation on the Palestine question. The topic had lost Horace more than one friend since the deep immersion he had undergone in Iraq had made him an uncompromising sympathiser with the Arab side. Only the exceptional British diplomat like Sir Dick would have been likely to admit to being one too. After losing Jordan, finding himself marooned in Beirut by his new employers and then expected to exercise a stiff upper lip over intolerable conditions in Khartum, Horace's convictions were even more bluntly enunciated than usual. The likelihood that Sledge did not share them, and the fact that Horace was in an emotional state, made this unfortunate:

'Lovely people, the Sudanese, but doesn't their fecklessness really give you the clue about the impregnability of Israel?'

'Perhaps it does, but the Palestinians can hardly be said to have had much of a chance.'

'What on earth do you mean?'

'Well, it's hardly been an equal contest.'

'I cannot imagine what you are suggesting.'

'The Israelis had the British, Hitler and finally the Americans on their side. How could they lose? British policies have much to answer for.'

'Are you British? You strike me as being more like a fascist, a communist and a racist.'

Horace refused to entertain the apologies Sledge offered him throughout the rest of the evening and for a long time afterwards. Next day when he told Ariel, a man generally non-commital, the response his upset condition induced was a statement that he 'assumed that relations were back to normal again'.

Sledge came up trumps when he took the same 'plane home as they did one leave. As so often, the BOAC VC10 overflew Khartum because of a 'hubub' and they had to take admirable Ethiopian Airlines instead on their first leg. This involved staying a night in an Athens hotel to which a promised bus failed to materialise when they landed. Horace was too encumbered with dependants, carrycot, golf clubs, bicycle with one tyre flat and thesis to seize control of the situation. Sledge, however, walked to the King's Palace Hotel, returned to report that space for all was booked in it and took charge of ferrying a large group of displaced air travellers thither. Horace admired his man of action performance and would on account of it have forgiven him if asked again.

His had not been the best start to make with new business colleagues. (They included, to Horace's nostalgic delight, an official whose wife was Bridget in the Arthur Ransome books on which he had been brought up.) Nonetheless, it seemed to have been overcome during their first two tours, marked of course by no communication with Sledge and not much more — but in this case for the very different reason that Horace could think of no subject to suggest for discussion — with Ariel. The situation was settled in Horace's disfavour, however, by his part in the Affair of the Russophile Registrar.

One of the liveliest people in the small British community in Khartum was Cliff, the Embassy Registrar, a self-taught, intellectual man who organised the amateur theatricals that — like Caledonian societies, Scots being much more amenable abroad than when they are north of the border — boost the morale of Britons overseas. Expatriate amateur dramatics were based on the Sudan Club of which, overriding their convictions, they had become members, habitually eating Friday lunch there. Horace did not know him well but could not avoid bumping into him as he took the lead in most of his own productions, in which Horace's wife was a regular performer. The Registrar and his wife were much missed by the nicer, more extrovert figures of the British community when they were transferred elsewhere. And yet, something must have felt not quite right. When, later in the year of their departure — which the ambassador had honoured with cocktails in his residence, — the BBC World Service included among its day's headlines news of the arrest of a British official in the capital concerned, Horace knew that it must be the ex-Registrar before he heard the name.

They were about to go on leave themselves and by the time they set off he had been placed, on remand, in Penham. Out of fellow feeling, Horace determined to visit him. The arrangements to do so were astonishingly casual, but he was disturbed on his arrival at having his name chalked up on a board.

Face to face, albeit through a glass partition, with a surprised Cliff, he did not know what to say:

'How are you, Cliff?'

'I'll survive.'

'We were very sorry to hear the news of what had happened.' (Conscious of surveilling ears). 'We aren't concerned about the story, only about you and your family. Is there anything we can do for you?'

'We'll be all right.'

It rapidly eventuated, however, that, in his resentment at this busy-bodying, he had oversimplified the situation. On re-emerging, Horace came upon Cliff's wife weeping against the prison wall and discovered that she was in fact homeless. He promised her that when they returned to the Sudan at the end of their leave she and their little girl could have their house.

Horace had made himself into a favourite of the ambassador in Khartum, a plain Mr, who beamed on him particularly when he was acting as head of the office and came to rely on him in a number of areas. Since leaving a situation with a first-class outfit to take up with one in the second division, this was just what he had wanted, in order to show the former that it could not manage without him. The days of approval were over now. It quickly became clear that, for visiting a fellow human being at his lowest point, Horace had been put on an Embassy blacklist. His crimes were major. First he had been found not to be British, now he had given succour to our enemies. When he grasped the reality of his changed position, he became contemptuous, and an eager collector of illustrations of ambassadorial pettiness.

Just before the end of his posting, after which he was retiring, the ambassador made a visit to the capital of Southern Sudan, and returned from it with such a bad bout of food poisoning that Juba had to be renamed Salmonella City. Horace could no longer address him, of course, in order to express a sympathy he didn't feel. His retirement journey was their first on leave from Khartum. Having travelled home on the same flight, Horace's final, savoured sight of him was as, like a Viceroy at Suez on his return from India, his extraordinary and plenipotentiary protection and props removed — compared with those of his knight ambassadors in Baghdad, they hadn't seemed many, anyway — he scrabbled for his luggage beside a Heathrow carousel. Their eyes met but there was no greeting. Horace's case arrived first.

Horace was delighted to read a newspaper account some years later of the ex-ambassador's involvement in a fracas at a West Country railway station, the entrance to which he appeared deliberately to have blocked with his car. He used to be driven around Khartum in an Austin Princess (the large earlier version, not the later smaller one), which — colonial habits being too pleasant to be easily jettisoned — was the same khaki colour as that of the one ridden in by the President of the Sudanese Republic. They had speculated about one being shot in mistake for the other. Like most British ambassadors, he was — correctly — concerned that British officials should run British cars. In a place where, as the British car industry waited for Honda to come to its rescue, this entailed a masochistic and ridiculous, Heath Robinson-type uphill struggle, he was more pedantic about it than most. The vehicle in which, Widmerpool-like, he had created a newsworthy scene was a Mercedes.

The Registrar's motives for accepting puny sums from the Soviets were complex. Horace had a theory that an uncaring employer played a large part in his downfall: Cliff used to claim that the ambassador had only twice visited his room, once when lost in his own premises, the second time to say, 'Strong smell of beer in here,' before moving on.

* * *

Horace played a lot of sport in Khartum. Squash was in a court open to the sky where the temperature habitually far exceeded 100 degrees. Cricket was much more important and, in a place where there was so little to do, treated with deadly earnestness. The ground was a large and pleasant green meadow, just past the prison in North Khartum. At other times, the cows grazed there which produced the milk delivered daily to their garden wall. A fine sight from the outfield on one of the weekend match days was the passage of a yellow and white Libyan Arab Airlines' 'plane, reported to carry on average a total of one passenger between Khartum and Tripoli.

Because of his ready access to clerical support, Horace was soon made secretary of the cricket club — too soon, perhaps, because the committee appeared to regret the speedy appointment when it discovered a rule in the constitution stating the holder of the position to be ex-officio vice-president as well. All went smoothly, however, until he undertook to escort to the ground an Egyptian who had recently arrived and whose reputation as a performer had preceded him. (Some of their most talented players were Egyptians, many of them old boys of the British-type public school

Victoria College, renamed Victory College by President Nasser after Suez.) When Horace called, he was not ready and coffee for which there was no time was pressed on him.

They duly arrived late for the start of the game. The team for which Horace had been selected was batting and two or three wickets had already fallen. He imagined that he would quickly be asked to put on his pads and set about arresting the decline. The call was delayed and further delayed, and Horace fumed on gathering that his unpunctuality had won him the number ten position in the order. As he walked in, he gave oral notice of his resignation from the committee to the president, who was fielding at mid-on. He then proceeded to bring the innings to a sudden end (they were a man short) by running out his partner. This had not been deliberate, though the charge was made, but no doubt it was an inevitable consequence of the hysterical reaction to a petty affront to his pride of an opening bat scorned.

Cricket seemed to Horace to be at the root of the other Embassy personnel problem to become known to the British community. They heard one day that a friend of theirs in the Embassy had left the country:

'Have you heard the news? You'll hardly believe it.'

'Whatever's happened?'

'Janet told me at the Club this morning that Peter and Alice have gone.'

'Gone? Gone where?'

'To UK. It doesn't sound at all as if they're coming back.'

'Whatever happened?'

'Apparently there was a sit-in at the Embassy yesterday. British staff at the University protesting about our Rhodesia policies.'

'I can guess who the organiser was.'

'Janet said Peter rushed down from his office on the next floor with a sword in his hand. Apparently he intended to set about the demonstrators and presumably had to be overpowered. I'm surprised you hadn't heard. Did no one at the office mention it?'

'I've been out at HTTTI all morning. Can you imagine Ariel saying anything anyway? I'm only his deputy, after all. Poor Peter and Alice.'

The ringleader of the demonstration was a teacher whose habitual drunkenness was encouraged by the leisure afforded him through the University being usually shut for political reasons. When intoxicated, he was in the habit of throwing his wife through a closed window into the Sudan Club pool. He certainly had no conception of the standards required in the game according to Peter.

Peter was one of Khartum's keenest cricketers. Whoever else could not make it every Friday and Saturday, Peter was there, with cheeks flushed in boyish anticipation. Every Friday and Saturday, when he was out for a single figure score, his disappointment was pitiful to see. Horace did not know him well enough to make a considered analysis. But his failures on the field were so deeply felt, he was so cut to the quick by the continual thwarting of his ambitions, that it was to the domino effect of his cricketing frustrations that Horace attributed the irruption of his spectacular final act. Peter's replacement was an interesting man who, though in due course far outshone by his son, was much better at cricket. He would take insultingly short singles to anyone whose arm was not accurate. Horace — a brilliant stopper of the ball, *à la* Washbrook, at cover point — possessed one which was not.

* * *

As a final fling before the birth of their second son, they went on a short trip to Eritrea in a rather less impressive Ethiopian Airlines' 'plane than their Khartum–Cairo–Athens one. During their stay, the waters of the Red Sea closed over Horace's engagement ring. (The Black Sea was to claim his wedding ring. His wife made no move to replace either.) Returning with Sudan Airways and hearing that their pilot was Captain Yusuf, they asked a hostess to inform him that Mrs Tension was on board. Yusuf is a very common name and, when she reached the cockpit, a Yusuf to whom she had not taught English shot them the apprehensive glance of one bracing himself for a hijack.

After arriving from Jordan by Sudan Railways — though not, like their lift van, falling off them, — their personal export Hillman had reached them with its battery in terminal decline. It could not be replaced in Khartum. Now, Horace imported a huge new Ethiopian one, which he had done all he could to conceal in the middle of one of their cases to avoid prohibitive Sudanese customs' duties. At Khartum Airport, although the case proved suspiciously difficult to lift and carry, the customs' scrutineer, who made a thorough peripheral search of it, failed — Horace thought out of post-colonial inhibition — to discover the battery.

* * *

Away from such happenings, making up for the dullness of Khartum, he intermittently complained of being chronically underemployed and at the lack of the prospect of having anything sensible to do. He spent a lot of time at his office desk working on his book. Short-term projects were given him in the expectation that they would mollify him, which in the short term some of them did. One was a visit by a famous British archaeologist, who came for a routine meeting with his Sudanese opposite number and agreed to deliver a public lecture during his stay. It was preceded by a reception which Horace, as the organiser of his programme, was the last to leave. Khartum streets are indistinguishable from one another, especially in the dark. Despite several attempts to find it, he lost his way to the lecture hall and had no alternative but to go home. The next day he asked Ariel how the talk had gone. The man who rarely vouchasafed an opinion on anything said, 'Terrible, he could hardly speak. He was so nervous, the whole thing was dreadfully embarrassing.'

Another visitor was Sir Christopher Cox, one of the founders of Western-style education in the Sudan and the mentor of many of the leading Sudanese higher educationalists of the day. He was equally famous as a furniture breaker. Rumour had it that, at a look from him, chairs would disintegrate, and this turned out to be no exaggeration. At the start of his programme, a buffet lunch was given for him by the Vice-Chancellor of Khartum University, whose closure on security grounds the government had just decreed after the opening ceremony of its medical faculty's fiftieth anniversary celebrations had turned into a riot. No sooner had Sir Christopher been directed to a seat than his advance towards it had reduced it to matchsticks.

He wasn't a big or hefty man. He was certainly nervous, not least as a passenger. Horace took him to his appointments in a

dismal-looking, small Fiat he had bought for the equivalent of
£618* as a stopgap until the Hillman arrived, which it needed four
months to do. (The wait for their heavy luggage lasted two
months longer.) Although the Fiat's gear lever collapsed at one
point and the boot key once had to do duty for the one meant for
the ignition when that snapped in two (as it did again when in due
course Horace was trying to hand it over to its new owner), the
ten-year-old car did not seriously let them down during the
waiting period. Nor should it have done, considering the
monstrous price paid for it. The prospect of riding in it must,
however, have daunted the legendary educationalist, whose chair-
breaking luckily did not function in vehicles. The first time Horace
chauffeured him, they had to halt at a junction only yards from
the collection point at the ambassador's residence. They
approached at a crawl with the passenger screaming at Horace to
brake when, if he had ceased to accelerate, the car would have
come to a stop at a point from which traffic to right and left
would not have been visible. They continued their journey with
Horace proceeding as gingerly as his passenger wished, and in due
course picked up the Director of the National Museum from his
place of work — the Fiat had never before had such a
distinguished passenger list, nor would it again — and took him to
the Sudan Club for lunch. (A number of Britons were murdered
there some years later, perhaps partly on account of its provocative
name, and Sudanese were so rarely seen in the Club that Horace
— like Wingate with the Maharana of Udaipur — once became
outspokenly irritated with one whom, in his Friday best, he
mistook for a waiter). The Director had a most uncomfortable
meal. Apprehensive throughout in the bastion of British imperial-

---

* This was a sizeable sum, especially for so unpromising-looking a vehicle in a
country which had almost no roads. The transaction provoked the utterance of
a never-to-be-forgotten dictum. The car had to be financed by a withdrawal
from a British building society, the resultant sum was caught up in a postal
strike and the countervailing funds failed to arrive before the manager of
Horace's Barclays branch in London bounced his purchase cheque and queried
with his employers his suitability to be a member of their staff. In reply to
Horace's protest that his record was the guarantee that matching funds were
on the way and that the strike was outside his control, he wrote, 'We are not
clairvoyant.'

ism and exclusiveness, he kept looking over his shoulder to make sure that his escape route to the street outside was still unblocked.

Two against whom it was rudely closed were workmen at the house. Horace carried a jacket to the office for use on calls. In his room, whose firewood furniture and lamentable decorative condition sharpened his regret for the one by the Tigris, he used to hang it on a nail in the wall behind his chair and lock his wallet in a drawer. Leaving for home, the process was reversed. On his return to the house on one particular day, he was unable to find the wallet and reported his loss to the local police:

'Do you suspect anyone?'

'No, I can't imagine how this occurred.'

'Is anybody working in the house?'

'Yes, there are three painters, but I don't believe any of them is involved.'

He would have done better to keep his mouth shut. The workmen were behind bars before he could say "Lord Kitchener".

Two days later he selected the same suit for work and had difficulty in getting his arm through the sleeve... He rushed to the police station, calling for the innocent victims of his carelessness to be freed immediately. Sudanese justice proved itself as speedy at release as at detention. Neither man sued or held his loss of liberty against him. One was a regular casual employee of the office who had always been friendly. After their shared experience, he became much more so. The Third World has a great deal to teach of forgivingness.*

A pleasant feature of the Sudan was the approachability of its leading figures. In their first year they met the country's first President, a descendant of the Mahdi who worsted General Gordon. A prominent member of the government, who eventually rose to the very top, came to all their film shows. A former foreign minister became a friend with whom Horace frequently discussed the past

---

* A First World example, however, is of a girl who once worked for Horace in London. He thought her incompetent, tried to quash a promotion granted her before his arrival and generally made his poor opinion clear to her and others, e.g. at annual interview time. The more damning he was, the more she smiled on him. When she accompanied her husband overseas, they parted the best of friends.

130

and present relationship of Britain and the Sudan and the quite different topic of the book he was writing. Sometimes, however, the country's rulers came too close for comfort and made a chillingly contrasting impression.

One day after the Hillman had at last put in an appearance, Horace's wife came with their four-year-old son to collect him from work. In an immature chauvinistic way he has since outgrown, he took over the wheel of the Hillman and they drove off. At the pastoral and uncongested ring road, they had to wait behind a white Beetle before being able to proceed. The other car backed into them two or three times. Although the Hillman bore little resemblance to the one whose victory in the East African Safari had persuaded Horace to buy it, when both were across it performed the feat — remarkable in a car totally devoid of performance — of allowing him to overtake and pin the aggressor into the kerb. Dressed in white robes, he was a sinister man with a patronising manner; beside him was a nondescript figure in a suit.

'May I see your certificate of insurance?'

'What are you?'

'*Ana ajnabi.*'

'*Ajnabi*? You give yourself colonial rights in independent Sudan?'

(Apprehensive). 'No, I'm just a foreigner. And I would like to see your licence.'

'Why you want see licence?'

'Because you have damaged my car by reversing into it.'

'I not give licence.'

'In that case, I will report you at the next police station.'

Horace was too recent an arrival to know that they were already at the next police station, that of the Ministry of Defence, at most 30 yards from where they were parleying. Having ascertained that the damage was slight, he drove on with no immediate intention of executing his threat. They had gone no distance along the diagonal road though the Airport Quarter, however, when he saw in his mirror that they were being pursued by lorryloads of armed troops. They caught his hopeless vehicle up — just after the junction with Airport Road, near Clergy House School where Andrew was a pupil — and encircled them with weapons brandished. It was patent that, for no evident reason, they were involved in an incident which was already bigger than them. Someone snatched the keys from his ignition:

'We go back to police station.'

This was the sort of situation he had always dreaded not having enough nerve for. But his wife, not newly pregnant, was as near hysterics as he ever saw her, their son was very frightened and someone had to keep cool. What he did next, as the convoy began manoeuvring in order to retrace its steps, was, however, neither calm nor collected. He was not sure how they expected him to return with them when they had taken his keys. He inserted his other set and drove off as hard as he could in the direction opposite to the one which they had indicated led to the police station. They overtook them again in a matter of yards. Surrounded once more, he pretended that his action had been designed only to facilitate their backtracking and they believed his preposterous story.

As he entered the building, a squad of men presented arms to the suited passenger ahead of him... They finally got away, hours later, when, to break the deadlock, Horace proposed that they shake hands like gentlemen and leave it at that. In the guardroom, the debate had passed back and forth between the police chief and the passenger with no conclusion being neared. To Horace's relief, his antagonist accepted the suggestion and left. He was almost free to go, abandoning his case for the sake of an earnestly desired return to normality. Before he could, however, he was required to reveal the full details of his name, address, place of work and 'phone numbers.

'You know all about me. Who was that?'

As though betraying a state secret, they said that he was the man who, until two months before, had been Vice-President, Minister of Defence and Commander-in-Chief of the Armed Forces. He had obviously retained effective links with the military and they in turn appeared to keep their vehicles well serviced.

They drove home, sapped of spirit. For days they expected a knock on the door. For months, their son was terrified by the sight of anyone in uniform and had to be dragged to school. The incident finalised their attitude to the Sudan as one not of affection. When he told him of the incident and its peaceful ending, with egregious self-justification Ariel said, 'So, you see, your Arabic does have its uses here after all.'

While dramatic events had been continuous in Baghdad, in Khartum they were on the one hand both less frequent and of almost no interest to Horace but on the other more prone to engulf non-combatants. Following a communist coup, a BOAC VC10 — full of British children released from their boarding schools for the holidays, and announced in advance to be carrying the new President as well, — was hijacked to Libya. Mothers and fathers spent anxious hours at Khartum airport when the only information available was that air traffic controllers had lost touch with the 'plane.

Quashing the coup was a bloody, frightening business: no decent martial music was put out on the radio, no curfew was imposed, and amphibious army vehicles, not under officer control, cruised about the capital terrorising Sudanese and foreigners alike. Horace — apprehensive against a background of machine-gun bursts — drove to the nationalised Barclays Bank for funds one morning and believed himself a dead man when a volley exploded, apparently in his ear. He flung himself through the doors of the bank and was helped by staff and customers, to whom he warmed, to join them on the floor behind closed shutters. The moment passed, he cashed his cheque and, as he got back into his car, noticed a section of soldiers laughing and joking down an alleyway, delighted at the effect of their irresponsible salvo.

Fifteen months later, the New Year, inaugurated with much ringing of church bells, soon went sour. A week after Andrew had indignantly told Princess Anne that he had been robbed of a place in the school sports' finals, the Black September murders took place. In the morning, as an ill omen, Ariel's dog had been shot during a cull of strays. In the evening, as they left for a cocktail party, they heard a fusillade. By the time they returned, the story was all over town: during a reception at the Saudi ambassador's house, the eponymous Palestinian group — named after the month in which King Husayn had put down the Palestinian movement which threatened Jordan's unity and future and stopped Horace getting to Amman — seized five foreign diplomats to avenge the shooting-down by Israel of a Libyan airliner (not on the Tripoli–Khartum run) in which 108 passengers had died a week before. A large area encircling the Saudi residence was cordoned off in response to the Black September threat to blow it and their captives up if their demands were not met. Horace's house was just within the perimeter and for the 60 hours the siege lasted their garden wall, which ran right round their premises, became a gallery for hundreds of spectators. They took care to keep their police guards — none remembered from the affair at the Ministry of Defence — well supplied with water, tea and beer and to maintain contact with nearby members of the British community who did not have the benefit of a ringside seat. The chief need was to prepare Andrew (now nearly six) for the possibility that, without warning, there might be shooting and explosions close by. This personal fear was, luckily, unfounded.

It was, however, bad enough that three men died. The hostage-takers killed the Belgian envoy, the incoming US ambassador and the man who had been chargé d'affaires until his arrival. Since the establishment of Israel, Americans have been the primary targets of Palestinian protest, but no convincing reason for taking the Belgian was ever given. Horace and his wife had been getting to know and like the chargé, with whom Horace (piano) had been playing in a trio only a few nights before his murder. They felt for their families while the captives were under sentence of death and grieved for their loved ones when it was carried out — so short-sightedly, for thereby was gratuitously thrown away the political gift the Israelis had presented to the Palestinians only days before.

It was perhaps partly as a reaction to such traumatic occurrences that some of the highest in the land sought and achieved oblivion through alcohol. Camel Beer, in bottles which gave the impression of being oversize, varied enormously in quality but was often quite delicious. Their minister friend was excessively fond of it and after cultural evenings with them had sometimes to be carried to his car. (Whether for allied reasons or not, many years later he failed to dismount from a train from King's Cross to Durham, where he was a frequent visitor to the University. A search party eventually found him in a snowdrift in Chester-le-Street.)

The paucity of leisure activities in Khartum was another reason why drink was dispensed so liberally. The Sudanis in general were fond of it. They must have suffered agonies (as if they had not had pain enough already) when, to celebrate one of the unwise extensions of Islamic law to cover the non-Muslim south of the country, alcohol was proscribed and President Nimeiri — reputed to be, in whisky terms, a two-bottle man — led the pouring of the nation's stocks into a Nile rapidly become inflammable.

Horace was once invited to a Bulgarian home for tea. It consisted of whisky, Courvoisier and cigars. A loosely attached member of the organisation's team once came to a never-to-be-forgotten lunch at Horace's house. Unskilled in such matters, he offered him an aperitif and, when he chose Noilly Prat and gin and indicated the size of glass he preferred to drink them from, filled it with neat spirit. The guest, presumably also a learner, drained it without taking breath and contributed nothing to the conversation during the whole of the meal.

An engaging colleague — continually ridiculed by the incoming British ambassador as 'the Irishman teaching the Sudanese English' — once had his brother, an ex-member of a Dublin government, to stay and gave a reception in his honour. The other guests were surprised to find the brother wearing, above the waist, only a string vest when the introductions were effected.

Khartum was a place where people cracked up. The Registrar and Peter were not the only ones. A British wife ran off with the British Butcher. A colleague, Acton, had a nervous breakdown. They had all been surprised when one of the staff — Herbert, a clergyman *manqué* who was in the habit of wearing gauleiter boots — invited Acton and his wife to stay for a settling-in night on their return from home leave rather than go straight into the business, in the early hours, of getting their house going again. The surprise turned to indignation when, letting the side down in an unprecedented way, Herbert next day denounced his colleague as a thief to the local police. The case developed and continued for some considerable time. Ariel seemed not to become involved. Their friend was caused almost fatal disquiet. When they were able to break a six-month silence imposed on them by Ariel, Horace and his friends asked Herbert what his evidence was and he claimed to prove the case by contriving it that a florin which he rolled along an upper banister rail in his house should land 'heads' on the floor beneath.

While this had been going on, Herbert one day made his usual battering-ram entry into Horace's room and asked to see the inspection report on the office which Ariel, now on leave, had not allowed to emerge from a locked drawer. Horace had been permitted to glance at it and had with typical carelessness forgotten its proposal that Herbert should be made redundant. In a spirit of ready cooperation, he handed it over. When, seconds later, Herbert crashed back in again, he did some of the quickest thinking of his life to explain the recommendation away.

Herbert had an expatriate Christian Lebanese assistant, a fat young man of attractive character, who suffered from asthma and regularly used a decongestant spray. He felt the full force of Herbert's terrorist methods. It was only grudgingly that he was allowed out of the building to perform his official tasks in town. When he returned, Herbert's grip on him was reapplied and in fear he resumed his seat in a corner of the office they shared. When Horace's heavy luggage had gone off to Turkey at the end of their posting, Herbert tried to hide the office emergency kit of basic cutlery, crockery and cooking utensils so that he and his family could not make use of it. Despite their strong dislike of him, the politically correct Ariel nonetheless added him to the list of friends they asked him to invite to the statutory farewell he hosted for them.

During his time in the Sudan, Horace's employers had libraries in four provincial towns, and offices in both Khartum and Omdurman, which are about five miles apart. Soon after sending Horace's monthly pay cheque to the wrong bank, causing him to have to go to law to recover it, the organisation transferred a colleague from Omdurman to the capital and sent him a document offering him guidance on the climate and local customs he would experience in his new post.

The first director Horace knew in Omdurman, Rite, had learned fluent spoken Arabic from his cook. After he left the Sudan, he took on responsibilities covering the Middle East in general and, as he received successive promotions, would arrive on 'familiar-isation' journeys — of the kind most commonly indulged in by people revisiting their favourite places of posting six months after spending five years in them — and be taken to meet the local Ministers of Culture, Education, &c. In an embarrassingly over-bearing way, he would harangue them in long stretches of kitchen Omdurmani colloquial speech which would have caused problems in Wad Medani and Suakin, let alone Amman or Damascus.

There had always been odd occurrences when Rite was about. In the Sudan, he and his driver twice disappeared on official journeys into the desert and re-emerged with stories of misfortune to tell. His wallet was lost in mysterious circumstances, an office vehicle returned with tyres of lesser quality than those the driver had set out with and, on one occasion, without any. The driver always seemed to be involved. When Rite was transferred, the driver went with him and they scandalised the local staff in their new country by living together in the official residence, which became one of Horace's better homes some years later.

An early successor of Rite's in Omdurman was an old Etonian called Alwis who, if he was not native on his arrival, very soon became so. He once asked for permission to be a little late at work because he wanted to start some decorators off in his house. Three days later, when there was a riot outside his office, he was nowhere to be found. Run to earth at home, he was discovered in his *jallabiyyah* with his feet up, supervising the painters. On the pretext of visiting British Voluntary Service Overseas' teachers, Alwis indulged in desert travel. His report on one of his lengthy forays was one paragraph long and stated his conviction that the Sudanese desert closely resembled that of Arabia.

Horace shared in the task of looking after the welfare of the volunteers. He visited them in dusty places with delightful names like Hassaheisa and marvelled that they seemed to revel in isolation and living conditions which, with no cooling and only rudimentary cooking facilities, he thought even in his hitchhiking days he could not have tolerated. Sometimes, however, they had problems.

When one was bitten by a dog, shrieking telegrams began arriving from medical advisers in London demanding to be informed — by lay people like Horace whose opinions they would have scorned at home — 'whether or not it is rabies, YES OR NO'. A sad case was that of one of the few girls, who was brought into Khartum after she had behaved strangely in her original place of posting, Atbara — the Crewe of the Sudan, — some way to the north. Though she took up residence with two volunteers experienced in the ways of the capital, it was not long before the abnormalities resumed. 'DEATH' was found written in the sand beneath the lavatory pedestal. More orthodox pieces of writing were left for her companions to discover which pointed in the direction of suicide. Finally, she was retrieved from the middle of one of the longer Nile bridges from which, in the small hours, she was staring fixedly into the water. In a rare example of untrammelled power, perhaps not exercised since as duty officer he had put two men inside for appearing dirty on guard-mounting, Horace decided to send her home. He escorted her to the airport, feeling high-handed and perhaps a little sadistic. Her papers, luckily, were in order — unlike those of the Noilly Prat victim who had shut up his house, emptied his 'fridges, sent his domestic staff on leave and arrived at the airport with his large family a month before to discover that the 'fixer' (the vestiges of whose last supper had not been cleared from Horace's first cooker) had omitted to secure exit permits for them.

The first secretary who worked for Horace was an elephantine lady, Selma Lloyd George by name, whose allure at the keyboard was as ponderous as her gait. When he was promoted — one of the only two occasions when this happened to him in a more than 20-year career with his new employers — he inherited a male amanuensis who was vastly superior. Of the Baggara cattle-owning tribe — accustomed, when peckish, to carving a slice from a passing quadruped, — Jibril supported Horace's efforts for the rest of his time in Khartum with exemplary fidelity. He once produced a marvellous howler when Horace explained to him his use of a foreign term in dictation and it came out, 'This French word volte-face will have useful consequences for our cultural work.' (When something similar occurred years later at the hands of a British secretary, Horace awarded Jibril silent exoneration.)

You could not get a suit made in Khartum. Just as Horace was due for home leave, Jibril asked him to bring him one back from Britain:

'How will I explain to the shop what you are like, Jib?'

'I'll give you brown paper with all my measurements to take with you.'

So Horace included in his case a large roll of sticky parcel-sealing tape, cut up into strips representing the lengths, widths and circumferences of Jibril's various members. He presented these to a gentlemen's outfitters in Croydon. 'Now I'm beginning to picture the man,' the tailor said as — entering with enthusiasm into the spirit of the game — he began to assemble Jibril from the clues he had so ingeniously provided. In due course, Horace's right-hand man had the dark suit he wanted. Even though he would have looked wrong in it among his cows on the plains of Kordofan, it gave them the smartest of colleagues.

It was after two years in Khartum that Horace's promotion came. Or he thought it had. When he had recovered from a homeward leave journey and called on the personnel department, he was informed that the elevation was temporary. No two employees of the organisation for which he had the doubtful honour to work were ever to be found in agreement with one another about how to interpret its regulations. The second ruling was overturned.

Things were mixed on the domestic front. While they found a nanny, Nini, from Eritrea, who very quickly began to provide all the help they could possibly require with their young children — including instruction in Tigrinya as the first language of the younger one, Swithin, safely delivered in Khartum a year before — the cook/houseboy position was not satisfactorily filled until three months before the end of their three-year stay. Every single one of the predecessors of the last incumbent, whom they were sorry to leave behind, had been equally hopeless, unreliable or vicious. The second had his employment terminated on his fifth day for refusing to babysit as contracted. Unlike poor Abbas in Baghdad, James received the award of a bicycle before departing. Robert, ejected for stealing their possessions, cheekily shouted, 'It's not your government now' as he took to his heels. Not all, however, were as spectacular or cunning as Khalid. On what turned out to be his last day in the job, a quarrel with Nini in the kitchen provoked him into hurling their rather expensive china at her. Sweeping their toddler up into the protection of her monumental bosom, she fled outside. When Horace arrived home from work, they were cowering in the carport pergola covered in blood. Khalid's resultant departure was so precipitate that he had no time to gather up his bundle of the references that are the vade-mecum of the Middle East's domestic servants. With studied deliberation, Horace forwarded them to him with a new one inserted out of order in the hope that it would do his career prospects no good. The hope was vain, for Khalid was quickly reported to be working, after no more than an insignificant break in the continuity of his employment record, for the US chargé d'affaires whom Black September later murdered.

They had a nice little dog, Jamilah, who suffered dreadfully from ticks. No matter how many times she was bathed in Dettol, no matter how many vets came to examine her, no lasting improvement was ever made to her condition and she was in due course put down. Nini had been fond of her and was sad at her passing.

Unaffected by weather or *coups d'état*, a daily delivery of milk was made, uniquely in their experience, to their front gate. Empties and full bottles had to tally and there was a good deal of arguing over arithmetic, as with milkmen everywhere. The supply of nearly all other necessities in Khartum was erratic. A hammer was needed to extract the local toothpaste from its tube. They were lucky in one respect, being able to import a periodic supplementary parcel from Nairobi which contained such items as bacon. In another, they suffered from the unwritten Foreign Office rule which appears to state that its diplomatic parcel bag may be used by people such as Horace had become only where — as would have been the case in Baghdad — it is not necessary. In Khartum, where life was close to unviable, they had no access to it. Their move from Beirut had come just before Christmas. None of their presents reached them on time and some failed altogether to appear. Gertrude Bell had taken delivery in Basrah of a box which 'ought to have contained a black satin gown'. They paid the Sudanese post office sizeable duty in return for a packet containing a bit of string with a rusty razor blade attached. Books for his wife's birthday in February were 14 weeks late.

Horace often could not obtain any of his favourite pipe tobaccos — Condor Ready-rubbed, Player's Whiskey Flake or Erinmore — and had to make do with Haggar's Fireweed, a product of the South. Well named, and probably years old when opened, it tended to set alight too quickly to allow the smoke to be drawn into the mouth.

Khartum well illustrated the housing situation for people like them. During their overseas career, they averaged three moves per posting, while British Embassy people seemed well satisfied from the start with the accommodation they inherited. In Khartum, Horace and his family lived in three properties. The second house was an improvement, but only intended as a stepping stone to their dream home. This was to have been a BOAC villa, suddenly surplus to requirements. The manager, known to them in Baghdad, invited them to inspect it, they were charmed by its lovely garden, beautiful appointments and decorative condition, and he seemed to accept their request to be allowed to occupy it in due course. Some days later they gave him and his wife a farewell buffet supper, which was not entirely unconnected with their anxiety to win his blessing as tenants. The following morning, 'their' house was advertised in the *Sudan Standard* at a price higher than their rent allowance and, of course, they never took up residence in it.

Sudan Airways during their time was actually British Midland flying their colours. (The same 'planes and crew had immediately before done the same service for El Al.) The arrangement seemed to work very well. So did a little scheme practised on board. Duty-free cigarettes which had been manufactured in Rhodesia (as it then was) were offered to unsuspecting passengers and then confiscated on landing at Khartum because the Sudan government looked with disfavour on Ian Smith's UDI administration.

Horace didn't like Khartum much. Besides being unsatisfactory as far as servants and housing were concerned, an everincreasing proportion of life had to be devoted to queuing and rationing. An average of three power cuts a day could be counted on. Much time was spent driving frozen food to houses whose power supply had not been interrupted and to retrieving it when the current had been restored. The climate was erratic. The hot weather was never consistent, as Baghdad's had been. In their first year they played tennis on Christmas Day and swam on Boxing Day, while Horace took part in a cricket match on 27 December, but such a pattern could not be counted on. It was, however, always necessary to jump up and down to keep warm when the temperature sank to 64 degrees indoors in the middle of January.

The Sudan wasn't Arab or Muslim enough for Horace's taste. Its spoken Arabic did not attract him, the way the Sudanese transliterated from their script into his irritated him. He had no work to do. There was nowhere to go. There were no telling or teaching for his wife. Health was rock-bottom. A new name — Dhobi Itch, which troubled him fleetingly — had to be added to the catalogue of the afflictions they had encountered. The city itself had little to commend it. Comparisons made with North Oxford, apeing Thesiger, merely demonstrated how Britons tended to lose their heads there. Iraq had been so magnificent that the country could hold little interest for them. One Independence Day, Horace noted in his diary that it was 'Sudan's great day, and I couldn't care less'. He didn't feel as contemptuous about it, however, as those expatriates appeared to, who, in the middle of a dinner party, would go outside 'to look at Africa'.

When the time came for them to move to Turkey, Horace decided to put their baggage in the hands of packers no one had ever heard of. Their effects arrived in Ankara in no worse a state than they had reached earlier posts, but the stressfulness of the operation remained unequalled. The firm had severely under-estimated the amount of time the job would take and there was continual strife between its representatives and their domestic staff.

The head of the company had been scornful about the small size of the load they were proposing to entrust to him:

'Where is rest of things?'

'Apart from the individual items I've pointed out to you in other rooms, this [indicating a heap of possessions on the floor of the *majlis*] is about all of them.'

(With a snort) 'Is hardly worth to come for such small amount. That's mean one half day enough for that.'

His men had hardly finished after a week. Their methods were lunatic. One of the containers Horace had dragged from country to country since the army was a small black trunk. He discovered a member of the packing team trying laboriously to inscribe their destination details on it with a twig dipped in black paint. Incensed after a week of frustration, wrangling and mess, he hurled the paint brush through the front door on to the lawn. Their cook appeared at that very moment, outraged that his toothbrush should be being subjected to such abuse.

It was ironic that a country they liked so little was nicest to them at the end. A lot of people went out of their way to mark their departure. Their final farewell party was given them by the Vice-Chancellor of Khartum University. They had to leave early to catch the VC10.

Gloom in Khartum

* * *

Many years later, Horace found himself embarking on a new career in Newcastle. One evening he was invited by his former employers to join the visiting Sudanese Minister of Higher Education and accompanying colleagues for dinner in the Civic Centre. He was pleased to note that an impressive printed menu had been produced for the occasion. He enjoyed the soup and read ahead to what came next: pork pie wrapped in bacon slices. He whispered to a waiter that the principal guests would not be able to eat the dish. The Sudanese gave a convincing display of noticing nothing as they sat for ten minutes with empty plates in front of them while an alternative meal was being improvised for them and fare prohibited by the Qur'an was served to the local dignitaries.

15

Mistaken Identity: London

Pooh-Bah: '... *of course we couldn't tell who the gentleman really was.*'
Pitti-Sing: '*It wasn't written on his forehead, you know.*'

(The Mikado)

After being softened up with smoked salmon in Carlton Gardens and having the opportunity of observing the Secret Intelligence Service in action in Baghdad, Horace had not said a clear 'no' or 'yes' to the suggestion that he consider espionage as a career. He received an annual 'Your papers have come up in the usual way' letter from MI6 but was otherwise only aware of having direct contact with it at positive vetting time. It was then that his past and present — like those of all people who might see classified documents — were scrutinised in order that any communist connections might be brought to light. Sometimes an interview was necessary. One he underwent during a leave from Khartum was notable.

It was conducted in a cell-like room containing only two chairs and a simple table separating him and his inquisitor. The first part of it was unremarkable except insofar as it seemed — 80 minutes out — to be unjustifiably protracted. There was no mention of the Slovenian Party Secretary or the visit to Penham. His interrogator's repetition of one particular query, however, struck him as significant. He gave his original answer again, adding, 'Why have you asked me that twice?' By way of reply, the investigator bent down and lifted onto the table a large pile of files which had up till then been invisible, for which, indeed, there had seemed to be no space in the room:

'If it is as you say, how do you explain all this?

Horace had been mistaken for, or mixed up with, other people

144

throughout his life. He was always being accused of pretending not to be Patrick McGoohan or Michael Aspel. When he had been in Baghdad, inefficient Foreign Office postal sorting had frequently delivered mail to him which should have gone to another official. No doubt some of his letters went to the other party and caused him similar irritation. Horace wrote to at least one company they both used and asked to receive no more bills not meant for him. He occasionally opened a wrongly-directed item in error, or read a postcard (his shadow probably did the same), and in this way began to piece his alter ego together. His knowledge now made him realise instantaneously that he was being confused with him and that it was his crimes that were being laid at his door:

'Not only am I not guilty of those things, I know who is and who you are talking about. He is at the moment in —.'

Collapse of embarrassed interrogator, let down by sloppy registry work. The interview came to an abrupt and unceremonious end:

'I apologise for this confusion. You may have every confidence that your future will not be affected. I request you to keep what has occurred confidential.'

Horace had, of course, no intention of complying. Fearful that his lack of success in his career had been caused by misfiled reports, he went straight to his employers to ask for their reassurance. It was duly forthcoming but, given their leading position in the unreliability stakes, he was no more convinced by it than he had been by Harold Wilson's claim, when two MPs were similarly confused, that the Secret Intelligence Service was incapable of making such a mix-up.

Only once, 11 years later, did Horace meet the person with whom his identity had been entangled. He had risen to an enviable height in his chosen service and seemed a nice enough chap.

The mistaken identification never completely ceased. Horace received a letter from a friend congratulating him on his appearance in a New Year's Honours' List in which he had not featured. Very recently, in the course of correspondence with the insurance firm they both used, he was sent a list of the jewellery owned by the wife of the Jekyll to his Hyde. He took some satisfaction from noticing that its total value was rather unimpressive.

16

Travails in Turkey

That singularly beautiful and
flexible tongue.
    (Gertrude Bell on Turkish)

The Arabs would not give up their
rich and flexible tongue for crude
Turkish: instead, they filled
Turkish with Arabic words.
    (T. E. Lawrence)

Within a week of his arrival in Canada to start his Ph.D., Horace had contemplated pulling out. He found himself attending classes on punctuation and writing footnotes. One day, the deputy director of the institute, in apparent complete seriousness, asked him the Arabic for 'engineer' and seemed grateful for his reply. His fellow-students, drawn from the four corners of the map but predominantly from some of its obscurer locations, were a set in which Horace did not feel that he belonged. Since, domestically, things were not as relaxed they might have been either (this had been anticipated), the overall picture was dark. Horace pondered a second application to Harvard, which had rejected him because he had no First at the time of his initial approach, but Khrushchev began to direct nuclear test fallout along the Canada–US border at just that moment and staying put became preferable to taking risks. He was rescued from the bleakness of his situation by his discovery of a Turkish professor on the staff of the institute who gave every appearance of having nothing to do except smoke. Horace asked him if he would help him to learn Turkish which — the natural advance from his Arabic and Persian — he had always intended to attempt one day. The professor readily agreed. During the year Horace remained, he made useful progress in the language and, with the aid of a dictionary, could read a difficult modern Turkish novel by the end of it.

He knew at the time that the professor had become an exile from his homeland after being the victim of allegations of communist leanings. 28 years later, flying to Turkey, that staggeringly over-politicised country, Horace recounted the origins of his familiarity with their language to a group of Turks on the 'plane. On hearing the name of his tutor, one of his fellow-passengers scoffed, 'Oh, that communist.' Horace replied that the tuition he received was in Turkish, not in communism — to which, indeed, the professor (later posthumously rehabilitated) at no time made allusion.

Between these two events, Horace's employers asked him if he would like, after the Sudan, to 'serve' in Turkey. (They did not need to be indirect about it, as the Ministry of Defence was to an officer who was to be posted back to the British Embassy in Ankara: before his move could be announced, he was informed that he would probably find his new defence attaché post 'right up his *sokak*'.) Since his student hitchhiking and rail and bus travel in Turkey, Horace had spent a lot of time in the country, driving across it on journeys between Britain and Iraq. Eager for a break from the Arab world and to broaden his basically Arabic horizons, and keen to leave Khartum for no matter where, he leapt at the chance.

It was a pleasing prospect — and remained so even when Turkey invaded the north of Cyprus just before they set out for Ankara. Because the effects of his Turkish tuition in Canada 12 years before had dimmed, the first job was to brush the language up. His employers arranged for him to do a crash course at a famous language-teaching establishment in London. 'Crash' was the word, for after a week of barely discernible progress Horace let on to his tutor, a Turk, how much his fees were — which told him how small a proportion of them he was taking home — and he did not appear at the school again. The direct method, which was *de rigueur* there and outlawed any use of English, had not in any case looked as if it was going to work. Opening the door one day, his tutor had said, '*dışarıya gidiyorum*', which Horace needed a week to remember did not mean that he was going into the corridor. On his first day, Horace exchanged a word with a class which was chanting, in Arabic, 'Good morning. Today is Monday. How are you?' On what turned out to be his last, he heard its members intoning the same chorus — with no greater understanding of what the direct method words meant than when they were first invited to repeat them. It was not until he arrived in Ankara and found a splendid teacher there that Turkish really began to yield again. Though not as tough as the structurally similar Hungarian he tackled many years later, it has points of great difficulty and demands continual upkeep on account of its obsessive precision, the astonishing ways in which parts of speech are forced into unfamiliar roles and its topsy-turvy sentence-construction. It is beautiful and somewhat effeminate and sounds like a gently cascading waterfall.

Next on the list was the car. Horace's previous public service postings had been to countries where BMC/British Leyland vehicles were either inadvisable because no service existed for them or blacklisted on account of their manufacturer's involvement in trade with Israel. To Iraq he had taken two successive superb Vauxhalls, to the Sudan his lifeless Hillman Hunter. To Turkey he could at last take a wholly British car, the first since the Mini he had driven from Montreal to Mexico City and back 12 years before, and show the flag. He chose a Rover. Against his better judgement, based on his knowledge of conditions in Turkey, he accepted the company's claims that Rovers were now exported there commercially and — crucial point — that the country was dotted with Rover agents. Telling himself, with typical optimism, that the law would recompense him if they turned out to be wrong, he went ahead because he had set his heart on the car, but with considerable misgiving.

From the start, the omens were depressing. He had expected to be treated with some deference as the owner-to-be of a Rover in the days when they were Rovers, but consideration was not to the fore in the communications which reached him from Solihull after he ordered, sight unseen, from Khartum. When he returned home on leave and the delivery date got later and later, bluntly worded notifications of price rises reached him with disillusioning regularity. When he asked to be taken for his first ever ride in a Rover, the salesman begged to be excused on the grounds that he didn't know how to drive. On delivery day, the lady in charge of the final rites (not 'rights') showed him BL's list of overseas agents, which made no reference to one closer than 370 miles from Ankara. The car could not be moved at first because of a jammed steering lock. The driving mirror fell off on the journey home. Nonetheless, the running-in period before they had to set off for Venice was not conclusively disturbing, though the car never felt happy, and it was only on the far side of the Channel that the disaster began with the simultaneous collapse of two shock absorbers and the complete loss of control of the engine revs. From Metz, where these chilling developments occurred, they drove on in two sorts of gathering gloom. The rev. counter needle, which the handbook warned them on no account to allow to enter the red zone on the dial, could now not be kept out of it. They bumped, bounced, roared and steamed into Pforzheim, fearing lest the car explode before they reached the Rover garage there. When they did, although he had never heard of their model and was unable to improve the ride, the proprietor at least managed to bring the engine under control. The journey to Venice was a long and worrying plunge and leap. Watching his dream car — now a nightmare — being winched on board the Adriatica Line's *Brennero*, Horace remembered the story told by one of the military attachés in the Baghdad Embassy of how, when his car was similarly poised above the Beirut quay, an official invited him to turn out his pockets in order to ensure its safe return to land rather than risk its precipitate entry into a watery grave. (A British ambassador to Lebanon had all his possessions dropped into the Mediterranean, perhaps through failing to treat a similar Beiruti welcome with sufficient seriousness.)

The *Brennero*'s crew declared a lightning 24-hour strike once the Rover was on board. The effect was to turn day into night. The Corinth Canal and the Dardanelles, the highlights of the voyage, were traversed in the dark. Once arrived in Istanbul, the Rover underwent further running repairs to give it a chance of reaching Ankara without additional mishap. It managed to complete the journey, but its condition had reverted to that of Metz by the end of it.

Like the car, Ankara was a great disappointment. Things were generally grim. There was little job satisfaction, accommodation and health were again major problems, the weather was mostly wintry, domestic help was hard to come by, opportunities for sport were scarce, the BBC was difficult to hear — there was no light to be seen anywhere.

Horace found that his boss was one of those he least enjoyed working with. 'Like dealing with a wet sponge,' an inspector said. Shipley tried at first to envelop him and his family in love, craving their affection and turning up at all hours at the cramped flat he had taken for them until their hearts sank at the sight of him. When he was making his farewell calls, he had to ask Horace the way to Ankara University. He once took the organisation's chairman, out from London, to lunch with the ambassador; Horace's wife gave a buffet for the chairman's wife and Horace (Shipley's deputy) was left to make shift with sandwiches in the office.

Erratic, Shipley put in the correct number of duty hours but rarely at the prescribed times of day. Just as Horace was packing up to go home after a hard morning or afternoon (or both), he would arrive, wide awake and eager to chat about how he had reached 100 m.p.h. in his Range Rover again. Horace rushed back from home leave one summer so that Shipley could travel round Turkey in the car and found that there was nothing for him to do.

It would, however, be misleading to suggest that his boss had no virtues. An outstanding one was his marvellous public speaking. He could fittingly introduce a lecturer or thank a departing colleague in two sentences. (People he was glad to see the back of he did in even less.) In his last post before retirement, he was radiantly fit for his age. He had immense self-confidence, addressing the ambassador, a knight, as Freddy, which not even his staff had dared to try to do. He was the closest friend of a notable athlete on the staff of the Embassy and acted as the great man's minder even though he was 15 years his senior.

He had obtained a Fourth at Oxford, about which he used to boast and which perhaps had something to do with his undeflatable ego. His marriage was probably more of a cause. He was embarrassingly uxorious. Despite the truths in Anouilh's *Antigone*, the public closeness of him and his wife was inhibiting to spectators, as it was later to be with the Reagans; one feared that they might at any moment start making love in full view. Horace found his pet name for her suggestive and could not use it.

They had another for their most revolting dog, which they loved as much as they loved each other. They delighted in it being sick, or indulging in other repulsive physical activities, when friends or official acquaintances could not easily excuse themselves. Horace and his family had a nauseatingly insanitary period one year when they had to live in their house and look after the dog while the Shipleys were on home leave.

Happily, the dog eventually began to bid for its independence, in the end successfully. Perhaps it felt smothered by their love. On a walk round the lake behind one of Ankara's reservoirs, it suddenly took to its heels and left its parents to make their desolate way home without it. Its master undertook a heroic tracking march to retrieve it. The next time it happened, however, there was no reprieve.

It took Horace a year each in two depressingly poor properties to obtain accommodation of a standard equivalent to that of their last Khartum house. Their second one had not much more to recommend it than a little extra space and a small garden where Horace and the boys could play football when the air was not too cold and the lignite fumes were not overpowering. They awoke one morning to find a dog dying in one of their flower beds, victim of a mayoral drive against strays. Their third and last Ankara dwelling, a flat, was much the best, not least through being the highest above the smog line. It was not without teething problems. Their beaming landlady quickly displayed a propensity to be mean with the central heating. Not far into the autumn the temperature in their sitting room made it uninhabitable. Nothing they could do persuaded her to raise it. They called the municipal assessors in. She learned of their impending surprise visit, turned the boiler full on, greeted them with collusive sanctimoniousness and reimposed Arctic conditions once they had departed well satisfied. Rescue came via their lady cook who went to the *hanım efendi* and informed her that she anticipated death by pneumonia for herself unless something were done. The temperature soared and the problem never recurred.

Problems with the flat's double glazing became a topic of family conversation just as a famous librarian called Glaister arrived for Horace to look after. They took him on a picnic to the nearby Beynam Woods, which sounded as if they were out of *Macbeth* and accordingly gave off an atmosphere of some foreboding. Glaister liked to tell stories against himself. He recounted how he was once in temporary charge at an overseas post when a VIP turned up:

151

I gave a reception for him as substitute for my boss who had never met him and was going to come along to the occasion immediately on his return from leave. The guest arrived first, as is proper, and I engaged him in apprehensive conversation. My boss made his entry. He took a drink from the tray by the door and started to approach in order to be introduced. As he drew near, I realised that not only had I forgotten the name of the guest, I could no longer remember that of my boss either.

As she was handing the lunch round, his wife was stung by a hornet. Her cry of pain turned to tears of hysteria as their Swithin, then aged four, asked, 'Double Glaister, do you have insects like that at home?'

Living in Ankara was no bed of roses. Indoors, there were frequent power and water cuts. Their first flat periodically had no hot water and no heating. There was a period when the city's gas plant broke down and deprived them of both for two months. Smog dominated the outdoor scene. It resulted from the wide use of poor quality coal for heating during the long and severe winter. It blotted out not only the sun but also the sky throughout one September–June period. At one point, while the front pages of newspapers frequently spoke of the 'Smog Crisis' in their headlines, the amount of sulphur in the air was claimed to be 37.5 times greater than was sufficient to cause death. There were frightening stories — a woman, not a smoker, went for a routine X-ray during a home leave and was sternly warned to give up by her doctor.

Partly in consequence, from the start their time in Turkey was an unending catalogue of fevers, migraine, sinus, stomach upsets, arthritis, insomnia and even stranger conditions. The insomnia was significantly contributed to by the beautiful street cry of a *simetchi* — a clown with a marvellous call — whose daily advertising of his pathetic bakery wares immediately followed the more restful dawn call from the local minaret. Though Horace and his family made the lives of the many doctors they consulted unbearable, it was not only them. At one point, every floor of their block housed someone resting a leg in the hope of regaining mobility.

In part for linguistic reasons, medical care was less satisfactory than anywhere else they went. Not that British medicine abroad was ever anything to write home about. A visiting specialist examined Horace for increased life insurance cover and failed him on the opening blood pressure test. After suffering an agony of apprehension in a two-day interval before a second try, Horace was both relieved and indignant to be told on his reappearance that the machine had been found to be faulty. (In Khartum, Acton's wife had asked the British doyen of the University's medical staff whether or not she were pregnant. He could find none of the signs of conception — and she gave birth to a rather large son a fortnight later.)

Rain cancelled tennis continually until June, and winter clothes were resumed in late September. The ice and snow were daunting and of only limited use for sledging on account of the encircling air pollution. A fault in the automatic choke of the car with which they eventually replaced the Rover caused it to remain on for far longer than necessary and made driving on the precipitous and icy hills of Ankara alarming.

Their most advanced country of posting, Turkey was not studded with cook-houseboys for them to engage at cheap salaries. The city was overflowing with "maids", but they were reputed to do very little rather badly. Their first domestic helper wept when they went on leave one summer, then hastened to bank the retainer they had paid him. On their return, he announced that he had obtained another position. The Embassy lawyer said, 'We'll knock that nonsense out of him,' but they heard no more from him and never saw their money again. The lady cook replaced him, did her best and babysat as well. Tools for cooking were unfamiliar and British food emerged tasteless in Turkey. But individuals were often good-hearted. (Even Rose Macaulay spoke of 'Turks being so kind'.) The cook and the block's dour janitor spread rice and water behind their car when they drove away from Ankara for the last time.

The city's mayor took over the only golf course in Turkey for building purposes, the only squash court was in Istanbul, it proved impossible to find a regular venue for cricket, and they had to fall back on the unfriendly British Embassy for tennis and rather poor swimming. Walking on the grass in a public park, let alone playing ball on it, caused whistles to blast. To fill a gap, Horace ran a weekly gymnastics' class for pupils of the Embassy school, a somewhat stressful undertaking. At its sports' day, the disorganised headmaster announced a fathers' race in which Horace was beaten into second place by someone who admitted afterwards to having no children, let alone any at the school. The following year, the head started the competitors off in mob formation. Horace, at the back of the ruck, saw no way of making his way through it and severely disappointed Andrew by not even setting off.

The political violence which culminated in the coup of September 1980 was some way short of its most spectacular flowering during their three years in Ankara. Nonetheless, the figures given every morning by one of the newspapers of people killed and injured in clashes in the previous 24 hours rose inexorably, and the day inevitably came when they included the assassinated editor himself. They themselves witnessed little. There was the occasional distressing scene — a boy beaten up on the street by his peers, a girl dragged into a car. Stories circulated which suggested that left/right strife was starting to develop at kindergarten level. Certainly, there was a well-documented account of a school inspector entering a class of 11-year-olds, taking one look at the assembled pupils, saying, 'Huh, leftists,' and striding out again. On his visits to the campus of the Middle East Technical University, Horace became used to running the gauntlet of army machine gunners lying tense behind their weapons in anticipation of a call to quell student unrest.

He only once got near to an actual outbreak of fighting. The occasion, at another campus, was a lecture engagement involving a visiting professor of English. Horace collected him from his hotel and drove him towards Hacettepe University, some of whose students he was programmed to address:

'There seem to be even more anti-riot vehicles around than usual.'

'I suppose you get used to all this military stuff roaming about. Sussex is certainly not like this.'

'These carry six different kinds of crowd-control weapon — water, rubber bullets, disabling gas...'

'They look like small tanks. Do the blue helmets show that their crews are in fact military police rather than troops?'

The gateway into the University was narrow and, as they

approached, their view through was blocked by a crowd milling around the entrance.

'Good heavens, is it safe to go on?'

'I think we'll be all right if we steer between those two lines.'

'They're students, are they?'

'Yes, and police. Keep your head down. Some of those guns were used not so long ago. Was this what you came for from Falmer?'

He slammed the car into the first remotely feasible parking place and they ran, with heads down and fully expecting crossfire to engulf them, to the office of the professor's host. Professor Etili, normally calm, sociable and jolly, was unrecognisable. Pale and wearing earphones, he was speaking into a walkie-talkie. He stopped and looked up in astonishment:

'You should not have come. There's been a riot. Three people have been killed.'

'We heard nothing in the centre of town. Professor Lerner is here to give his lecture.'

'There will be no lecture today. Go home as quickly as you can.'

They fled, peering cautiously from behind pillars to make sure that no one was pointing a gun in their direction before sprinting beneath the pillars holding up the University's first floor. Retrieving the car, they drove off the campus as a Turk would and felt that the opposing forces had only held their fire until the interruption by two pitiably anachronistic strangers — like third parties at a Roses' match — was over and they could get on with their battle once more. For a brief space Horace dined out on the adventure, a hero of the moment.

Atilla Etili was typical of one kind of Turk. Urbane, a leading medical man, a pro-vice-chancellor of his University, he had been welcoming to Horace from the day of his arrival in Ankara. He and his wife came to their receptions, they went to dinner at their home. It was not precisely with amusement, however, that Horace heard him say that it was the skeleton of his former closest friend which was propped up in the corner of his sitting room. The connection survived the shock. Illogically juxtaposing two macabre subjects, Horace wondered what Atilla's view would have been of the Armenian massacres. He did not ask him, eschewing the topic as he did Palestine with people whose friendship he wished to keep.

The arts were among Horace's responsibilities in Turkey. A visiting British ballet promoter laddered her tights on the stairs at the Ministry of Culture and could not be persuaded thereafter to maintain her interest in the question of possible British participation in the infant Izmir Festival. Energetic programmes were mounted in Ankara. The President of the Senate made an unscheduled exhortatory speech at a choral evening in the organisation's theatre. A trumpeter from Istanbul played 'Jesu, Joy of Man's Desiring' ever faster until he lost control and ran out of puff. The most prestigious offerings were staged before sadly sparse audiences in the concert hall of the Presidential Symphony Orchestra, which during one season gave performances under the baton of some half dozen visiting British conductors, one of whom described it as 'not the worst' he had worked with. The first five went on to their next country *sans* fee, Turkish bureaucracy being too ill-organised to produce the payment with the same efficiency as the performances were delivered. The last of the batch, however, had heard about this tradition of delay and covertly planned a counter-attack. The members of the orchestra had settled behind their music stands, the leader had taken his place, the audience had lowered its anticipatory murmurs — and the Maestro, not proposing to make his entrance without his cheque in his pocket, began a sit-down strike in the wings. So fast can red tape be untangled if the need is sufficiently great, the performance was in the end very little delayed. It is unlikely, however, that the artiste in question was invited back, or cared whether he was or not.

The Turkish character contains a generous measure of the unthinking, which is one reason why Johnny Turk is such a good soldier. There was the news item in *The Times* about the two Turkish fairground attendants who grew tired of seeing their customers having all the fun while they just operated the machinery. One day, at close of business, they decided that their moment had come and, pressing the switch, jumped on to the big wheel. It was only the following morning that — the municipal electricity having behaved itself — the local muezzin, mounting his minaret at dawn, was surprised to see the fair in full swing at such an early hour...

Freya Stark gives a marvellous example. An Istanbul *müdür* in the Ministry of the Interior, pining for an appointment by the sea

(Istanbul is sea-girt), asked to be posted to Seki, in the south of the country. To his long-lasting chagrin, he discovered on arrival that it was well inland and that snow made roads to the Mediterranean impassable for four months of the year.

Not so catastrophic was the case of Horace's teacher of spoken Turkish. Ali had been joint founder and owner of Incekum, an idyllic private resort motel near Alanya, until the stress of managing the staff became too great for him. Years after his resignation, he and his wife were invited by the residual owner to help him celebrate the completion of a new top storey. In the middle of their night as honoured guests, they awoke to the thump of picks and the scraping of spades as the municipality set about demolishing a development for which it had not received its percentage.

Behaviour behind the steering wheel exhibits more of the Turkish personality than it does of many other nationalities. Turks are desperately awful drivers. The fatalism Islam is accused of fostering plays a part, no doubt. In Ankara motorists were bad enough, regularly ignoring red lights and displaying indignant surprise when they collided with vehicles failing to make it across their bows. There was more scope on the open road. A bus driver killed two of the British Embassy's staff when — with a fingers-crossed recklessness which seems to be ingrained in his kind — he overtook a car at the top of a hill on the Ankara–Istanbul road, entirely filling their half of it as they reached the crest from the opposite direction before careering down a steep embankment. When apprehended, he said that he would not have hit them if they had not been in his path.

Turkish traffic accidents had an inevitability about them. Friends in Baghdad, travelling the length of the Turquoise Coast — the name the Turks have invented for their lovely Mediterranean shore — before the road was asphalted, had had their car severely damaged by the only other vehicle they encountered.

* * *

Ankara being rather grim and haughty, they got out of it as often as they could despite their ever increasing nervousness about going on picnic journeys even in the immediate vicinity of their home. They rarely ventured abroad without seeing a bus on its roof in a gorge, a taxi on fire or bodies in blankets. (At that time, Turkey produced its own car, the Anadol, made from a type of glass fibre which appeared to go up in flames at the slightest impact.) Istanbul quickly ceased to be their favourite destination as the driving on the road separating the two cities became more and more fearsome. They preferred to head for the sea on quieter routes with little traffic, though they always had to keep a weather eye open for marauding buses.

During a winter journey to the Mediterranean, they had hardly unloaded the materials for an icy picnic when two cars arrived at a great pace and shrieked to a halt behind theirs. A civilian and a soldier leapt out and came across to the uncomfortable spot where they were preparing to begin a rather stony repast. (His wife never had anything ready and the wind chilled them as they waited irritably to be fed.) Arrest, though for no imaginable offence, was the least of the consequences they feared. The civilian had the worst possible one on his mind. His bureaucrat's dark suit and spectacles clashing anachronistically both with the pistol he carried and the pastoral surroundings, he harangued them, speaking over their heads and addressing the horizon. They thought him either a lunatic accompanied by his attendant or a character somewhat eccentrically rehearsing his lines for a play. His soliloquy began, however, to make sense after a time and Horace understood that he was advising them to leave the place as speedily as possible because the locals had murdered someone exactly there only the day before. They wolfed their meal down and fled the scene in something of a panic. They marvelled as they sped away at the total lack of self-consciousness of their declamatory messenger. While speaking in public is an unremarkable matter for Arabs, who seem to quote poetry and proverbs in every conversation, the Turks are much less self-assured and significantly less happy about — as the British would see it — making fools of themselves.

* * *

One of their most eventful short breaks from Ankara was to Aleppo at the end of a summer. The first night was spent in Konya, the whirling dervish city Horace had not visited for 16 years. The whole place reeked of death and felt like a cemetery. His father had died the previous year, and the atmosphere of their hotel brought the memory of his last, undignified days — and the smell of his terminal medication — forcibly back. The sheets in their hotel room, which Horace described in his diary as 'nasty', seemed dank, as though the last occupant of the bed had passed on in it. The music playing in the restaurant had a melancholy character which reinforced his dejection. He was in any case depressed about the Armenian massacres, which he had just seen hurtfully scorned by a brazenly positioned, smashed Armenian gravestone at the Roman Baths, one of Ankara's few historic sites. He would not subscribe to the Rose Macaulay generalisation that 'Turks do not care' for 'classical antiquity', let alone to the easily disprovable charge by Beverley Nichols that 'the Turks ... have raised more scars on the face of civilisation than any other people', but the refusal of even close Turkish colleagues, when others brought the subject up, to admit that the massacres had indeed happened was difficult for him to reconcile with the refinement and fellow feeling of many of the people they knew.

To his surprise — to his delight, indeed — he was not the only one finding the Saray Oteli oppressive. The main course had hardly reached them when Andrew suddenly burst into tears. The *Dr Zhivago* theme tune had made him cry when he was two years younger. Now the hotel music had recalled to him, too, the grand-father he had been fond of.

The following morning was drizzly. His wife was stung by another hornet at their first pit stop. Just before Silifke their new car experienced one of its many Michelin punctures. Under weigh again, they caught up a Skoda van which appeared to be having difficulty in going straight. It wandered to the right and pulled back, it crept all the way across the wrong side of the road before struggling away from the brink. Finally it dived at the margin and tumbled over the edge. They thought the driver was going to be a prosaic successor to Frederick Barbarossa, whose drowning in the Göksü (Cydnus) River at about this point knocked the stuffing out of the Third Crusade. They were shocked at the spectacle and could not imagine the feelings of the victims even when it became thankfully clear that a tree ten feet below had broken their fall and saved them from a fatal drop. They helped pull them back up and tried to offer words of comfort to the occupants, — an old man, his wife and a little girl, — but they were too shocked to respond. Horace left them to the care of fellow-countrymen who had also kindly stopped. They could not be sorry at the destruction of their lethal vehicle. Horace was for some time apprehensive about the possibility of them being caught by an oncoming one with the same defect.

After they left Iskenderun, Andrew (approaching eight) began to take shots with a camera Horace had given him because he was unable to use it himself. (He pitied him, knowing that the results would be no good, but rejoiced in due course to discover that they were better than any he had achieved himself.) A new, broad high-way had ironed out Macaulay's 'wild steep mountain zig-zag', the alarming Belen Pass to Antakya, where the tyres would not grip on the hairpins and fierce gusts made it a struggle at the wheel. Passing through Bab al Hawa', they stayed at the Barun, Horace worrying neurotically about the possibility of rats in their dusty room.

Although, shut off from the west since the Six Day War, the Syrians welcomed them warmly, Horace felt that Aleppo ('... complete chaos, filthy, lacking any sign of public authority or civic pride, continual hooting of an intensity I remember nowhere else') was showing signs of chronic neglect. It was not the lively, uninhibited place he had first known 15 years before. The area of the post office where he had found a satisfactory number of non-engagement letters awaiting him then was greatly run-down.

* * *

They had been marooned in Iskenderun for a short time on their first drive to Baghdad. Approaching Ankara, where they stayed in a hotel which was aptly called the Uğur Palas,* they began to hear rumours about trouble in Syria, which — with the Kurdish war in

---

* Though even the Turks themselves can become confused about it, as when the *Turkish Daily News* once spelled the English word bogus 'boğuş' in error, the Turkish ğ is pronounced y in a few contexts but otherwise functions only as a silent indication that the preceding vowel is a long one. The Turkish habit of calling hotels of whatever category 'palaces' is only now becoming less fashionable as a consequence of the greater prosperity and realism brought about by the late President Özal's Thatcherite dispensation.

full swing as usual — was unavoidably on their route to Iraq. There was frequent politico-military instability in Damascus during the period and they did not possess the information to judge whether or not this particular bout needed to cause them special concern. With the British Embassy in Ankara reinforcing its reputation for being unhelpful, they drove on. They sought out the Nominal Consul on arrival in Iskenderun.

Though it is certainly a striking spot, they felt that Rose Macaulay's description of it in French mandatory times no longer held true. Very hot and extremely humid, with bad mosquitoes, and hotels and restaurants which are erratic at best, it was neither 'Frenchified' nor 'gay' and probably not somewhere to remain for longer than strictly necessary. Jammed, like Beirut, between mountains (the Amanus) and the sea, it occupies the spot where the Mediterranean coast does a 90-degree turn south towards Lebanon. In naval warfare terms it is so attractive that Churchill's hesitation over it before choosing Gallipoli as the landfall for his First World War thrust at Turkey should cause no surprise. Its name, linked with that of Alexander the Great, reveals it as a place of considerable antiquity. Now it is the chief town of the Turkish province of Hatay, which Syrian maps still show as belonging to Damascus, as they probably will indefinitely. No great feelings of anguish are seen on the faces of the inhabitants of the province which was taken away nearly sixty years ago but no doubt deep sorrow would not be difficult to find. Perhaps it shows itself in the irritability of the officials at Bab al Hawa', which commands the clearest and most lofty view of the lost land on the plain below.

As though to divert minds away from bereavement and nostalgia, the Turkish authorities mount a non-stop programme of martial events in Iskenderun. There are always bands, parades and celebrations of landmarks in the life of Atatürk. Naval ships, dressed overall, line the harbour. The beat of the drum and the rasp of bugles, controlling the jerky movements of uniformed automata, give the town an alert and disciplined, but chocolate soldier, air. If you step off the kerb at the wrong moment, you are likely to be tapped on the arm by a dapper private in white spats and peaked helmet whose whistle is at the ready in his mouth. A further false move and that army Alsatian will be encouraged to take a closer interest in you.

With his patrician air, unseasonal three-piece suits and over-polished hall tiling, the Nominal Consul looked incongruous against the simple backcloth of Iskenderun. Though not called on, as Macaulay's had been, to fight the Syrian consul on their behalf, he had no option but to be more civil to them than the faceless colleagues in Ankara to whom he was loosely connected — no doubt not loosely connected enough for them. He directed them to the best of the indifferent set of hotels and restaurants, which Horace had not needed to sample three years before. Over a quarter of a century later — when they had introduced the kind of shower which is no more closely connected to the corporation drains than via the carpet, the floor and the room beneath, — Iskenderun's hotels remained the discerning tourist's emergency choice only. (Off the beaten track, but only a little to the south, even worse could be encountered in a 'newly built' hotel which had continuously self-flushing toilets in every room, sheets too short for the bed, no protection against mosquitoes and no provision for the encashment of traveller's cheques.)

The best of Iskenderun's hotels is the Güney Palas. There, none-theless, if you eat outside, you are the target of a large population of cats which rub themselves, insistently yowling, against your legs. You strive with one hand to keep them from jumping onto the table as you do the best you can with the only main course on the menu and try to dismiss thoughts of tummy upsets and rabies from your apprehensive mind.

* * *

Surprising, if not macabre, was the occasion, some five years earlier, when Mark had taken on the responsibility of guarding Horace's camera while he swam from a beach near Silifke and contrived to allow it to be stolen. A significant proportion of the Middle Eastern traveller's time is spent in police stations. Though mysterious in their responses, the local law-enforcement officers were completely confident that they would be able to track the camera down by the following day. Communicating with them was via a prisoner whose cell door was opened to enable him to interpret:

'Please tell him that our camera has been stolen.'

'"Crime, where did commit?", he asks'.

'On the beach. You can almost see from here. The other side of that large rock. When we swam, we left it by our clothes.'

'Taking it who you think?'

'We have no idea. One minute it was there, then gone.'

'Officer say he know who taking. Back in morning you will come.'

They were not required to describe the camera or even declare its make. It had disappeared so magically that they were not entirely convinced that it had ever been in their possession. The policeman lent them hope by giving a light-hearted emphasis to Turkish's put-down word *yok* — 'a discouraging word', in Macaulay understatement: he felt that a thorough investigation was quite unnecessary, perhaps (they felt) because this was a performance repeated regularly by some well-known malefactor or because the camera was already on his premises. His demeanour was shady and they had no idea whether or not to be as sanguine about the outcome as he was.

In the morning, the prisoner was given another door's width of freedom so as to permit Horace to reclaim his property. It felt eccentric for them all to be so totally dependent on a criminal (Horace and Mark had no idea what had led to his incarceration), but he and his captors handled the negotiation as though both sides felt their cooperation to be the most normal thing in the world, an unstrained and perfectly natural negotiation by partners. Macaulay's largely uncomplimentary opinions of Turkish policemen, obsessively held, received no endorsement whatever.

* * *

On another holiday, many years later, Horace took Andrew and the son of a colleague to the private beach of the Alanya motel where they were staying. On their way down, an ancient retainer removing leaves from the stream in front of it told them not to go into the pool which it fed and which separated the motel from the strand above the sea. This was their object, and the children had had many memorable cruises there in their inflatable Czechoslovak boat. True to form, Horace reacted to the warning by indicating that they could manage without unsolicited advice and by launching Andrew onto the water. In due course, he handed over to Edward Campbell, a less sturdy boy who — before any of them had time to credit what had happened — was 150 yards out to sea. Horace realised in a flash that the rain which had fallen overnight must have dug a channel joining the pool to the sea where there had been none before.

The sea was rough. Edward lost his grip on the paddles. The boat turned over. Horace was imagining breaking the news of his drowning to the boy's parents when a Turkish guest in the motel sprinted down the beach, flung him his watch, dived in and — provoking unimaginable relief — brought Edward out. Their rescuer retrieved his property and returned to his parasol pursued by heartfelt thanks. (Only then did they realise that the tide had been coming in fast.) Edward was quite unmoved, seeming to have noticed nothing amiss even during the few seconds when he was alone and oarless on a boiling ocean.

Turks are splendid swimmers. (Even ladies of the old school, dressed completely in black, get dragged in by the younger members of their families.) The most remarkable was one they observed when they were on holiday in Marmaris, near the country's south-west corner and at the head of a bay which widens out so prodigiously that the claim that the whole of the British fleet anchored in it during the Napoleonic Wars is entirely plausible. Each morning he waded in and disappeared over the horizon. As they were withdrawing from the beach at nightfall, he would resurface, having completed yet another Heroic course.

* * *

On a visit to Turkey from Jordan, the family drove out east from Incekum to a favourite swimming spot — one of many on the Mediterranean coast where good waves scour firm, scrubbed sand excellent for long jumping. They were established on the beach, half in and half out of the water, when a motorist parked his car, scrambled down the cliffs from the road above and proceeded to dig a hole beneath a sheltering bush, which was exactly deep enough to accommodate him — like Simeon Stylites in the monastery garden — up to the neck. Fully clothed, his face serene and the whole of his buried surfaces cool, he relaxed into sleep with a smile. They could not but admire his unembarrassed self-assurance and his confidence that the world outside would leave him unmolested while he recruited his forces.

* * *

This absence of self-consciousness is reflected in Turkish surnames. Atatürk decreed in 1935 that to be called Mehmet Ibrahim Süleyman, each of these being — after the Islamic fashion inherited from the Arabs — 'first' names, was no longer adequate for the twentieth century. In complying, many Turks took the opportunity to select surnames which made statements about themselves, so Hiçyılmaz and Korkmaz (fearless) are common. Of sociological interest is the widespread Balyemez (does not eat honey). Much soul-searching and debate, such as the Turks expend on detail, must have gone on before decisions were taken as to whether to adopt Çeligel (steel fist) rather than Bayraktaroğlu (son of the flag-bearer) or Kahvecioğlu (son of the coffee-maker). The national rethink also made people conscious of given names. Atilla, chosen by the begetters of a leading Ankara dentist, gave some of his culturally alert foreign patients pause before they agreed to be conducted to his chair.

* * *

Termessos was the most appealing site they visited. Just north-east of beautiful Antalya on the south coast, it stands a mile high. It was one of the few cities Alexander could not conquer. At the very top is a marvellous theatre with nothing beyond it but the sky. Of a number of unfenced landmarks on the walking route the guidebook says, 'It is impossible to climb down those wells.' It would, however, be only too easy to fall into them and never see daylight again.

* * *

Their car saga lasted throughout their posting. After their arrival in Ankara, a long and acrimonious correspondence began with BL. It did no good. On its day, their Rover could break all their land speed records, but with its intermittent over-revving defect —

the only short-term antidote to which was to switch off — it was always liable to endanger them, as when immobility became necessary with a Turkish bus doing 70 behind. The problem got worse and worse. After one repair by an appointed workshop, they were warned that it would be hazardous to engage reverse gear with the engine warm and the ignition on. They seemed never to go on a journey without a new symptom appearing. One time they lost part of the exhaust system. On another occasion a cigar lighter fire put the horn, clock and interior lights out of action. A Rover man arranged to look in and came six weeks later than promised. Following his visit, Solihull offered, if Horace drove home a car which could not be counted on to get to the outskirts of Ankara, to put it into 'normal operating condition'.

Horace's earlier travels in their country had persuaded him that, as mechanics, Turks were inspirational improvisers. He was sadly disappointed by their efforts with the Rover. Rose Macaulay claims that 'road-menders, brigands, etc., ... can usually ... produce from their pockets spare parts such as fan-belts, differentials, and those kinds of things..,'* but the only example of this during their Turkey period was not a Turkish one. On a drive home for leave, the Rover's successor gave out, not for the only time, and, in the middle of nowhere in Jugoslavia, Horace wound down his window and shouted, *Mehanik*! A man appeared from behind a hedge on a hillock directly above them and ran down with a bag of spares which included a suitable replacement dynamo, the spent one turning out to have been made in the country.

They never came across anyone who could fathom the Rover. Getting rid of it became a matter of urgency. The last straw (not attributable to the car itself) was when Horace collided with a water-seller and a traffic police stand in the space of five minutes during an Ankara power cut brought on by a thunderstorm. The Rover found a ready buyer in an agency which traded in diplomatic vehicles on which Turkish duty had not had to be levied. Its initial offer of TL 80,000 seemed, under all the circumstances, too low. The representative asked to look at the boot again and added

---

* The picture conjured up by this claim is of the order of, though not as comical, as that of the Erewhonian who, under doctor's orders, had to conceal a shoulder of mutton about his person.

an acceptable TL 10,000* to his bid. Although Horace had made no claims for the car, and the purchaser did not deem it necessary to try it out, he was racked by guilt and fear over the transaction for some time afterwards.

Replacing the Rover landed them in further trouble, though this time of an employer relations' kind. They gave a lift to the Embassy person who decided these things just as the car was reaching the acme of its troubles with a slipping clutch. It had to be abandoned on the monumental Ankara hill where they lived, Cinnah Caddesi, named for the founder of Pakistan, and he and his wife had to walk a near vertical half mile home. Displaying unusual sympathy with their sufferings, he sent to advise them to replace it with anything which took their fancy.

As in the Sudan, in both Turkey and the UAE, whither they were bound next, there were virtually no British cars because servicing arrangements for them were either makeshift or non-existent. Opting for a Peugeot, they ordered a red one. When Horace went to collect it from the Croydon delivery garage, he noticed a garish orange one standing at the gate. Learning that it was destined for him and querying the change of hue, he was informed that the makers considered it something not to get worked-up about: 'The purchaser may detect a small difference in colour.' Whatever their thoughts on its paintwork might have been, Horace's employers required him to bear the cost of shipping the car to Abu Dhabi himself because it neither was, nor looked, of British manufacture. Once it had gone off, however, they made it clear that they were not going to allow their principles to inhibit them from requiring Horace to use it in their official business there.

---

* Since then, Turkish inflation has been so uncontrollable that TL 90,000 are now worth 20 pence, enough only for a small packet of chewing gum from an Istanbul Hilton Hotel minibar.

17

Bob Serjeant: Cambridge

... a scholar, and a ripe and good one; Exceeding wise...
(Shakespeare, *Henry VIII*)

After Baghdad, when he was trying to decide on something on which to spend the rest of his life — he had by now given up all thought of being famous, — Horace kept an appointment at London University. The McGill one had never got started but he still thought that a Ph.D. would be useful. The purpose of his call was to talk about research topics with an eminent Arabist professor at the School of Oriental and African Studies. His suggestion to Horace was to consider spending some time in the Istanbul archives, deciphering Old Turkish documents with the aid of his knowledge both of Atatürk's Turkish and the Arabic script. Although some money might have been attached to the project, Horace allowed his family responsibilities to persuade him that he could not afford to take up the recommendation.

Still reluctant to abandon the idea of a Ph.D., however, he came across the Cambridge external regulations which provided for its award to Cambridge MAs like himself who published a suitable book. As a result, during leaves, he got into the habit of returning to Cambridge to acquire relevant facts in the Middle East Centre (new since his day) and at the University Library. Sometimes his old tutor, Augustus (Gus) Caesar, invited him to use the spare bedroom of his college set. The SOAS professor had succeeded to the Cambridge Chair of Arabic and Horace naturally renewed contact with him, feeling it important to combine his research expeditions with calls on Professor Serjeant.

He would arrive by appointment at the Centre. The secretary

would have no knowledge of any arrangement made. The professor would in any case have somebody with him. His visitor would finally emerge and Horace would make a tentative entrance:

'Good morning, Professor Serjeant.'

'Good morning. You're Prince Ibn ...?'

'No, Horace Tension.'

'Tension? Oh, yes. Of course. When did you get back from Sudan?'

'Turkey, actually.'

'How's old Ekrem Bey? Do you see anything of ... in the Embassy?'

'I'm with the ... organisation now.'

'Of course, I remember that breakfast we had with Abd Allah. When I had that awful cold.'

'Yes, you arrived with it from the Yemen. The worst one I've ever seen. Abd Allah's wasn't much better.'

'How about lunch? There's quite a gathering today. You know Peter Clark? Just moved to Tunis. A bit off my route. I'm expecting ... to turn up. Promising Arabist. You must tell me about your book on the way.'

Though not a large man, the professor gave the impression of being one. It was a surprise, therefore, to be introduced to his latest car, which — old, of course — seemed much too small for him. He was an alarmingly jerky driver, with not much in the way of control over levers and pedals. It was always a relief to reach Grantchester safely. A semicircle of Arabists awaited them in the garden. A barmaid tripped back and forth between the group and the lounge, bearing pints of beer. The professor, an engaging man now in his element, beamed on the company:

'This is Tension. On leave from Khartum.'

'What brings you to Cambridge?'

'Well, I don't feel I need to search for an excuse to come back, particularly on a day like this. I'm hoping to make a Ph.D. submission to Professor Serjeant in due course.'

'Indeed. What on?'

'The life and works of Tawfiq al Hakim.'

The barmaid sat down beside the professor. Horace eventually gathered that she was their host's wife. At least, she joined them on the journey back, when his driving — after several pints — was even worse than on the outward run. Horace pulled at his seatbelt but it didn't work.

Bygone Heat

* * *

Although most of the book was written in the Sudan, it took several years for Horace to find a publisher for one which had at the same time to be a thesis. Its prolific subject, nearing the end of his life, became if anything more profuse and — before the invention of the word-processor — Horace's text was in continual need of revision. Peter Clark having fixed a meeting with a publisher friend of his at a pub that was part boat on the Thames, the transition from type to print was at last effected. As soon as he had his author's copies in his hand, Horace sent one to his professor. Professor Serjeant moved fast, short-cutting all the regulations so that Horace could be invited to defend his publication a year earlier than he had anticipated.

As he arrived at the Centre, his mentor was just negotiating his way into a parking space. Horace's heart leapt, and he knew it would probably be all right, when, by way of greeting, the professor said, 'What a marvellous piece of work you've done.' Nonetheless, a severe viva followed at which, for a couple of intense hours, he was thoroughly grilled, especially by the external examiner. It emerged that this formidable Orientalist was travelling on by rail. So, to ensure that he did not miss his train, the last part of the interview took place, convivially, at the station pub. His judges were moved to tell him that he had passed. He drove back to London, delighted that a process which had lasted many years had finally been so triumphantly concluded.

He saw very little literary assessment of his book. One by an Arab exile foreshadowed the strictures on his pro-Palestinian convictions which were to make him so indignant in Jordan. Culturally ungenerous in the manner of the author of *Orientalism*, she gave him little credit for — no doubt imperfectly — trying to tell the English-speaking world about a marvellous modern Egyptian playwright and novelist whom her fellow Arabs had done little to promote in the West, where his works should be much better known. It was not flattery when Nagib Mahfuz said that Al Hakim should have received the Nobel prize for literature before he did.

18

Illegal Pioneer: UAE

... Abu Dhabi, ... an Arabian Night-mare, the final disillusionment.
(Wilfred Thesiger)

Abu Dhabi is now an impressive modern city.
(Wilfred Thesiger)

Following the discovery of oil in marketable quantities there two decades earlier, the Arab shore of the Gulf had been catapulted overnight from Stone Age poverty to the premier league of international riches. Abu Dhabi had sprung up from the sand to be an imitation Benidorm or New York.

Nonetheless, the Gulf had gone about its development all wrong. It decided to spend much of its sudden wealth on expatriate middlemen and workers rather than get down to the task of pulling itself into the twentieth century by its own efforts. Like Iran and Iraq, the six countries which now make up the Gulf Cooperation Council — Bahrain, Kuwait, Oman, Qatar, Saudi Arabia and the United Arab Emirates — imported huge numbers of *gastarbeiter*. In accordance with the rule that ex-colonial masters are preferred as guides by newly independent states, their advisers were mostly British.

The administrators and managers were non-Gulf Arabs, the foremen Indians, and the labourers Egyptians, Filipinos and Pakitanis from the North West Frontier. The foremen and labourers received pay which was just sufficiently greater than their home salaries, or than they could have expected to get if there had been jobs for them at home, to make worthwhile the exchange of their self-respect for second-class citizenship far away. They had no right to own property and no possibility of a Gulf passport. With very rare exceptions, they were not allowed to bring their families

171

with them and, as a result, during a third of their lifetime commonly saw them only every other year. Many of the 'labourers' had no proper jobs, but spent their prime opening doors, summoning lifts, cleaning toilets or dusting main roads; those who followed the first of these careers tended to possess degrees. Their living conditions were squalid and their status was little removed from that of slave.

How much these hordes contributed is debatable at best. The least well remunerated group could usually speak neither Arabic nor English (the second language of the Gulf) and spent most of their exile in a daze, getting in the way and being more of a nuisance than a help. Thousands of the Pakistanis in particular became taxi drivers, depriving the natives of the Gulf — except in Bahrain and Oman — of sensible, respectable work they should have done themselves. The rulers and shaykhs always overestimated the number of foreigners they needed and their civil servants were easily hoodwinked when residence permits ran out. Accordingly, crowds of aliens of ambiguous status are regularly to be seen sitting around in the sun hoping to be hired. It had been imported labour with time on its hands which had brought down several early Muslim dynasties.

The oil and, especially, gas will take so long to run out, however, that for the foreseeable future, and despite the tiny proportion of its income which has been devoted to establishing a manufacturing base, much of the Gulf will be able to continue to purchase the services of foreigners indefinitely. It shows every sign of intending to maintain the time-honoured Arab tradition of paying other people to do the work. Like most of their neighbours, the Kuwaitis certainly have no serious intention of being self-reliant in labour. They must have been glad of the excuse for a purge of their Palestinians which was presented by Yasir Arafat's foolish alliance with Saddam Husayn, Kuwait's invader in 1990. On the other hand, they have done nothing to cut the numbers of imported Filipina and Sri Lankan nannies who — trying to read their immigration papers upside down — arrive by the 'plane load.

It would have been much better, and far less wasteful, for the Gulf to catch up slowly and steadily by obtaining core training for key people abroad and selecting a severely restricted number of experts to lend a temporary hand on the spot. The progress of the shaykhdoms is impressive, but — inexperienced at Western-style negotiating — their rulers, like the Shah, have been mercilessly cheated, too, notably by bandits disguised as builders who seized with both hands an unrepeatable opportunity to become doubly rich through first working with cut-price, substandard materials and then replacing them when they failed. Many of the thousands of British expatriates who were posted to the Gulf seemed eager to do little more than cash in on the oil-price boom, no matter who they trampled on in their chase towards Eldorado. They granted their co-nationals few favours.

At Bandar Mashhur, his glimpse of the Gulf on his trans-Iranian drive had induced fear in Horace. It was an indication of his improved psyche that, a dozen years later, a posting to one of the least known and furthest Arab regions — living mysteriously in history's shadow on the opposite coast until 20 years before — was an exciting prospect. Like the Sudan, the Gulf was at the edge of the Semitic world but, unlike it, on one of Islam's internal Sunni–Shi'i frontiers. Comparatively close to where Islam and Arabism had begun, it had been largely cut off from the rest of humanity — even from brother Arab areas, as Horace had seen in Baghdad — for centuries.

Horace's despised employers led him to understand for six months that it was to Bahrain that they wished him to go after Ankara. When in due course he got to the capital of the United Arab Emirates he found that the country was worth every anticipation. It has features — like its lovely Gulf of Oman coast — which are not eclipsed anywhere. After Turkey's dreariness and rain, the balmy air and clear views were a joy. Following Khartum and Ankara, he needed a good posting, and here he seemed to have landed one. He had the thrilling task of setting up an operation in territory where he knew nobody.

Opening up in Abu Dhabi turned out to be a struggle. His optimism was immediately affected by an unwelcome surprise. They found their airfreight from Ankara spilling out all over the tarmac at the airport when they went to clear it through the customs. One of Horace's allowances, allegedly designed to compensate them for the vagaries of their peripatetic existence, never seemed to recompense them adequately for the loss of treasured possessions, particularly books. One never to be seen again was a prize Horace had been awarded by his college, a pleasing English–Turkish–English dictionary.

They had no special privileges or protected position and had to compete with everyone else who was trying to set up or survive in Abu Dhabi. The famous British firm of estate agents, which pocketed Horace's deposit for a flat suitable for an office, collaborated brazenly with a rival bidder to gazump him. On the day when, unbeknown to him, that had occurred, he had returned to the hotel full of the news of the ideal premises he had found. They celebrated at dinner that night by treating themselves to one drink each. At the next table, however, was a group of foreign businessmen:

'It's a marvellous building — 55 flats, well finished, landlord no trouble. I snapped it up first thing this morning, no bother at all.'

'What company did you say you represent?'

'PETCO.'

'Oil? Then money's no problem for you. You should try working for a foreign government.'

'I only had to pay the agents three years in advance. We start moving in on Saturday.'

The building under discussion turned out to be the one in which Horace thought he had just taken a set of rooms. It made him feel no better about the destruction of his puny illusion that the self-satisfied oil company executive who had vanquished him by making a down payment which goes some way to explain the cost of petrol was the son of Tahir Yahya of nostalgic Baghdad memory — a slimmer, smarter version of his father.

Visitors too made the most of the prevailing ethos. The founding of the Abu Dhabi Cultural Society was one of the few early attempts to garner the artistic and literary heritage of the emirate. Horace brought out a famous Arabist to address the Society. He mocked ones like Horace for speaking a hybrid classical/colloquial Arabic, by which he and his fellow teachers of the language had done nothing to stop them from being contaminated. Hindsight suggested nationally motivated content in his criticism. It seemed particularly uncalled-for when Horace had arranged a 60-minute talk for him that earned him the equivalent of £1,250, of many times more than that now.

The shock of Abu Dhabi prices for newcomers who did not have the financial backing to cope with them was not only felt in the most basic spheres of existence. In due course, the question of a haircut arose. Horace buys his on grounds of price (almost) alone. He therefore selected his barber with care, choosing the least pretentious-looking establishment he came across. The proprietor was from Damascus:

'So, you have visit Suriyyah?'

'Yes, I've been there many times, but always transiting the country quickly. Afraid of coups!'

'That was why I came this place: in Suriyyah instability, no freedom, *mukhabarat*. No one have money to buy professional services.'

(Suddenly apprehensive) 'How long have you been here?'

'I here since ten year. No culture then, no culture now. But at least these people rich. You know, there are three kinds of haircut in Abu Dhabi. First, Hilton Hotel type, like mine...'

One side of the Embassy was bounded by a lane which playful inspiration on the part of a former colony (in all but name) had — tweaking the tail of its erstwhile rulers — named Shari' al Istiqlal (Independence Street). The Embassy was expected to offer him substantial support whether it wanted the organisation to open up in Abu Dhabi or not. The transitional office arrangements it made were, however, unsatisfactory. Prompted by remembering that the bookcase in it belonged to his employers, it first had the impractical idea of loaning him its waiting room. Though the accommodation was palatial compared with that occupied by Ronald Storrs as Oriental Secretary in Cairo, the idea did not outlast the day of its inauguration as he was jostled by a stream of visitors. He moved to the stationery store — the stationery 'cupboard' in popular mythology — and was able to use it as a secure base from which to strike out into Abu Dhabi. If not via secretarial help which was not forthcoming, his advance was supposed to have been eased by the loan of one of the Embassy cars, but it wouldn't start and he had to hire one instead. It went against his conscience that only Japanese makes were available. He was able to resume normal transport arrangements when, after queuing for days outside the harbour in a line of ships which stretched right across the horizon, the *Strathaslak* at last brought his Peugeot, surrounded by shaykh-destined consumables. He gave it the warm welcome due to a long-awaited friend and son-substitute. The UAE was too hot for its malfunctioning automatic choke to present further difficulty.

He finally found a flat which would do as an office and no one else wanted and commissioned a street sign for it. He forbade the artist to erect it before he had approved of the finished article. They returned from Dubai one Friday to see it stuck drunkenly in the sand outside and with part of the organisation's name spelled wrongly in the English portion of the bilingual text. Horace's telephone was red hot next day as British expatriates, beside themselves, rang to accuse him of dishonouring their country.

A major early irritant at work was the attempt by inadequately supervised junior colleagues in London to make him personally responsible for the finances of the organisation's long-established Dubai branch, which was under his general control. It was run day-to-day by a colleague who could not have shown more fellow feeling or been more helpful. Horace had problems enough of his own and firmly refused to have anything to do with its cash. He kept the Abu Dhabi budget in a Strepsil tin. When an auditor came out on an inspection they could not agree the value of its contents.

The organisation sent him no communications at all during the first seven and a half weeks when he most needed its support. A new year began and his employers still had not added him to the distribution list of their weekly house newsletter. Refusing to admit that boom-time Abu Dhabi needed a special approach, they gave them the cruelly tight deadline of a month to find a house to rent. During that period they paid them allowances which, though in theory handsome, were quite inadequate in relation to the cost of living. As a result, Horace and his family could not afford to eat properly in the first of their two hotels. The second, the enjoyable Al Ayn Palas, had a lovely pool in which, though not a good enough swimmer to be generally keen, he did record numbers of lengths. Even then, an eagerly anticipated tin of Carlsberg blue in the evening after a marathon performance was a guilt-inducing treat.

Despite the pool, getting a house had to be top priority if bankruptcy were to be avoided. Ankara had cured them of flats.

Houses were scarce, however, and competition for them among expatriates was cut-throat. With their allowances running out, they bid for the unlikeliest of places and obtained the title to at least one villa which, when they arrived to claim it, already contained tenants who had perhaps had a larger advance than them at their disposal.

They had fancifully imagined that in a fabulously oil-rich state housing would be free or very cheap. They were surprised to end up renting at unprecedented cost. This was doubly galling since the house they had finally to settle for was just as awful to live in as it looked from outside. In due course, their successor gave it one glance and refused to occupy it. It had major problems. There was no water pressure and what water did reach them was unpleasantly discoloured. Downstairs was a playground for mice, which ran races up the curtains and were found dead under the dining room table at breakfast time. No poison, no cat, could eradicate them. The garden was a rock-strewn sandpit, surrounded by a crumbling wall beyond which camels were kept until it was time for them to be ceremonially slaughtered at '*Id al Adha*, the festival which commemorates Abraham's preparedness to sacrifice Isaac; Horace had not met the killing of camels before and was shocked by it. They put a lot of work into the garden, obtaining free plants from the municipality and doing what they could to improve the view from their windows while they had one. It was all useless. Their surroundings never lost the character of a construction site and the salinity of Abu Dhabi's soil meant that most of the plants with which they tried to civilise it disappointed them by dying.

Finding consolation in minor satisfactions, they converted a balcony on the east side of the house into a place to catch occasional cool zephyrs late at night. They got into the habit of repairing there to hear Sports Round-up and the World News on the BBC World Service — a comfort despite its insistence on mis-stressing Iranian names from the moment Ayatollah Khomeini appeared on the international stage.[*] The balcony was a fine vantage point from

---

[*] The habit is catching. BBC newsreaders now regularly stress the last syllable of all foreign names which end in 'i'.

which to watch 'planes preparing to land at Abu Dhabi airport. Their 'plane-spotting acquired enormously added poignancy when they were counting the moments until their elder son would come back to them from boarding school.

Horace's employers, unconcerned that their alternatives had been to stay in a hotel they could not afford or occupy a house with no innards, looking as if it had been badly shaken up in an earthquake, had neglected to order them, let alone ship, any furniture. Inside the house, makeshift things borrowed from friends were all they had. Swithin had to sleep on the floor. When at last a container came with furniture for them, Horace (having no staff) unloaded it himself and did long-term damage to his back.

The organisation had not covered itself with glory. No office, staff, accommodation, furniture or transport was a notable performance. Horace would not have minded his situation so much if his employers had shown any interest in his problems or been grateful for his efforts in the face of odds they had themselves piled up against him. He felt like an exile — 'no sort of understanding or sympathy in London,' as Sir Arnold Wilson remarked — and, being fairly senior and a long service member of the staff, resented being so badly treated. In terms of continuing civilised relations with principals whose administration had shown itself to be laughably bad, and as uncaring as when he was stranded in Beirut seven years earlier, the Abu Dhabi expedition was of course a disaster. It was for this that they had lost a son! They discussed what attitude to adopt and decided to make no secret of their displeasure.

Considerateness was a commodity in short supply in London, and in Abu Dhabi too. His employers found a headmaster for the local British-type junior school (Al Khubayrat, called Alcu-by-rat by the local British, who considered it affected to pronounce Arabic names correctly and stressed this one on the wrong syllable) whose board proceeded to eject him from the country without notice — and without consulting Horace, his sponsor — on the grounds of alleged inadequacy.

Their landlord, Khamis, who was gruffly friendly in the Gulf manner, once brought his wife across. She became the only unveiled Abu Dhabi woman Horace ever saw when her husband said to her, 'Take that thing off.' That secret revealed, however, he

178

made no allusion to a far-reaching reconstruction project he had
in view.

* * *

At 115°, it's as hot as it will get now. Everyone has had about
enough. The banks are emptying markedly and the traffic congestion has eased because expatriates have begun to go on leave
and their wives have laid up their Honda Civics until September.
The indigenous inhabitants of Abu Dhabi are anxious to be off,
too. The end of the year examinations at the University and in
schools are nearly over. The school sessions have followed their
normal course, with the Ministry of Education assuring pupils in
Al Ittihad, the official daily, that the average student will be able
to pass, examinees countering next day beneath headlines
shrieking, 'Pupils Say Geography and Physics Questions were
Hard and Long' and an invigilator being beaten up in Dubai for
detecting a case of cheating. The University, now completing its
second year, has been quizzed for months by the press about the
arrangements it plans for its students in the summer vacation — a
difficult one to field because, as Rameses might have put it, the
summer in the UAE is undoubtedly longer than anywhere else and
students of all levels have five months' holiday. To the relief of
critical journalists, it is hoped, the University has recently said that
it has arranged English courses in three Arab universities for
selected students to attend and practical attachments in ministries
and other government establishments for others. It is not true that
Abu Dhabi translates itself *en bloc* to Kensington in July, August
and September, but it is not easy to see the secondments being of
tremendous assistance to civil servants of the future.

What circumstances those involved in the great exodus will find
awaiting them on their return are uncertain, but they look a bit
sombre at the time of writing. The UAE has been blowing hot and
cold about pork for at least the last eighteen months and the
presence of its derivatives in toothpaste and other essentials has
been fanfared. The Dubai agent for Brylcream has denied that the
product he represents bears any relation to the offending,
unfortunate article. Will the expatriate who purchases pork from
shelves labelled 'FOR NON-MUSLIMS ONLY' be able to resume the

habit when he comes back? Much more basic, and at present provoking as much social stress as the shortage of petrol on the M6, is the question of alcohol. Its purchase in Abu Dhabi has always been limited to permit-holders, but recent statements suggest that the UAE may be heading for total prohibition. The lead in this is, surprisingly, coming from Dubai, where until now the ruler, Shaykh Rashid, has taken a lenient view along with a useful cut. His appointment as the UAE's prime minister a month ago may have something to do with it, but the influence of Ayatollah Khomeini is the most likely reason for his sudden hard line. The three British pubs in Dubai, and even the bars of the dozens of first or luxury class hotels there, are under threat as a result of this volte-face. If the cause of it is unclear, its consequences are a snook cocked at Shaykh Zayid, the federal president, who has always been the more dour in his attitude to this kind of question, and frantic queuing by Abu Dhabi expatriates at the two licensed drink shops. They obviously believe that Zayid's emulation of his prime minister will be swift and swingeing, and they may well be right. One cannot but hope that, if British exiles are deprived of one of the UAE's compensations, reciprocal action will be forthcoming in certain London boroughs.

It is all of a piece with decision-making procedures in this country that, at this very moment, tourism should be a prominent topic of newspaper discussion. The UAE has high ambitions for its touristic future, and it is certainly realistic in this: its Gulf of Oman coast is worth travelling a long way to see. But will visitors come if alcohol is forbidden them?

Since cars are so expensive to hire, the hypothetical tourist is not likely to be affected if another expatriate hunch becomes reality. The foreign community has always been afraid that one day Saudi Arabia, whose convictions are paid much attention here, would convince the UAE that it should remove the affront to Islam represented by ladies who drive. Such a development would make life very difficult for families, and women at the wheel in the UAE are not in noticeable league with death. Indeed, being cut up on one of Abu Dhabi's scores of roundabouts by a sternly veiled and *burqu*'ed local chauffeuse is a periodic experience to treasure.

The UAE has several internal problems of a much less superficial sort. It has been caught up in a political crisis for at least the last three months. Which of the big emirates is to be top is the theme of this drama. There are only two real competitors, Abu Dhabi, which has held first place until now, and Dubai. Sharjah is the most weighty supporter of Shaykh Zayid, Ra's al Khaymah of Shaykh Rashid. The country is in a tricky position, with Iran peering critically across the Gulf, Saudi Arabia prompting from the rear and Oman in league with Egypt. The last is perhaps the crucial point at the moment. Without Egyptian expatriates by the thousand holding the civil service and the education system together, the country would be in a perilous state, yet a report in *Al Ittihad* claims that the UAE, which has sided firmly against President Sadat over his peace agreement with Mr Begin, has begun to discuss with Kuwait and Saudi Arabia a proposal to prevent Egyptians from sending their savings home. If the report is true, Cairo is likely to administer a swift riposte, bringing serious consequences to the UAE.

* * *

At the start of their second year, ominous marks began to ring their perimeter which indicated that a large building was to engulf them. In due course the house Khamis occupied behind them was bulldozed. The operation took no more than 30 minutes. Even the smashing of a human habitation in which chicken bones were flung into the corner at mealtimes was a sobering spectacle. The ensuing works hemmed them in in the ugliest and most intrusive way and eventually cut off all the light from their dining room, whose windows were less than a yard from those of the new building. Khamis saw no need now to be nice to his foreign guests, or to give them value for the seeming fortune they were helping him to amass.

The building site watchman (charmingly, *natur* in Gulf colloquial) improved his situation with picaresque ingenuity. He was not provided with electricity for light or — in temperatures of up to 115 degrees — cooling. One day, like Colonel Nicholson in *The Bridge on the River Kwai*, they noticed a suspicious cable running through the sand. It led to his accommodation — too rudimentary to deserve the names 'hut' or even 'box' — from the quarters which Dawud, their excellent Pakistani cook, shared with a paramour and which were none too grand themselves. The watch-man's electrical needs were being met, courtesy of them, as Islamic solidarity outwitted both landlord and tenant.

They were not the only ones with housing problems. The ambas-sador also had an undignified phase. He and his wife were lying in bed in their residence one night when a faint scratching noise was heard coming from the loft above their heads. By the time its cause had been eradicated, the corpses of 957 rats had been taken away.

Though one year they turned the air conditioning off in mid-January before restoring it four weeks later, the heat in Abu Dhabi was nothing like so great or regular as Baghdad. The humidity, however, was formidable. A ready appreciation of the ridiculous was an asset in coping with it. Horace had always determined to be the fittest person of his age, no matter how many years he had attained. In Abu Dhabi he had to abandon tennis when he could persuade no one to play with him in July; he was pleased to be able to prove the theory to which he subscribed that wringing out a shirt could fill a bucket with sweat. Nor did the demonstration demand much preparatory exertion. As one of his many grudging contributions to the alleviation of their domestic problems, Khamis was one day unable to avoid sending a new water tank round. There being little subject matter for a camera in their immediate vicinity, Horace strolled 50 yards down the road to make a photographic record of the arrival of the new acquisition, soon lolling self-satisfiedly on their roof. By the time he had taken refuge in the air conditioning once more, the crisp shirt he had started out in was completely drenched.

The climate was not a difficulty. Though successful at squash and tennis, however, he was prey to continual illness. He was also prey to the British community, which was otherwise Abu Dhabi's only unattractive feature. It seemed mostly to be made up of aggressive people with red faces, and the 'dull fat eyes' observed by Kipling's Kim, who took no interest in the society surrounding and subsidising them as they scrapped for projects to make them *nouveaux riches* and for membership of the haughty British club. Horace needed several years to become reconciled again to being of the same nationality. Ungenerous comments reached him from his very first day. They were perhaps provoked by misplaced impatience for Horace to be doing things for them, as well as by contempt for the organisation which, in their opinion, had taken too long to send him. It was a deep disappointment to find among his critics people — like the test drive Jaguar owners — who had been friends in Baghdad, where he had of course represented an employer whose style at least provoked respect. Two others in particular, a husband and wife, sneered vocally at his efforts. He was a former diplomat who had not risen high and had spent most of his working life in the Gulf. From a distance, he had been involved in regional aspects of Horace's work in the Embassy in Baghdad. Now — ironically in view of the fact that it had done, and continued to do, so little to help him, — he objected to Horace's determination to be as independent of the Embassy as was feasible. While Horace was still homeless and had no furniture or staff, the wife was putting up to him the most impractical suggestions of cultural events for him to organise for the British community. Since he had at least gathered that part of his vague brief was to do business with the government and people of the UAE rather than the local British, he declined to cooperate and earned her scorn. In the week his desk arrived, she called him 'inactive and useless to the [British] community'.

She was not the only imperious British spouse. At one point there were widespread rumours that Shaykh Zayid, the ruler, would in due course move the capital of the UAE from Abu Dhabi to his birthplace, Al Ayn. Horace volunteered this at a cocktail party to the wife of a Briton high in the petroleum industry, one of the class of 'intolerably snooty women' identified by Falle as products of the overseas life — who according to Storrs can hardly bring themselves to acknowledge those of the country of their husbands' posting although these are 'as likely as not better born, better bred, better read, better looking and better dressed' than themselves, — she responded by saying, 'The oil companies would never allow it' in a manner which defied him to suggest again that the UAE enjoyed any kind of independence. With the recent opening of a new international airport in the oasis city, however, the transfer is still a possibility.

Among the Baghdad companions-in-arms to resurface in the UAE, Shanks had become Consul-General in Dubai. All fun extinguished, he looked completely wrong in the role of pin-striped, sober public figure, like Lawrence of Arabia seen (by Alec

Kirkbride) in a lounge suit. His successor was Derek. Hamid Ansari reappeared as Indian ambassador. Their friendship resumed and, 12 years on, as in Baghdad, they captained opposing cricket teams. A Turkish diplomat, universally liked in Iraq, arrived to open his country's first Embassy in the UAE.

The British ambassador could not have been more supportive — invitations to meals and receptions came with embarrassing frequency — or less interfering, making him seem a model. In due course, however, he too revealed the usual spots. Horace went round one day for a periodic chat and had his breath taken away to be told — shades of Cromer and Wingate's Sudan annual report for 1900 — 'I've just produced a despatch on cultural diplomacy. Sorry I didn't show you it before it went off.'

Horace's employers sent several inspectors out while he was in the stationery store. The first reacted to his complaints by warning him that it was unwise to fall out with London. Though, as it turned out, he was quite right, Horace was gratified to hear that, after visiting his Dubai sub-office, his pompous superior had had to spend 18 hours at the airport before being able to get away.

A very tall, nice colleague had touched base even sooner. Horace put him up in a hotel which had recently had a fire. His room was on the sixth floor, which the brigade's ladders had been unable — as he delighted in telling him — to reach. Occupying his room, Horace's guest flung open the French window onto the balcony and came to a screeching halt when he realised, almost too late, that only a wall nine inches high guarded the drop.

The task of opening the new office was doomed to initial failure, though Horace did not realise it for six months. There had been depressing pointers. Suggestions of a kind he had heard nowhere else were commonly made that his employers and, by inference, he were in the espionage business. An ominous quotation from Shaykh Zayid reached his ears: 'If those people come here and ask me for land to build on, they can forget it.' Such signs discounted his surprise when, in due course, he learned that his masters had not bothered to clear the way for him at all. The things that had been said, the rumours and hearsay — all was now seen in a different light. He came across papers in files which explained what had happened. One in particular minuted a conversation, between the predecessor of his colleague in Dubai and a bumptious member of the staff of the Abu Dhabi Embassy, which made him gasp. It recorded that the latter, asked for his final opinion as to whether or not the organisation should try to set up an operation in Abu Dhabi, gave a non-committal reply. On such a foundation, Horace and his wife had travelled a great distance for almost no purpose, incurred disproportionate expense, lived in squalor and (the first step towards the breakdown of their marriage) sacrificed a son. Horace and Swith were miserable playing cricket without him and spent all Andrew's school holidays anguished at the prospect of losing him again.

A contact-making call on the Director-General of Cultural Affairs in the Ministry of Foreign Affairs, an Iraqi, had been the final piece of the jigsaw. As he crossed the threshold, he was struck amidships:

'How dare you come to the UAE without authority? I understand that you have been calling at ministries.'

'I have been carrying out the duties of my post, as I have done in three or four countries before.'

'You will cease them immediately in the absence of my prior permission.'

He had to face the fact that he was illegal. In being determined to seize a share of the oil wealth despite Abu Dhabi's reluctance, his employers had overplayed their hand. He immediately went to the ambassador and asked him to declare him his cultural attaché, but he declined. The title was only conferred 18 months later, after Horace had extracted himself from a tunnel with no light at the end and handed over to a successor. No heads rolled in London for their ineptitude. His superiors, however, criticised him for — as they found it convenient to interpret it — becoming gratuitously involved with the Ministry of Foreign Affairs. They did nothing to right the situation and had obviously hoped to get away with their trespass on the UAE indefinitely. A particularly wounding and unjustified rebuke arrived by telegram on Christmas Eve.

After his initial paroxysm of fury, the Director-General did all he could to regularise Horace's position. The MFA's Chief of Protocol, the son of a former Syrian prime minister, went out of his way to lend a hand, not always productively. At one point he asked Horace to pursue legality through the under-secretary of one of the ministries. This official accordingly called a meeting to try to hammer out an acceptable status for Horace's office. He asked him and several other people to attend. At the time appointed, the only absentee was the convenor himself. Even this non-meeting was more than was happening in London. Joint British–UAE talks took place there, involving a long table of people for the whole of a day while two did all the talking. Exactly as in Beirut, no reference was made to the problem which had taken the stuffing out of Horace's mission.

Thanks to the forbearance of the authorities of the UAE, being illegal did not tie his hands completely. When the Queen and the Duke of Edinburgh came out, the principal object of their visit was to inspect the University newly opened, a year early, in Al Ayn; Shaykh Zayid had said, 'Why wait till next year? Let's open it now.' It was still at the stage when expatriates delighted to claim that the students were served breakfast in bed and the girls followed lectures on closed-circuit television to keep them from contact with male teachers.

The Queen and the Duke flew in one of their Andovers to the artificial city of Al Ayn, charming, idyllic and bestrewn with beautiful gardens and parks for the citizenry. The 'plane taxied up to a red carpet placed beside the airstrip. At the head of it waited Shaykh Zayid, and down both sides stood his tribal followers tapping little drums with their drumsticks. As the Andover came to rest, Zayid and his men began to skip in time to the beat. The Queen descended the steps and he started to dance, inviting her to join him. Sadly, she declined.

Because embassies take the lion's share, Horace had been gratified to be asked to give the Queen and the Duke a guided tour of the University. He enquired what the dress would be and was given the advice — again, non-committal — to wear whatever he chose. On the day, he donned brown shoes and a grey suit. After he had been driven the 100 hot miles from Abu Dhabi to await the royal party in the ambassador's charming Al Ayn bungalow, he was embarrassed to find himself the only one not in dark things. Great, accordingly, was his relief when Prince Philip arrived from his hotel in the capital — a new one, afterwards said not to have had its water connected in time for the visit — wearing ox blood shoes and a suit of matching informality, possibly ginger in hue.

The convoy of royal party and accompanying officials progressed to the University at breakneck speed. It became so utterly split up that Horace completely lost contact with the Queen and the Duke and never regained it. The group touring the University was to have numbered six in all but turned into a cast of thousands. Security was non-existent, Prince Philip was on several occasions alarmed at losing sight of the Queen in the throng, and Horace's moment of glory was denied him. He was also denied a seat at the top table for the ensuing lunch at the Hilton Hotel, but found himself in good company. The Embassy official who had allowed him to be illegal had planned things so well that, while there was a top table place for him, Sir Hugh Boustead, a British legend in those parts, was likewise overlooked — and Shaykh Zayid's eldest son joined the groundlings in order to be with him.

The University finding a way to get round governmental objections, Horace was asked to place parties of its students on specially arranged summer courses in Britain. While on leave, he visited the girls at Colchester, the boys at Plymouth. The boys were unreasonably demanding and not grateful, and even by rising at 5.00 a.m., the college cook was unable to satisfy them that everything possible had been done to fortify them against the Ramadhan fast.

The Ministry of Education also succeeded to some extent in turning a blind eye to Horace's lack of status. It asked him to find it a Chief Inspector of English. Horace explained that there were forms which needed to be filled in to enable a contract to be drawn up. The Assistant Under-Secretary waved the requirement away with typical Gulf haughtiness. When Horace returned from a home leave, Salim expressed surprise that the recruit had not reported for duty. (If there had been any question of him doing so, Horace's splendid Dubai colleague would have terminated his own leave early in order to receive him.)

In due course, the exercise went through in orthodox fashion. Horace (6' 2") and his colleague (5' 7") came to meet the new arrival in London. Horace's irritation that he did not stand up to greet them was forgotten when it was only with considerable difficulty that he was eventually able to lever his 6' 8" frame from his seat.

As in their garden, everything in Abu Dhabi was either going up or being pulled down and all the final touches (landscaping, vermin control &c.) were lacking. But the city already had its splendid, broad promenade ('cornish'), with a waterfall at the end of every block and, at one point, a control box surmounted by an intriguing sign reading WHEN FLASHING PLEASE TELEPHONE ABU DHABI MUNICIPALITY TOWN DRAINAGE DEPARTMENT. The western edge of the island, where the channel is widest and most mettlesome, is a striking amalgam of sea of ever-changing colour, sand of a dazzling white and diver birds engaged in serious, unselfconscious fishing.

All the major roads of the capital, criss-crossing in grid formation, were dual carriageways connected to the rest of the network by roundabouts. These were often half a mile apart, which called for careful journey planning. If you got your calls in the wrong order through recollecting that somewhere was on the left which was actually on the opposite side, parking regulations might require you to add an extra hot mile to your journey.

* * *

Dubai — the attractiveness of its name obscured by the ugly British expatriate stress on its first syllable — rises impressively astride one of the world's watermarks, the broad and lively Creek, which labourers in their thousands pay pence to cross backwards and forwards all day, on miniature, motorised, open dhows (called *abrah*s) with nothing to hold on to, in order to visit the *suq* or return to their accommodation, such as it is. Dubai is grand and sophisticated: its hotels give fewer dinars for Scottish than for British pounds and clients of the pub called Thatcher's spill out in the early hours, making a most unIslamic noise.

Despite his agoraphobia, Horace adored the bucolic and friendly yet mysterious desert road there from Abu Dhabi. Like Al Ayn, Dubai is about a hundred miles away. Now disfigured for more than half its length by a continuous line of advertisement hoardings which no doubt pay the merchants of Dubai handsomely, the road ran parallel to the coast and only a short distance from it. On the desert side, there were occasional tantalising glimpses of mansions built in the centre of artificial oases. The highway was littered with large American cars which oil shaykhs had abandoned at the first sign of unreliability. (Horace knew an ordinary citizen of the UAE who owned 11 Mercedes.) Its construction postdated the Dubai–Abu Dhabi land speed record, set when its surface consisted of not much more than sand by the brother of the shaykh who has dominated British horse racing in recent times. Their father, Shaykh Rashid, the then Ruler of Dubai, master-minded the city-state's controlled prosperity. Horace's Dubai colleague ridiculed many of his projects, such as the Jebel Ali dry dock and the Trade Centre, but in every instance Shaykh Rashid's foresight and ambitious thinking have been vindicated. Even the Dubai Classic golf tournament is owed to his inspiration.

It was in Dubai that Horace decided to abandon his 13-year-old boycotts of the pro-Israeli Marks & Spencer and Selfridges when he witnessed nationals of the emirate driving their new Mercedes away after unloading them from a ship with its Hebrew name carelessly painted out and clearly visible to their Nelsonian eyes. In any case, it was common knowledge that the first stop for UAE nationals in London was the Marks & Spencer in Oxford Street.

The territories of the seven emirates which make up the UAE form a patchwork. A beautiful road joins Dubai with the Gulf of Oman coast. It passes through Sharjah, where in Trucial States' times there was an RAF base. More recently, it erected many large hotels to cater for tourists before introducing prohibition, turning itself into a ghost city by driving them away the few miles to comparatively liberal Dubai. Past inland oases, the road skirts the black Hajar mountains beyond which lie Fujairah (capital of the emirate of that name), the idyllic Indian Ocean and Khawr Fakkan, a possession of Sharjah which reclines at the head of a white sand bay, in one diplomatic view 'the most beautiful beach in the world'.

Al Ayn, where Horace loved to go, is a modernised oasis where the ambassador's bungalow, when free, was available to other official British people. Booking it became considerably easier when sleeping policemen were installed on the Abu Dhabi–Al Ayn road and HE's official Jaguar, low on the ground, could no longer complete the journey. He was not so keen to travel there in an undignified Hillman which gave out entirely in due course.

As elsewhere in the Emirate of Abu Dhabi, to which Al Ayn belongs, the road humps were not initially announced by warning signs, and a number of speeding motorists — including some on Horace's street — were killed through not knowing that they were there.

Before their upgrading, two roads of contrasting character led to Al Ayn. In 1902, it took the admirable Sir Percy Cox five days to ride to the oasis of Buraymi, of which Al Ayn is part. It was humbling to think of him having to start by negotiating 'the dangerous sea-ford of Maqta with the tide up to his camel's girths'. Now one leaves the island of Abu Dhabi by the Maqta' Bridge, which takes only seconds to cross. The road, though dusty, open, straight and flat, desolate at the start and featureless for the most part, had several dramatic stretches. At its highest point, Indians have established the Restaurant Zamzam, named for the spring whose discovery led Abraham to found Mecca beside it. Nearby, they have recently opened the High Taste Restaurant. A new, parallel route is, though a motorway, defaced by frequent clusters of sleeping policemen which make a taxi ride along it a nerve-racking experience.

From Dubai, the highway to Al Ayn meandered. It was washed by a desert of a deep, rich red whose stately sand dunes undulated like a fairground switchback. The motorist had to be wary because it teemed with camels. Strictly dromedaries, having only one hump, they do not look — on their skinny legs — like a threat. Impact with a car's bonnet, however, upends them in a way which almost guarantees that, with just the right clearance and windscreen-shaped bodies, their solid, podgy forms squash the life out of the driver.

Now, Dubai and Al Ayn are connected by a luxury motorway, illuminated throughout its Abu Dhabi Emirate section and with camels still abounding on the Dubai stretch. There are regular nostalgic glimpses of the old road. The new one's three lanes either side are so empty of traffic that Shaykh Rashid's judgement has to be given extra benefit of the doubt. The desert flanks the road throughout its length. Suddenly, a sign announces 'Parking in 500 metres'; a maintenance man appears on a lorry-mounted ladder, repairing a gantry in the middle of nowhere. From near the halfway point, the black and jagged Hajar dominates the view to the north and the dunes through which the road passes turn an even deeper red.

* * *

Despite the frustrations and disappointments marring his posting, Horace was able to derive a great deal of satisfaction from coming to what terms he could with a new country, aided only by a colleague 100 miles away. He ignored the MFA's strictures whenever he could get round them and continued to enlarge the circle of the ministries and institutions where he was known, persuading them, and private persons, to make use of his limited wares. His employers eventually took pity and asked if he would like to transfer to Jordan. Although in the end Horace accepted the suggestion, they did not really want to go at all. The only place now for them was home, so that he could look for another job and alternative schooling for the boys.

Horace put a 'For Sale' notice on their car's back window. Until very close to their departure date there was no flicker of demand. Right at the end, a taxi driver waylaid them in the street and talked them into reducing their reserve price. He paid a deposit, then the balance, and drove the car away. The deal called for him also to take over their remaining insurance and convey them to the airport. To save himself £11, he didn't turn up on their final morning and they had a panic before catching their 'plane. Luckily, their driver was one of the kind they normally had to reprimand for breaking the speed limit and for once they ignored the warning bells clanging in the cab.

They had asked for the supply of electricity and gas to be resumed to their London house and for the 'phone to be switched on for their return. When they arrived back, none of them was functioning.

19

Hotel of Character:
Damascus

Since our arrival on these coasts, Christopher and I have learned that the cost of everything ... can be halved by the simple expedient of saying it must be halved.

(Robert Byron in Damascus)

They flew in from Abu Dhabi by Tunis Air, the nearest he had got to his desire to visit the land of Hannibal. It was wonderful to be back in Syria. He preened himself at the airport, confident because he knew the language and feeling immediately at home. He remembered people saying that arriving where the script was familiar but had no meaning for them, as in Turkey or Norway, was worst.

Warmly greeted by the Syrians, as usual, they swept into town in a Pontiac taxi with an attractively expansive driver. Damascus looked as exciting as ever. It was good to be in the centre of the Arab world once more after so long on the periphery, engaging though the UAE was.

They registered at the HMG-approved hotel. At first glance it seemed standard Middle Eastern mediocre, though extraordinarily gloomy and dusty, but the Kattan quickly began to display unusual personality traits.

The lift had two doors, both of which opened at each stop. On some floors, carpeting led off in two diagonal directions to the bedrooms. On others, one door was the threshold of a fall through space. When Horace learned that the hotel's location had been selected because of the grandstand view it afforded of public executions, he regarded this macabre feature as peculiarly appropriate.

A notice on their door recorded the absurdly low price of their room: 12 Syrian pounds for bed and breakfast for three. He ran downstairs:

'Is the price of our room really only what it says on the door?'

'For you, sir, 10 per cent discount.'

Abba hits were broadcast non-stop throughout their stay. He had not heard the numbers before. They were all about the black sheep of the family and Fernando. They went round and round all day and began to drive them mad.

The deliberations of him and his colleagues held greater interest for him than normal. The local man on the spot (Richard, organiser of the Diwaniyyah expedition 13 years before) had a profound knowledge of Arab culture and traditions of which some in the British Embassy were jealous. At lunchtimes, he guided them to restaurants in the vicinity of the conference venue. By the end of the second day Horace had begun to feel unwell. His upset stomach and dreadful head kept him out of circulation for the greater part of a week. They had to cancel their flight back to Abu Dhabi. 'What did he expect,' his wife reported the Embassy as saying, 'from following Richard's advice?'

They were to go straight to the airport from his sickbed. He woke early, washed-out and weak. A voice was speaking loudly in English in the next room:-

Syrian markets have to be approached with caution. Everything depends on making contacts in the *suq*. Your attitude must be one of deference. He knows that you know he's got reservations, but you must on no account allow him to suspect that you've penetrated his disguise. He has got to approve of you more than vice versa. The veriest rogue may be just your man. Your needs will of course differ according to your product. The agent who adopts a straightforward policy and is well known to the leading politicians of the day could turn out to be ideal for certain kinds of transaction, the more devious operator for the larger contracts. And then there's the question of commission. This too must be carefully reconnoitred lest any suggestion of bakhshish or bribery arise. ...

193

When this had gone on for some minutes, Horace suddenly realised that it was not a conversation, in the flesh or on the 'phone, but a monologue. He rapped violently on the wall. As in the sad case reported by Beverley Nichols, the speaker ceased immediately and did not resume his soliloquy.

When they got down to breakfast, served in a bare, barn-like vault, there were quarrelling and fighting in the kitchen and no bread. Suddenly, a man dressed in shabby khaki and spotted with perspiration burst in from the street with a brown paper bag under one arm. Plunging his hand in, he crashed a thin French loaf on to the first table. Likewise the second. The next loaf escaped his clutch and rolled on to the floor beneath the third. Retrieving it, he blew on it before banging it down in front of the alarmed residents. Swithin was sick.

20

Disillusion in Jordan

... you meet only dreadful, unrepresentative people in Amman.
(Jonathan Raban)

Horace's period of residence in Jordan got off to a difficult start. The London GP they had been with for years retired and, before leaving home, the family had to transfer to another, recommended by Horace's employers. First impressions had not been encouraging. In Abu Dhabi, their younger son had fainted several times and become the first patient in one of the city's new luxury hospitals. Although the episodes were diagnosed to be a symptom of growing, they sought the view of the new man. He knew of the case by the time they telephoned and began their conversation and relationship by identifying Swithin, whom he had never seen, as 'the little epileptic'. Worse was to come. Three weeks before, Horace had undergone a Treasury medical examination (required before taking up official work overseas) and passed it with flying colours. He needed a routine blood test, however, to make sure that his uric acid level had stayed normal. When he went to receive the result, the GP confirmed that it was, but added, 'You know you're a diabetic?' He assured him that, while he might have no symptoms then, he certainly would within 12 months. He pushed across his desk pamphlets with names like *Living with your Diabetes*. Ridiculing the diagnosis, Horace nonetheless drove home expecting to descend into a coma at any moment. He spent the first year in Jordan proving the sentence wrong. He could do nothing, however, to persuade the regional NHS administrators to withdraw their claim that no diagnosis had been made or to have it expunged from his medical records.

Most people considered Jordan a posting in a million but — though he had been depressed at not being able to get there earlier in his career — Horace had never ceased, from his first encounter with it, to consider it his least favourite Arab country. Whether because of its Jordanian/Palestinian ethnic mix or not, it never lived up to the welcoming promise of its balmy, scented air as you drove across the Syrian frontier. The garage attendant who had overfilled your tank would laugh at the pool of petrol widening on the ground at your expense. Keeping doors locked seemed to be a national obsession. Police at the airport would unmercifully beat and kick the poor and illiterate Egyptian workers who helped Jordan become wealthy during the Iran–Iraq War. Newspaper and cigarette kiosk proprietors would reply in broken English to your Arabic because they believed no foreigner capable of tackling their language. (During Horace's period of posting, the Jordanian authorities gave their name to an illustrated book called *Jordan as I See.*) A staff member claimed that conditions were too difficult for him to try to get to the office through a hundred yards of snow when Horace had battled to his desk across three miles of drifts. (Early one March, when Horace's house was cut off, it seemed as if the whole of Amman had come out to throw snowballs.) A senior official Horace had always got on famously with ran him down to his boss, visiting from London. A very senior Jordanian was in the habit of telling jokes ridiculing Christianity, and for some reason St Paul in particular, at Jordan University lunches. While they were sometimes coupled with anti-Arab ones such as that about the 'Arab brain — never been used,' Horace — though not a convinced believer — objected to them and wished that he dared counter in kind. Finally, an unforgivable insult. In other Arab countries, especially Iraq, people had been delighted that a Briton — sprung from the land of Balfour — should go out of his way and risk his career to side with them over Palestine. Not so Jordan where, after espousing the Arab cause for the whole of his adult life, Horace was indignant at finding himself charged — in a spirit which anticipated the unjustified innuendoes (not directed at him personally) of Edward Said — with being lukewarm in his support.

There were things to savour, nevertheless. Five thousand year-old Jerash, Jordan's second most famous antiquity, exerted a consistent charm. Horace passed through the modern little Circassian town beside it almost weekly on the lovely run to the country's second university and never tired of seeing the columns of the Roman provincial city striding golden across the valley to the west of the road. On foot, its grandeur could overpower. His boss, out on familiarisation, expressed a desire to visit it. Horace wanted above all to show him the perfection of the South Theatre. He had forgotten its size, however, and — only when they had climbed to the highest row of seats and vertigo had seized him — realised that he would have to ask his already disapproving senior for aid if he were ever to reach ground level again. Luckily, before humiliating himself, he espied a way out at the back, involving the conquest of no drop.

Horace hadn't been to Petra for 21 years when the Ministry of Education suddenly invited him (and Andrew) to visit schools, and a University — Mu'tah — under construction, in the south of the country and to take the Nabatean city in on the way. They provided a car which punctured *en route* and a self-important driver who boasted of his equestrian prowess. If you do not feel like walking through Petra, you can hire scrawny, flyblown geldings whose spirit has long been knocked out of them. The driver looked precarious all the way from the mounting block, and was finally thrown off in the Siq when his horse began ramming him backwards and forwards against the rock face at its narrowest point. Horace revisited Petra three weeks later.

Mushattah, where Gertrude Bell archaeologised soon after setting out on her journey to Hayil, was a favourite picnic spot. The most compact of Jordan's Umayyad desert castles, it was constructed on an absolutely level site and thus excellent for cricket. It would be a pity if the proximity of Amman's over-shadowing new airport turned out to offer an environmental threat to the charming structure, a millennium and a quarter old.

Humphrey Lyttelton brought his band to Amman, wearing MCC ties in Horace's honour. Good friends — known before in Baghdad, Khartum and Ankara and, in one case, in each of their places of posting — reappeared in Amman, and new ones were made there. The Jordanian head of scientific research was really a professor of English who was rarely allowed to engage in the work closest to his heart. Later on, he was made an ambassador.

Overweight and never without a cigarette in his mouth, Horace prayed for his longevity with exceptional fervour.

Favourite neckwear was replaced in Jordan. One day in a supermarket Horace met a Jordanian friend wearing a tie indistinguishble from his Achilles Club one which had just fallen to pieces. When he made the mistake of admiring it, it became his so fast that he has never been able to remember the identity of the tie he swapped with it.

Amman was not without character and incident. A colleague who came out to inspect Horace's office shot himself soon afterwards. The Embassy spy was undecided about what sort of car to order for his return to Britain. Discussing the problem in his office one day, Horace was surprised when he suddenly threw himself on to the floor to gauge whether or not an Astra's advertised dimensions would give him enough legroom. Horace had been fond of him throughout his stay. At one of his farewell parties, however, his British oilman host, also apparently a fan, issued a verdict on him which caused Horace to leave without saying 'goodbye':

'Pity to lose our friend.'

'Indeed, I've not met a nicer chap anywhere.'

'Only a hired killer, though. Rub you out without a thought.'

The British ambassador worked day and night on Jordanian–British relations and his effectiveness in the short term struck Horace as being the greatest he had known. It did not, however, prevent Jordan from siding with Saddam Husayn in his Kuwait grab. Many of his staff hated him. Whatever you do, be nice to the Jordanians, was his rule. A consul who was not prepared to implement a policy he considered damaging to his own professional standards was very quickly returned to London. At 'prayers', the other participants cringed as, week after week, the ambassador and his brave commercial attaché squabbled with barely controlled mutual loathing over the latter's alleged shortcomings. Oddly, however, the attaché rejoined the ambassador's team at his next post, which he could hardly have done without his approval. A peripheral member of Horace's staff, to whom the ambassador had particularly objected, also apparently basked in his favour there.

One evening when the ambassador came to his premises for an event, one of Horace's *farrash*es began shrieking and yelling at him as he got out of his official Jaguar. Much though Horace disliked the man, this was embarrassing and potentially worse. He was on the point of roughly quelling the seeming insubordination when they realised that Ahmad, with typical fecklessness, had allowed his fingers to become trapped in the closing electric windows of the extraordinary and plenipotentiary car.

British ambassadors had no luck when visiting his office. Overcome by the stress of a guided tour, Horace's predecessor, making the introductions, claimed his guest's driver as his own librarian.

* * *

It was nearly twelve years after his posting to Amman before Horace set foot in Jordan again. The capital had grown so much that — even allowing for the fact that road signs were never very generously provided — it was only with difficulty that he could recognise his former haunts. Jordan's sustained pro-Iraq stance had earned it a considerable degree of isolation in the Arab world, it had had to absorb huge numbers of additional Palestinian refugees, now from Kuwait, and adverse outside opinions of its security arrangements had ruined its tourism. Petra and Jerash were silent and unexpectant. Nothing remained of the ambassador's former brooding and fearsome presence and Horace noted with satisfaction that the British Embassy had gone from Third Circle. The ambassador went on to a different career some years later which at one point occasioned an extraordinary appearance in Peterborough in *The Daily Telegraph* as an exemplar (wearing — unimaginably — a roll-neck sweater and no tie) of parliamentary sartorial style.

21

Salman Rushdie Strikes: Qatar

It's perfectly delightful getting hold of Persian again, the delicious language.

(Gertrude Bell)

Once you really get the run of the Sporting Club, and make friends with a few nice people, you can forget you're in Egypt altogether ... you really needn't get to know any Egyptians.

(Beverley Nichols)

Horace took up his Doha posting much against his will. It seemed an unworthy job in an unimportant country. Who had heard of Qatar? His employers had asked him to make the move in 'late summer'. Suddenly they defined this as late July. Bang went his holiday plans. The hottest period in Doha, when no one would have returned from more temperate summers abroad, would replace the climax of the cricket season at home. The excuse given for this characteristic piece of employee-unfriendly short-sightedness was the need to find new premises for their work in Qatar.

The office building had been condemned by visiting inspectors. It was in an insecure, Shi'ite part of town — Islamic fundamentalism was nearing its high tide — and it was indefensible. In particular, it had numerous open balconies onto which, it was fancifully stated, an attacker could easily hurl a grenade. No move to somewhere more suitable had taken place by the time Horace left Doha 18 months later.

Qatar's Arabism was vastly less diluted than Abu Dhabi's had been. The British community was far more conscious of being in

200

the Arab world and interested in trying to establish a cultural *modus vivendi* than it had been there. Mercifully, there was no British club. Extreme expatriate attitudes were muted. It was indeed with some justification that some of his co-nationals objected to Horace having a Peugeot as his official car. Since his employers had refused to pay for the shipment of the Peugeot he had used for their work in Ankara and Abu Dhabi, he objected too. For himself, he bought his predecessor's Range Rover, which he had noticed standing unsold, rusting and neglected, in the grounds of the obsolescent property. He had some initial difficulty in persuading himself that owning it would not breach the permanent personal embargo he had placed on its manufacturer after it had let him down so badly in Turkey.

Doha offered Horace another chance, almost a quarter of a century after failing to turn up in Shiraz, to see if Aghdas — of a prominent family — had survived the Khomeini era. It was withdrawn before he could take advantage of it.

The UK's longstanding poor relations with Iran and Syria (no diplomatic ties and no normal ones, respectively) were being re-examined as he set out for Qatar. Before leaving, he had made a point of reminding his employers that, after pioneering Abu Dhabi, he would be the man to reopen their operations in either country. Less than five months after his arrival in Doha, a 'phone call from London asked if he had been serious. Within the month, he was interviewed at home for the task of starting things up once more in Tehran and he was delighted to be selected to perform it. He basked in his employers' approval (for once) and promotion (at last!) might follow. His would be a triumphal return to Iran after 24 years... Best of all was the prospect of remedying his neglect of the third of his oriental languages, the Indo-European one which had the useful advantage that it was far the easiest. He began to brush up the language, to think about packing and — because the Iran–Iraq* War had severed air and sea links — to thrill at the prospect of driving his old lady of a Range Rover to Tehran. Although he had been unambitiously happy there, he

---

*   The names of the two countries are very different in Persian and Arabic and, strictly, should be transliterated Iran and Al 'Iraq.

became dismissive about Qatar. His private maximum intended length of stay had been two years, and moving after eight or nine months was far preferable to risking missing his deadline.

The whole thing went up in smoke with astonishing rapidity. One morning, soon after the posting was confirmed, the BBC World Service relayed Ayatollah Khomeini's call for Salman Rushdie to be murdered for his unpleasant and scurrilous *Satanic Verses*. Horace knew immediately that his hopes, so recently built up, were in desperate jeopardy. In a matter of days the move was cancelled. The imminent despatch of a flood of British diplomats (including him) to Tehran was countermanded, staff already working in the well-remembered Embassy he was eager to renew acquaintance with were brought home, and diplomatic relations — which had begun to ripen exponentially — were cut once more. The British–Iranian landscape was left bleaker even than before and the scene was completely devoid of cheer. Thanks to an ill-judged attack on Islam, Horace had to be satisfied with Qatar.

* * *

In theory, Qatar is overshadowed by its neighbours — Bahrain has maturity, Saudi Arabia size and the UAE grandeur. But it is saved from insignificance by qualities of its own. The people are delightful. The climate is mostly idyllic. The countryside — crammed with rich Qataris practising farming, one of the two pursuits available to gentlemen — is pleasing, some of the beaches are lovely, the dunes are difficult to beat, there are ample jaunts for Fridays. The capital itself is picturesque, self-confident and growing apace, driving big roads never-endingly into the encompassing desert and reclaiming ever more of the multicoloured sea. The story about Doha's dustbins containing three times as many rats as Abu Dhabi's is a canard. Life is orderly and problem-free and expatriates never seem to tire of seeing each others' faces in one identical context after another. Apart from the exceptional one who downs your bottle of brandy before leaving your house unimpaired, the Qataris hardly engage in the whirl (ladies virtually not at all) of which — from behind their palace walls — they are amusedly scornful and anxious spectators.

Drinking in public places is prohibited, which makes many

expatriates fitter than at home and renders negligible the chance of being hit by a drunk driver. Of course, the unavailability of alcohol in hotels and restaurants sounds the death knell for tourism, even the short-stay kind which visiting travel agents (by no means disoriented by landing on the second longest runway in the world) frequently and correctly recommend. Though a meritocratic government may be considering a change, Qatar has so far preferred its principles to that particular source of foreign currency.

The fall in the oil price has hit hard a country with five cars per household. Government servants have recently started to earn their pay according to the Gregorian Calendar. Free water and electricity used to be taken for granted, but real or threatened scarcity means that now they are not always available for new properties, and consumers are beginning to receive quarterly bills.

Getting a driving licence keeps people occupied at the beginning of their stay. British licence-holders, swallowing their pride, have to undergo the Qatari test and — if they fail it, as many do — to enrol for courses of driving lessons which start at 4 in the morning. (Their colonial forebears hoodwinked the Qataris into becoming cruelly early risers, like the Kuwaitis; the rest of the Gulf starts work at 7 a.m. at the very earliest.) The availability in the UK of automatic British licences for Qatari citizens is not the supreme manifestation of Qatar's postcolonial revenge: as a constant reminder to it of who the masters are now (they are not the much-maligned "Egyptian mafia"), the British Embassy has been given an Independence Street address; one of its tasks — of arguable prestige — is to issue eligible foreigners with drink permits. Qatar's sense of humour is not always so evident: it is a crime for an expatriate to affect the national costume.

Of course, there are far more immigrants from the Subcontinent and further East than from the UK; few drink permits for them. They appear to live pitifully, in their single-sex (AIDS-riddled?) simplicity, but presumably earn better than they would at home. They have mostly kept Qatar running in useful ways, opening establishments with names like Youth Butchery or Salah Punchry [puncture repairer] and turning the arid Doha of the '50s into today's green Doha by patiently standing in the gardens of Western expatriates, on a regular and surprisingly costly basis, and often in the dark, with hosepipes in their hands. Sometimes, however, their efforts bring the capital to a complete halt. Its streets seem to be comprehensively 'up' at the best of times. A recent notable achievement was their total encirclement of the Ministry of Public Works' Engineering Department by a maze of giant pipes, deep trenches and impenetrable wire. With Qatar in recession, they are increasingly being taken on as senior managers — at middle management salaries. They put the British to shame with their linguistic talents. At a more fragrant level, guest workers from across the Indian Ocean provide guest workers from the USA with secretaries with names like Lolita.

For so small a country, Qatar pulls its weight well. It did remarkably at the last Olympics. It recently beat China, away, at football. It has introduced a number of innovations which could be of benefit to mankind. Two make driving safer. Another is *Shai Sulaymani*, tea made in a glass with a mandatory Lipton's teabag.

The 5000 British stand out a mile, often in shorts in defiance of local convention and of the Embassy. They are all going to retire to Australia. They have their own supermarket, the Centre, which has been run successively by a number of British retail firms, at present Tesco and BHS jointly. The local wish to make them feel at home and to please them where possible (as, despite the generous number of Arab mosques in the UK, has not been the case over their desire for Christian worship and the public celebration of Christmas) has resulted in a newspaper and radio and television channels in English; on the last, synchronisation between picture and sound is somewhat better than on the Arabic channels. To the distaste of the seeker after Arabism, shoppers in Arab supermarkets are treated to the British football results broadcast in English.

The position of women is enigmatic. Post offices have counters marked STAMPS–LADIES–POSTE RESTANTE, which suggests that the local female of the species has some of the characteristics of a commodity. In fact, she has improved her lot faster than in the UAE and in a few locations — notably the Hamad, the Gulf's finest hospital — has insisted on being seen in uncovered splendour. (Expatriates who teach girls in the segregated University speak highly of their beauty.)

The various races making up Qatar hardly mix. It is only

through a minority interest like rallying that they come together and disregard the conditions which normally separate them. Cars are the other respectable hobby for gentlemen.

* * *

Being satisfied with Qatar was not especially difficult. Though Doha produced little in the way of career-enhancing achievement, the job was pleasurable even if he had at one point to finance it out of his own pocket. His Range Rover greatly enhanced his self-esteem as he swept in it to work. Relations with ministers and officials were rewarding and — though not, again, with the ambassador — free of stress, the way of life was undemanding, the country — a jewel of a peninsula topped by opal and ruby dunes — came to seem a miniature paradise. Swimming and writing made his out-of-hours' time pass satisfyingly enough. He loved the air, the heat and the humidity. He relished continuing a habit of coming to terms unaided with countries which were completely new to him and where he knew no one.

Rite* had built a nice official house, but one with a cockroach problem. The bathrooms in particular suffered from it. The rat surfacing in the Baghdad toilet bowl was of course the worst thing possible of its kind, but cockroaches lying in wait there he found unnerving. Endless repeat visits by pest controllers effected no solution and the deposits left by their sprays were a worry when there were children about or things were dropped on the floor. Leaving for work one morning, he encountered a cockroach on his front doormat which was writhing from the effects of the poison. Friends mocked him when he told them that it had seemed to appeal to him for succour as it made an unsteady terminal dive indoors. His secretary shrieked with a contrary emotion when, on an earlier occasion, two cockroaches inadvertently carried from home scuttled out of his briefcase as he opened it on his desk.

At the end of his first year in Qatar, there was a British trade fair at the Sheraton Hotel. In this remarkable, pyramid-shaped edifice the rooms cling to the sides and colourful, opaque, bullet-

---

*   See Chapter 14.

shaped lifts silently rise and descend. A whole community seems to live out its existence beneath the hotel's shade. Most of its members are Qatari males who are not allowed to reside in it or in any of Doha's other hotels, and use it for seeing and being seen or as a means to keep their large families entertained. Some of them remain until midnight, when they go outside to picnic under the hedges beside the roads which radiate like spokes from this dominant feature of Qatar's topographical, social and touristic persona.

Most of Doha seemed to visit the fair on one of its days of opening. Horace and his staff had a stand, local agents of British firms displayed their products and — with the skill at which the British seem to be unrivalled — VIPs were intercepted on more important missions and persuaded to stop over. Little Qatar felt duly flattered.

There was an enjoyable moment of personal nostalgia. The two people with whom Horace had successively shared the room beside the Tigris in Baghdad 25 years earlier flew in from different directions — one on secondment to an aircraft manufacturer, the other accompanying the Foreign Secretary — and they had a fleeting reunion.

In Doha, immigrant workers from the Subcontinent had a higher profile and status than in Abu Dhabi ten years earlier. Their liveliness showed in their shop signs. There are two ways of putting names from other languages into the Arabic script. The first is to do a straight transliteration, so that 'White House' and 'Jemima's Pantry' written in Arabic come as close to their original pronunciation as the Arabic script will allow. The other is to translate the name, 'White House' becoming 'The House the White' (*Al Bayt al Abyadh*) in Arabic. The Indians (mostly from Trivandrum), Pakistanis and Bangladeshis of Doha often, with frequent happy results, chose an inaccurate or inapposite variant of the latter method. There were 'Goldilocks Cakes and Sweets', which appeared in Arabic as 'The Golden Lock for Sweets and Pastry' (*Al Qufl adh Dhahabi li'l Halawa wa'l Bastri*), the 'Lock' being the kind you turn a key in. Though inter-tongue complications were not necessarily involved, the 'feel' of English was often missing. Baghdad had led the way with a brand of matches called the 'Scissors'. (Col. Bailey noted that cigarettes in Bukhara bore the same anachronistic name.) A plastic bag, frequently seen in Doha transporting items of gentlemen's clothing, advertised 'King of Elegance — All Kinds for Elegant Man'. A popular but limited eating place called itself 'Restaurant and Casino* Kitchens and Happiness Bruce Lee'; its menu featured 'Mutton Making Charge With/Without Rice QR 25/200'. Doha offered little scope for eating out, but there were also the 'Youth Satisfy Restaurant' and the 'Sham Restaurant'** among others. On your way to one of them — in your best suit, perhaps run up in the Dubai *suq* while you were doing a return transit of the Creek there in an *abrah* ('Pant per Piece DH 40') — you could buy a 'Sewer Playset' made in China and then, if authorised, leave your car on land marked 'NO PARKING OTHER THAN CONCERNED VEHICLE BELONGS TO RABBAN BUILDINGS'. You hoped that the basic materials of your menu choices had not been provided by Al Manyoor Foodstuff Est. The best example Horace saw of a signboard going (heroically) wrong announced 'Al Ghandi [sic] Electronics– Iliktruniyyat al Kindi'.

In Doha, there was no need to be apprehensive, as in Baghdad, about political instability. The Ruler and his family were not particularly popular, but political consciousness had not developed to an extent which made their violent overthrow a serious likelihood. Nonetheless, since a bomb had been left on one of his garden walls in his predecessor's time, Horace was careful about security, exaggeratedly in some views. He always allowed his office gate-keepers to check under his car with a mirror before he drove off (Qataris would have had no patience with this procedure) and he never alighted from it before making sure that he had not been followed.

It was not only security doubts which led him to be cautious. He had had to address a large group of overseas students just before being transferred to Doha from Britain. Lacking inspiration, he decided to tell the Arab Brain story, suitably adapted to his audience. It came out wrongly:

---

* In the Arab world, a casino is a shop specializing in the sale of gaseous drinks.
** *Sham* means Damascus or Syria in Arabic.

207

Assistant at second-hand brain shop: We've all kinds of brain here. Suit every budget. There's a Japanese brain in that corner: $500. Chinese brain, Malaysian brain: $250. Australian brain: $150.

Customer: Have you nothing cheaper?

Assistant: Well, at the lower end of the market you've got a Ruritanian brain: $75. Then there's an Arab brain. Never been used...

Two spokesmen for the Arab contingent whom he deeply regretted hurting by this piece of carelessness came at his invitation so that he could apologise to them. In vain he stressed that he had frequently heard this anti-Arab story told by Arabs in the Arab world, like the anti-Christian raconteur in Jordan. One refused to forgive him and said that his story had hurt him so much that he had been unable to sleep since hearing it. Horace consequently travelled to Doha in some fear of the long arm of Islamic fundamentalism. He had not forgotten the murder in Athens of a friend in the organisation who was shot in the street, it was thought by Arabs, at the end of a perfectly ordinary morning at the office.

When he returned 30 months later to work in another capacity in the British city where he had committed the gaffe, he one day needed the advice of a foreign student leader. To his consternation, he found himself talking to the Egyptian he had been unable to sway and who had still not completed his Ph.D. Having escaped without a scratch from Doha, he found his head in the lion's mouth once more.

22

Detained at Saddam's Pleasure: Qatar

Spite of ye all, he is free — he is free!

(W. S. Gilbert)

We had eleven hours and a change of carrier at Gatwick. We arrived in Dubai, still amazed that the Gulf Education Fair had not been cancelled. It remained scheduled to last until three days before President Bush's deadline. Although the Baker–Aziz talks failed during it, I decided to keep to my original plan of going on to Qatar, where there was a job to be done. Casual contacts advised caution, but official opinion was not unfavourable. Friends drove me to Abu Dhabi along a road now almost completely lined with hoardings. I spent a nostalgic night with them. In 11½ years, the city had not changed much but matured and acquired a verdant elegance.

13 January
My Doha leg was given a prompt start at dawn by the mosque behind the house. Even when curtailing sleep, the call to prayer ('God is great … Come to prayer') never fails to charm me.

It had been clear and sunny in Dubai. Doha was dark and dead. Only six of us disembarked from my uneasy flight. To be on the safe side, I swapped my 17 January return booking for one on the 15th. An unkind friend greeted me with, 'Trust you to come at a time like this.'

14 January
A lady accepted for a Ph.D. visited me at the hotel, seeking details

of the University and city. A copy of our new video, imported with some difficulty, should set her mind at rest. I called on an old chum at the Palace who thought Saddam would still surprise us by withdrawing at the last minute. The Minister of Education was on good form, still hoping for the implementation of projects we had started in the past. I went on to the University for discussions with the Chairman of Civil Engineering and the Dean of Economics.

William and Ken took me to lunch to the place which serves the best food in the capital, the government's Doha Club. The spectacle of 'planes clearing its roof by inches before landing at the airport behind had always been impressive. Now we had to cover our ears as formations of F-16s, some giving victory salutes, roared back from their missions. The gentle Qataris will not relish their macho anachronism.

My flight tomorrow has been cancelled but I'm booked for the 16th. The talks between Pérez de Cuellar and Saddam have ended bleakly. Both William and Ken thought that the deadline might well affect their Qatar University midyear break plans. Ken is now toying with the idea of driving to Oman. I could accompany him as far as Dubai if the worst happened and catch my flight to Istanbul that way.

I was tense on my return to the hotel from dinner. Fewer cars than normal were on the streets. On the eve of deadline day, Doha had an expectant air.

15 January

After another morning at the University, I visited Gulf Air to learn that now my flight tomorrow has been cancelled. They waitlisted me for another and confirmed a booking for the 17th. I'm apprehensive about getting stuck here, perhaps for ever, thanks to my risk-taking.

There appear to be fewer than ten other guests in my 440-room hotel and all of them are permanently stationed by the Reuter tickertape machine.

16 January

When I awoke, to my relief Doha seemed normal. I may still make it. President Bush's deadline (8.00 a.m. here) passed without incident. This morning I completed my official business but have brought plenty of work to do. My lecture on the 'Rise of Islam' would look odd coming from someone who had contrived to get himself marooned in Arabia.

The airline cannot give me so much as a first-class seat on today's flight and has cancelled tomorrow's. I taxied to discuss my prospects with them, but to no avail. My driver expressed interest in taking me the 400 miles to Dubai and said that, if his sponsor agreed, the journey would present him with no difficulty. Dave, another refugee (stranded *en route* to leave from a North Field natural gas platform) is also keen to move to Dubai by land; his company would provide a car at least to the border. He claims that, out of apprehension, many offices are closed today.

I ascertained from BA that Emirates, the Dubai airline, still proposed to take off for Istanbul on the 19th. I hope to be on board.

I registered at the Embassy and received instruction from a lieutenant-colonel in the use of a gas mask, now placed within easy reach of my pillow.

Ken is concerned that his exit visa letter, addressed to the airport commander, may not be valid for the frontier. The British Council, who have been generous in their assistance, offered their car to take me to the border tomorrow. The hotel's front-of-house chief got me waitlisted for an Abu Dhabi flight in the morning which the airline earlier told me did not exist. A friend rang to urge me to forget about Turkey and go straight home by the Gulf Air 'plane tomorrow. Dave is booked on it and believes there is a spare seat.

17 January

Reading the tapes on the way to breakfast, I discovered that the war, which I reckoned would be won quickly, had begun at 3.00 a.m. our time. My tension lifted now that the uncertainty was over.

The airport is shut. My taxi driver came to admit that he couldn't obtain a visa. The Council, understandably, withdrew the offer of its car. There is, of course, nothing stopping me from taxiing to the border to try my luck.

In the afternoon, I went down to the airport. A Gulf Air Tristar was manoeuvring but there was no other activity. In the evening, I inspected the other two luxury hotels and thought them even more lifeless than my own. One of Qatar Television's channels has been given over to CNN 'War in the Gulf' coverage and I watched events unfold.

18 January

It seemed impolitic to kill a bit of time by using my new VCR to film the fine corniche. I sat by the hotel pool in hot sun; the water was too cold to swim. I lost an ally when Dave was reposted offshore.

I did a lot of writing today. Scared by Saddam suddenly firing missiles, apparently, in all directions including this one, I turned off the television when my feeling grew that the ones aimed at Israel were imaginary and slept untroubled beside my respirator.

19 January

Doha looks as usual. Ken is working on his Oman visa. The Embassy confirmed his understanding that the Saudis were manning their checkpoints on the road to Dubai and turning people back. I consider the attempt well worthwhile and Ken agrees.

BA told me that Emirates were still serving both Istanbul and London. The first claim turned out not to be true and Turkey will have to wait until May. Home, however, has jumped back unexpectedly into focus, provided that I can reach Dubai.

I faxed my secretary about a new overseas student-attracting diploma. Another North Field employee confided to me that his employers might be laying on a bus to Dubai and that I would be welcome to a seat. ...

23

Farewell: Egypt

'I wish it wasn't over', said Roger.

(Arthur Ransome)

The ancient Greek ferry, the TSS *Ionia*, transported them away from the Lebanese coast, which stood up cold white against the autumnal blue of the Mediterranean as they got into their stride, skirting Israel. How infuriating the Arabs can be! Early during the first dinner served to deck-class passengers, a neighbour plunged a hand into Horace's meal and re-emerged trailing a sliver of pork, which he held aloft for his companions to ridicule. As if the whole point wasn't that he knew, he asked, 'What do you call this?' Horace reacted angrily to his interference and wondered at the shipping line's inclusion of pork, anathema to Muslims, in its Levant menus.

Their finances could not stretch to the purchase of a share in a boat to shore at Port Sa'id. During the night sail to Alexandria, the last Arab world stop, Horace found one of the passengers struggling to join him under his mosquito net. He could not remember afterwards whether or not ladies had been admitted to their class of accommodation, but this certainly wasn't one. He kicked him out with such force that for a moment it seemed, in the bright moonlight, as if his momentum might carry him overboard.

It was Sunday in Alexandria and they visited the area near the port while the ship spent the afternoon preparing to depart for its next anchorage. The occasional droshke reeled by; no one attempted to deal with the droppings, and the aromatic air was soporific. This did not feel like the country which the Syrians had claimed was so cruelly oppressing them.

They sat in the bows as they passed Crete to the west, Horace reading *The Ambassadors*. Around them, a British group with cine-cameras — won, Horace and Mark thought, on the pools — exclaimed in Lancashire accents at dolphins cavorting under the prow.

References

Foreword

p. xiii   'Why hanker ...', Horace, *Ode 16*, Book 2
p. xiii   '... how couldst thou take ...', Doughty, p. 1
p. xiii   *Persian Pictures* by Bell
p. xiii   *Eothen* by Kinglake
p. xiii   'free from all details ...', Preface to Bell (1928), p. 7
p. xiv   Macaulay, p. 133
p. xv   Storrs, p. 339
p. xv   'Edward Said view ...', in *Orientalism*
p. xv   'The East looks to itself ...', Bell (1928), p. 27
p. xvi   'seldom erred on the side of charity', Winstone (1978), p. 74

Chapter 1

p. 1   'How big the world is ...', letter of 18 June 1892, in Bell (1927), vol. 1, p. 25
p. 1   '... I am really more surprised', letter to Penelope Kerr from Hamadan of 20 April 1930, in Moorehead, p. 263
p. 3   'An imagination ...', Lloyd, p. 1

Chapter 2

p. 8   'Certain words ...', Lambton, p. 43
p. 8   'Give me the haunch ...', Borrow, p. 126
p. 8   'black mischief', Horace, *Ode 9*, Book 3

Chapter 3

p. 13   'The landlord asked ...', Fermor, p. 33

p. 19   'unfortunate companion, Methley, ...', in Kinglake's *Eothen*

p. 20   'the unexpected happens ...', Stark (1986), p. 5

p. 20   'in their pit in Bukhara', in Hopkirk, p. 279

p. 20   the 'cruel city ...', Nichols, p. 109

Chapter 4

p. 22   '... perhaps, no country ...', Morier, p. 5

p. 22   'Themselves they consider ...', Herodotus, p. 69

p. 22   'extremus finis ...', in footnote to Polo, p. 35

p. 23   'Gertrude Bell's steamer', in Bell (1928), p. 142

p. 23   'they were the prey of rumour ...', in Byron, pp. 108–9

p. 23   'There would be something eccentric ...', Stark (1958), p. 3

p. 24   'their personal disqualifications', Bell (1924), p. 103

p. 25   'Gertrude Bell had felt similarly about Tehran', in Bell (1928), p. 27

p. 26n 'Anthony Powell's coincidences', in *A Dance to the Music of Time*

p. 27   'which Ibn Battutah travelled', in Ibn Battutah, pp. 79, 347

p. 27   'lasting nine months in Tabriz ...', in Polo, p. 29

p. 29   '... that which seems a backwater', Bell (1928), pp. 178–9

p. 29   'fragmentary state of its historic ...', in Byron, p. 62

p. 29   'Ibn Battutah's visit ...', Ibn Battutah, p. 101

p. 30   'thinly-clad and shrouded forms', Bell (1928), p. 46

p. 31   '"Patience"-like entourage', in Gilbert

p. 34   'the coldest of cold water ...', letter of 18 June 1892, in Bell (1927), vol. 1, p. 25

p. 34   'Robert Byron's Marjoribanks', in Byron, pp. 55 *et seq.*

p. 34   'Persian was "extraordinarily easy" ...', letter of 30 August 1918, in Bell (1927), vol. 2, p. 461

p. 36   'rather refreshing to the spirit ...', letter of 18 June 1892, in Bell (1927), vol. 1, p. 25

p. 36   'to favour hotels with *Palas* in their titles ...', in Macaulay, p. 89

Chapter 5

p. 38   'Now, I can talk a little Arabic ...', in Marlowe, p. 59

p. 38   '... when I tested him ...', Ibn Battutah, p. 137

p. 42   'like Arthur Ransome ...', in Brogan, p. 106

References

p. 42 'the one thing that never pays ...', letter of 27 May 1930
to Flora Stark from Qazvin, in Moorehead, p. 290

p. 42 'Lord Cromer would not ...', in Storrs, p. 55

Chapter 6

p. 43 'Here is the East ...', Byron, p. 38
p. 43 '... what a different history ...', Stark (1986), p. 109
p. 44 'an old stick-in-the-mud ...', Altounyan, p. 149
p. 44 'a far finer city', Brogan, p. 202
p. 45 'homogenous yet ... strange', in Fedden, p. 96
p. 49 'none of the politeness', Stark (1951), pp. 315–16
p. 49 'demanded of Layard', in Waterfield, p. 35
p. 51 'great Jewish opportunity', Stark (1990), p. 182
p. 51 'a capital whose appearance ...', Byron, p. 38
p. 51 'as it had not', Storrs, p. 284
p. 52 'violence witnessed by Layard', in Waterfield, p. 33

Chapter 7

p. 57 'A signpost pointing ...', Raban, p. 326
p. 57n 'as Margoliouth and Freya Stark agree ...', in Margoliouth, p. 19 and Stark (1951), p. 286
p. 57n 'the Andalusi poet Ibn Jubayr ...', in Duri, p. 901
p. 58 'Dr Grantly and Ripton Thompson', in Trollope, p. 69 and Meredith, p. 120
p. 61 'Freya Stark had thought it "horrid"...', Stark (1951), p. 71
p. 63 'for the construction of the walls of Babylon', in Herodotus, p. 86
p. 63 'Xenophon and the Ten Thousand', in Xenophon, p. 36

Chapter 8

p. 65 'We sat in the garden ...', letter of 4 May 1924 to her father from Baghdad, in Bell Archive
p. 66 'din made by Baghdad's dogs', in Storrs, p. 220

Chapter 9

p. 71 'But with it all, the ...', Trevelyan, p. 205
p. 71 'I have for months ...', in Marlowe, p. 113
p. 72 'paper-handling described in ...', Stark (1990), p. 226n

217

p. 76   'according to Philby père', in Philby, p. 143
p. 76   'Gertrude Bell's noisy negotiating', in Marlowe, p. 116
p. 76   '... stimulated as Storrs had been by working ...', in Storrs, p. 218
p. 76–7 'Arab suspicions about MECAS', *Daily Telegraph*, 5 March 1994
p. 77   'Bell's one-time daily job ...', in letter from Baghdad to her mother of 16 July 1924, in Bell (1927), vol. 2, p. 704
p. 77   'Residence of the Ottoman Vali of Baghdad', in Collins, p. 158n
p. 78   'the most certain way in diplomacy ...', Grey, p. 72
p. 79   'the tragedy of British–Iraqi relations', Glubb, p. 169
p. 79   'against overwhelming odds', Stark (1990), p. 127
p. 79   'Gertrude Bell doing the same', in letter to her father from Baghdad of 7 February 1921, in Bell Archive
p. 80   'Layard's travel by Embassy caique', in Waterfield, p. 106
p. 82   'whose skill Sir Humphrey Trevelyan had witnessed', Trevelyan, p. 150
p. 83   'As Freya Stark noted', in Stark (1990), p. 99
p. 84   'zone of Indian influence ...', Butt, p. 82
p. 86   'they had, like Gertrude Bell ...', in letter of 14 June 1918, in Bell (1927), vol. 2, p. 459
p. 87   'as well perhaps as Freya Stark', in Izzard, pp. 188–92

Chapter 10

p. 89   '... men know best about everything ...', Eliot, p. 736
p. 90   'a more malodorous little dirty spot', Bell (1924), p. 108

Chapter 11

p. 92   'Journeys are a trial', Ibn Iskandar, p. 59
p. 93   'Nothing is colder than the East ...', Kipling, 6 May 1904, to Mark Sykes, in Leslie, p. 99

Chapter 12

p. 96   'Esmé Dobbs and I ...', letter of 9 April 1924 from Baghdad to her father, in Bell Archive
p. 96   'Of course the British Embassy ...', Stark (1986), p. 161
p. 97   'something quite indescribable ...', Stark (1990), p. 110
p. 99   'unstable, being made of mud brick', De Gaury (1966), p. 27

p. 99 'I could hardly follow the Test match ...', *Daily Express*, 4 July 1996

p. 100 'Iraq's last best hope', Falle, p. 158

p. 101 'better service than Ronald Storrs had enjoyed', in Storrs, p. 238

p. 102 'packs of wild pi-dogs ...', in Storrs, p. 220

p. 105 'which Gertrude Bell was unable to approach', Winstone (1993), p. 114

p. 105 'as far as it was possible for an imperialist ...', Falle, p. 123

p. 105 'Gertrude Bell had ... done the same', in letter of 28 November 1918, Bell (1927), vol. 2, p. 463

p. 105 'Layard had campaigned', in Waterfield, p. 101

p. 105 'indulged in by Glubb', in Glubb, pp. 114–15

p. 106 'the iniquity of oriental journalism', Stark (1990), p. 82

p. 107 'like Storrs before him', in Storrs, p. 225

p. 107 'Freya Stark's fulminations', in Stark (1990), p. 82

p. 110 'since Freya Stark's day', in Stark (1990), p. 105

p. 113 'baleful and magnetic influence ...', Stark (1986), p. 203

p. 113 'the fire and brimstone ...', Stark (1990), p. 216

p. 114 'It was vodka with which Sir Roger Stevens ...', in Stevens, p. 131

Chapter 13

p. 116 'Back at Oran ...', in Leslie, p. 199

p. 116 'During my long absence ...', Bailey, p. 290

Chapter 14

p. 119 'Khartoum looks like ...', in Butt, p. 63

p. 119 '... a provinciality, a Khartum ...', Storrs, p. 207

p. 125 'Widmerpool-like', in Powell's *Dance to the Music of Time*

p. 131 'one whom ... he mistook', in Wingate, p. 32

p. 140 'ought to have contained a black satin gown', letter of 20 January 1917, in Bell (1927), vol. 1, p. 395

p. 142 'apeing Thesiger', in Thesiger, p. 30

Chapter 15

p. 144 '... of course we couldn't tell ...', Gilbert, *The Mikado*, Act II.

Chapter 16

p. 146 'That singularly beautiful ...', Bell (1924), p. 327

p. 146 'The Arabs would not ...', Lawrence, p. 45

p. 153 'Turks being so kind', Macaulay, p. 162

p. 156 'Freya Stark gives a marvellous example', in Stark (1958), p. 194

p. 159 'Turks do not care', Macaulay, p. 32

p. 159 'the Turks ... have raised ...', Nichols, p. 239

p. 160 'wild steep mountain zig-zag', Macaulay, p. 171

p. 161 'Macaulay's description' reads '... the charming pretty Frenchified town curving round the gulf, set with palm trees and very gay', Macaulay, p. 171

p. 162 'Though not called on, as Macaulay's had been, ...', in Macaulay, pp. 174–5

p. 163 'a discouraging word', Macaulay, p. 25

p. 163 'Macaulay's largely uncomplimentary opinions', in Macaulay pp. 28, 29, 31, 32

p. 166 'road-menders, brigands, etc. ...', Macaulay, p. 24

p. 166n 'the Erewhonian who ... had to conceal a shoulder of mutton', in Butler, p. 169

Chapter 17

p. 168 '... a scholar, and a ripe and good one ...', Shakespeare, Act 3, Scene 2, p. 456

Chapter 18

p. 171 'Abu Dhabi, ... an Arabian Nightmare, ...', Preface to Thesiger (1984)

p. 171 'Abu Dhabi is now ...', Preface to Thesiger (1991)

p. 175 'compared with that occupied by Ronald Storrs', in Storrs, p. 113

p. 178 'no sort of understanding or sympathy in London', Sir A. T. Wilson to Sir George MacMunn, ex-Commander-in-Chief in Iraq, on 10 September 1920, in Marlowe, p. 230

p. 179 'as Rameses might have put it', in Rameses and Roly, p. 87: 'The Egyptian Army is very large and is probably the largest Army in the world. ... Seniority is entirely by weight'

p. 182 'dull fat eyes', Kipling, p. 131

p. 183 'intolerably snooty women', Falle, p. xiv
p. 183 'as likely as not better born', Storrs, p. 79
p. 183 'like Lawrence of Arabia', in Kirkbride, p. 10
p. 184 'I've just produced a despatch ...', in Daly, p. 145
p. 189 'the most beautiful beach in the world', Glen Balfour-Paul, in Butt, p. 107
p. 190 'it took the admirable Sir Percy Cox', in Graves, p. 78

Chapter 19

p. 192 'Since our arrival ...', Byron, p. 41
p. 194 'the sad case reported by Beverley Nichols', in Nichols, pp. 26–33

Chapter 20

p. 195 '... you meet only dreadful ...', Raban, p. 325
p. 199 'an exemplar ... of parliamentary sartorial style', in *Daily Telegraph*, 29 March 1995

Chapter 21

p. 200 'It's perfectly delightful ...', Winstone (1993), p. 76
p. 200 'Once you really get the run ...', Miss Smythe-Brown in Nichols, pp. 184–5
p. 206 'Col. Bailey noted that cigarettes', in Bailey, p. 241

Chapter 22

p. 209 'Spite of ye all, he is free ...', Dame Carruthers in Gilbert's *Yeoman of the Guard*, Act II

Chapter 23

p. 213 '"I wish it wasn't over," said Roger,' Ransome, p. 374

Bibliography of Works Cited
or Quoted

Altounyan, Taqui, *In Aleppo Once*, John Murray, London, 1969

Bailey, Lieutenant-Colonel F. M., *Mission to Tashkent*, Jonathan Cape, London, 1946

Bell, Gertrude, *Amurath to Amurath*, Macmillan & Company, London, 1924 (2nd edn)

Persian Pictures, Benn, London, 1928

Bell, Lady, *The Letters of Gertrude Bell*, Benn, London, 1927

Bell Archive, Letters of Gertrude Bell, Gertrude Bell website

Borrow, George, *Lavengro*, P. R. Gawthorn, n.d.

Brogan, Hugh (ed.), *Signalling from Mars: The Letters of Arthur Ransome*, Jonathan Cape, London, 1997

Butler, Samuel, *Erewhon*, Everyman's Library, London, 1932

Butt, Gerald, *The Lion in the Sand*, Bloomsbury, London, 1995

Byron, Robert, *The Road to Oxiana*, Picador, London, 1981

Collins, Robert O. (ed.), *An Arabian Diary: Sir Gilbert Falkingham Clayton*, University of California Press, Berkeley and Los Angeles, 1969

Daily Express, London

Daily Telegraph, London

Daly, M. W., *The Sirdar: Sir Reginald Wingate and the British Empire in the Middle East*, American Philosophical Society, Philadelphia, 1997

De Gaury, Gerald, *Three Kings in Baghdad*, Hutchinson, London, 1961

Doughty, Charles M., *Passages from Arabia Deserta*, Penguin, Harmondsworth, 1956

Duri, A. A., 'Baghdad', in *Encyclopaedia of Islam*, E. J. Brill & Company, Leiden, and Luzac, London, 1960, vol. A–B (new edn), pp. 894–908

Eliot, George, *Middlemarch*, Folio Society, London, 1994

Falle, Sam, *My Lucky Life*, The Book Guild, Lewes, 1996

Fedden, Robin, *Syria and Lebanon*, John Murray, London, 1968

Fermor, Patrick Leigh, *A Time of Gifts*, Penguin, Harmondsworth, 1979

Gilbert, W. S. and A. Sullivan, *The Savoy Operas*, Macmillan & Company, London, 1978

Glubb, Sir John Bagot, *Arabian Adventures*, Cassell, London, 1978

Graves, Philip, *The Life of Sir Percy Cox*, Hutchinson, London, 1941

Grey of Fallodon, Viscount, *Twenty-five Years, 1892–1916* (vol. 2), Hodder & Stoughton, London, 1928

Herodotus (translated by Aubrey de Selincourt), *The Histories*, Penguin, Harmondsworth, 1959

Hopkirk, Peter, *The Great Game*, John Murray, London, 1990

Horace (translated by James Michie), *Odes*, Hart-Davis, London, 1964

Ibn Battutah (translated by H. A. R. Gibb), *Travels in Asia and Africa 1325–54*, Routledge & Kegan Paul, London, 1957

Ibn Iskandar, Kai Ka'us, *A Mirror for Princes*, Cresset Press, London, 1951

Izzard, Molly, *Freya Stark*, Hodder & Stoughton, London, 1993

Kinglake, A. W., *Eothen*, Blackie, London, n.d.

Kipling, Rudyard, *Kim*, Macmillan & Company Ltd, London, 1965

Kirkbride, Sir Alec S., *A Crackle of Thorns*, John Murray, London, 1956

Lambton, A. K. S., *Persian Grammar*, Cambridge University Press, Cambridge, 1957

Lawrence, T. E., *The Seven Pillars of Wisdom*, Jonathan Cape, London, 1926

Leslie, Shane, *Mark Sykes: His Life and Letters*, Cassell, London, 1923

Lloyd, Lord, *Egypt since Cromer*, (vol. 2), Macmillan & Company, London, 1934

Macaulay, Rose, *The Towers of Trebizond*, Reprint Society, London, 1956

Margoliouth, D. S., *Mohammedanism*, Thornton Butterworth, London, 1936

Bibliography of Works Cited or Quoted

Marlowe, John, *Late Victorian: The Life of Sir Arnold Talbot Wilson*, Cresset Press, London, 1967

Martin, Theodore, *Horace*, Blackwood, London, 1870

Meredith, George, *The Ordeal of Richard Feveril*, Dent, London, 1945

Moorehead, Lucy (ed.), *Letters of Freya Stark* (vol. 1) L. Compton, Russell, Salisbury, 1974

Morier, James, *The Adventures of Hajji Baba of Ispahan*, Dent, London, 1927

Nichols, Beverley, *No Place Like Home*, Jonathan Cape, London, 1936

Philby, St John, *Arabian Days*, Robert Hale, London, 1948

Polo, Marco, *The Travels*, Everyman's Library, 1958

Powell, Anthony, *A Dance to the Music of Time*, 12 vols, Heinemann, London, 1951–75

Raban, Jonathan, *Arabia Through the Looking Glass*, Fontana, London, 1979

Rameses and Roly, *Oriental Spotlight*, John Murray, London, 1944

Ransome, Arthur, *Swallows and Amazons*, Jonathan Cape, London, 1944

Said, Edward W., *Orientalism*, Penguin, Harmondsworth, 1991

Shakespeare, William, *King Henry VIII*

Freya Stark, *Alexander's Path*, John Murray, London, 1958
  Beyond Euphrates, John Murray, London, 1951
  Dust in the Lion's Paw, Arrow Books, London, 1990
  East is West, Century, London, 1986

Stevens, Sir Roger, *The Land of the Great Sophy*, Methuen, London, 1962

Storrs, Sir Ronald, *Orientations*, Nicholson & Watson, London, 1943

Thesiger, Wilfred, *Arabian Sands*, Penguin, Harmondsworth, 1991

Trevelyan, Sir H. *The Middle East in Revolution*, Macmillan & Company, 1970

Trollope, Anthony, *The Warden*, Penguin, Harmondsworth, 1986

Van Ess, John, *Spoken Iraqi Arabic*, Oxford University Press, Oxford, 1956

Waterfield, Gordon, *Layard of Nineveh*, John Murray, 1963

Winstone, H. V. F., *Gertrude Bell*, Quartet Books Inc., New York, 1978
  Gertrude Bell, Constable, London, 1993

Xenophon, *The Persian Expedition*, Penguin, Harmondsworth, 1957

Index

225

Index

Index

Baghdad, xiii–xv, 18, 27, 29, 54–
7, 59, 62, 64–5, 67–8, 70–1,
73–5, 77, 79–89, 92, 94–7,
99–106, 108–11, 113–15,
120–1, 124, 133, 139–41,
144–5, 149, 157, 160, 168,
173–4, 182–3, 197, 205–7
Baghdad Hotel, the, 82
Baghdad News, The, 75, 88, 106
Baghdad Radio, 80, 88, 96, 110
Baghdad Television, 96
Bahrain, 171–3, 202
Bailey, Lt. Col. F. M., 116, 206
Baku, 33
Balfour, Arthur, xiv, 53, 65, 196
Balkan Trilogy, The, xiii
Baluchis, 118
Balzac, Honoré de, 8
Bandar Mashhur, 173
Bandar Pahlavi, 33
Bangladeshis, 206
Barbarossa, Emperor Frederick,
159
Barclays Bank, 69, 129, 133
Barnard Castle ('Barney'), 7
Barrie, J. M., 73
Barun Hotel, 41, 160
Basrah, 40, 92, 95, 111, 140
Ba'th Party, xi, 96–8, 101
Bazzaz, Abd ar Rahman al, 98,
99, 106
BBC, 80, 110, 111, 116, 149,
177; BBC Arabic Service, 111;
BBC World Service, xv, 14,
62, 123, 177, 202
Beaconsfield, 76
Begin, Menachem, 181
Beirut, 18, 54–5, 59–62, 67, 71–
4, 76, 110–11, 116, 119, 122,
140, 149, 161, 178, 186
Belgrade, 14, 60
Bell, Gertrude, xv, xvi, 1, 23–5,

29, 34, 36, 40, 65, 76–7, 79,
86, 90, 96, 104–5, 140, 146,
197, 200
Benidorm, 171
Bethlehem, 53, 56
Beverley (aircraft), 6
Beyazit, Sultan Yıldırım, 20
BHS, 204
Birmingham, 6
Bismarck, Otto von, 78
Black Sea, 9, 127
Black September, 116–17,
133, 140
Blue Mosque, 21
Blue Nile River, 120
BMC, 148
BOAC, 110, 122, 133, 141
Borrow, George, 8
Bosphorus, 21
Boustead, Sir Hugh, 187
Bridge on the River Kwai, The,
181
Bridgestone, Dr, 9–11
Bridget, 123
Britain, 14, 31, 51, 65, 68, 78,
82, 92, 105, 107–8, 111, 113,
118, 131, 138, 147, 187, 198,
207
British, 13, 16–17, 27–9, 40, 48–
50, 53, 56, 61–2, 64, 67, 69–
73, 76, 78–81, 84–5, 88, 98,
100, 103–5, 107–8, 110–13,
116, 120, 122–6, 128–9, 133–
5, 137–8, 149, 153, 156, 158,
167, 171, 174, 178, 180, 182–
4, 186–7, 189, 198–200, 202–
4, 206, 208, 214; British–Iraqi
relations, 79, 103, 111;
Butcher, 135; conductors, 156;
Embassy, 34, 81, 96–7, 99,
103, 108–10, 115, 121, 140,
147, 153, 157, 161, 193, 199,

227

Index

203; Empire, 6; expatriates,
61–2, 67, 106, 142, 173, 176–
7, 179–81, 186, 188, 202–3;
fleet, 164; imperialism, 83, 98,
107, 130; mandate of Iraq, 72,
84; medicine, 153; Trade Fair,
205; women, 94, 183
British Club, 182, 201
British Council, 73, 115, 211
British Institute (Tabriz), 26, 30,
36
British Leyland (BL), 148, 165
British Midland Airways, 141
British Schoo l (Baghdad), 69, 90
Britons, 5, 63, 79, 123, 129, 142
Brooke, Celia, 89
Brylcream, 179
Buhayrat Qatinah, 44
Bukhara, 20, 206
Bulganin, President, 101–2
Bulgaria, 14–19; Bulgarians, 16,
17, 66, 83, 135
Bumadyan, President Huwari, 97
Buraymi, 190
Bush, President George, 209–10
Byblos, 55, 119
Byron, Robert, 23, 29, 34, 43,
51, 192

Caesar, Augustus (Gus), 168
Cairo, 107, 111, 118, 127, 175,
181
Calais, 15
Calderbank, Mark, 8, 18, 35–6,
40, 43, 45–8, 50–3, 56, 62,
162–3, 214
Caledonian societies, 123
Cambridge, xiv, 1, 8, 10–11, 27,
29–32, 34–5, 57–9, 76, 168–9
Camel Beer, 134
Campbell, Edward, 164
Canada, 59, 146, 147

Canal Zone, Suez, 1
Carchemish, 41
Casablanca, 98
Caspian Sea, 9, 32, 33
Castelbenito, 3
Central Asia, 22
Centurion tanks, 98
Chaldeans, 84
Chalus, 33
Charlie Sue, 66
Cheake, Sir Marcus, 112
Chester, 5
Chester-le-Street, 134
Chic Tailleur, 101
China, 100, 107, 204, 207
Chomsky, Noam, 11
Chopin, Frédéric, 101
Christ Jesus, 50–2, 56, 103
Christianity, 196
Christie, Agatha, 41
Christmas, 68, 83, 85, 88, 98,
121, 140–1, 185, 204
Chtawra, 62
Church of the Nativity, 53
Churchill, Winston, 78, 100, 161
Circassians, 197
Civil Service Commission, 77,
112
Clark, Peter, 169–70
Clergy House School, 131
Cliff, 123–5
Clouds Hill, 37
Clough, Sir Dick, 75
CNN, 212
cockroaches, 30, 68, 205
cocktail parties, 81, 107
Colchester, 187
Colonel Bogey, 79
Comet (civil aircraft), 120
Commonwealth War Graves'
Commission, 79
communism, 147

Index

Index

Index

Index

Index

Index

163; surnames, 165; swimmers, 164; Turks, 20, 36–7, 71, 113, 147, 153, 157–9, 164–6
Turki, 28
Turkish Daily News, 160
Turkish Railways, 25, 27
Turquoise Coast, 157
Twin Rivers, xiv

UAE, 167, 171, 176, 179–80, 183, 185–6, 189, 192, 202, 204
Udaipur, the Maharana of, 129
UDI, 141
UK–Israel Association, 111
Ulbricht, Walter, 107
Umar, Caliph, 50
Umayyads, 46, 197
Umm Qasr, 112
Union Jack, 13
United Arab Republic, 44
United Nations (UN), 80, 112
Ursie, 66, 67
USA, 69, 108, 204
Üsküdar, 21
USSR, 29
'Uyun al Akhbar, 10

Vale, Major, 2–6
Van Ess, the Rev. John, 40, 55, 88
Van Waggoner, 88
Vancouver, 37
VC10 (civil aircraft), 122, 133, 142
Venice, 149
Versailles, 29
Victoria/Victory College, 126
Vienna, 15
Voluntary Service Overseas, 137
Wad Medani, 136
Wadi Musa, 48, 49, 53
'Washbrook', 8, 13, 61

Washbrook, Cyril, 8, 127
Washington New Town, 26
al Watan, 106
Watani al Akbar, 97
West, The, 41, 45, 113, 170; Westernisation, 81
West Bank, 56, 78
West Germany, 15, 18, 87
Wheeler, Sir Mortimer, 10
White Nile, River, 120
Widmerpool, 125, 219
Widowers' Houses, 115
Wilson, Harold, 145
Wilson, Sir Arnold, 38, 71, 76, 113, 178
Wimper, CSM, 2, 6
Wingate, Sir Reginald, 129, 184
Winnie the Pooh, 58
Wisden Cricketer's Almanac, 83
Wolson, 116–18
Woolly Bear, 67
workers, guest, 204
Wright, Sir Michael, 73

Xenophon, 63

Yahya, Tahir, 101, 174
Yam, 29
Yatta, 56
Yazidis, 84
Yemen, 169
Yeomen of the Guard, The, v
Yusuf, Capt., 127

Zagros Mountains, 92
Zayid, Shaykh, 180–1, 183–4, 186–7
Zenobia, Queen, 45
Zionists, 43
Ziyad, 88, 105
Zora, 66
Zubayr, 112